5/02

D0075696

MYTH AND FAIRY TALE IN CONTEMPORARY
WOMEN'S FICTION

Myth and Fairy Tale in Contemporary Women's Fiction

Susan Sellers

palgrave

First published 2001 by
PALGRAVE
Houndmills, Basingstoke, Hampshire RG21 6XS and
175 Fifth Avenue, New York, N.Y. 10010
Companies and representatives throughout the world

PALGRAVE is the new global academic imprint of
St. Martin's Press LLC Scholarly and Reference Division and
Palgrave Publishers Ltd (formerly Macmillan Press Ltd).

ISBN 0–333–72014–8 hardback
ISBN 0–333–72015–6 paperback

This book is printed on paper suitable for recycling and made from fully managed and sustained forest sources.

A catalogue record for this book is available from the British Library.

Library of Congress Cataloging-in-Publication Data

Sellers, Susan.
    Myth and fairy tale in contemporary women's fiction / Susan Sellers.
      p. cm.
    Includes bibliographical references and index.
    ISBN 0-333-72014-8 – ISBN 0-333-72015-6 (pbk.)
      1. English fiction – 20th century – History and criticism. 2. Myth in literature. 3. Women and literature – Great Britain – History – 20th century. 4. Women and literature – United States – History – 20th century. 5. American fiction – Women authors – History and criticism. 6. English fiction – Women authors – History and criticism. 7. American fiction – 20th century – History and criticism. 8. Fairy tales – Adaptations – History and criticism. 9. Feminist fiction – History and criticism. 10. Feminism in litera-ture. 11. Women in literature. I. Title.

PR888.M95 S45 2001
820.9'15'08209045–dc21   2001033108

10   9   8   7   6   5   4   3   2   1
10 09 08 07 06 05 04 03 02 01

Printed in China

Contents

Preface

My parents took me to the London Planetarium when I was eight years old. I have no memory of this trip other than a vista of stars in a night sky which may be no memory at all but merely the picture conjured in my mind by the word 'planetarium'. Indeed my mother insists that I spent the entire visit with my eyes floorwards as I tried in vain in the darkness to untangle the knots in the string of my yoyo. The point is that what should have been my first fervent encounter with the wonder and mystery of the heavens left me detached and bored. It was too scientific, too packed with information my brain could not take in, too remote from my own experience. An outing to the same Planetarium today is a very different proposition. The setting has not changed: there is still the domed ceiling with its panoply of stars, but now there is a story to help you through. A space craft navigates the sky looking for a planet on which to land. Those aboard have had to leave their home which is under threat from an exploding star. There is plenty of detail about the distances between planets and the precise gaseous mix of different atmospheres: a plethora of facts and figures to satisfy even the most curious. But this time there is also a narrative, with its usual ingredients of identification and drama which impel us finally to care about Mars' freezing temperatures or that Neptune is swept by raging hurricanes.

There is something else. Watching the face of the little boy I had taken with me, I realised that the story he was hearing connected to stories he already knew. He was perfectly familiar with space craft and unknown voyagers from television and books. On the way home he told me a tale he had read about a family lost in space whose ship did not have enough fuel to return to earth. The story of the London Planetarium gained impact from its relation to the tales and images that already created his cultural mindscape. There was yet another level to the Planetarium's decision to use narrative that set me thinking about myth. In a context of global warming and nuclear and chemical warfare the tale of a disintegrating planet strikes a pertinent and terrifying chord. The prospect of having to abandon the earth now lies within the realm of possibility. The portrayal of voyagers searching a hostile universe for a new home voices a contemporary configuration of the fundamental fear of survival.

This book is about the power of myth in giving expression to our common experiences and about the role of narrative in enabling us to undergo, shape and survive those experiences. It takes the view that stories play a formative part in creating who we are since they present a medium through which we can organise, communicate and remember our experiences, proffering ready-made schemata that equip us to understand and evaluate our lives by connecting what happens to us to a wider community and other points of view. It is also, more specifically, about the questions and alterations to existing paradigms generated by Western feminism in the final decades of the twentieth century and the imaginative, sometimes provocative, always interesting responses of women fiction writers to that interrogation. This is a vast topic, and one which is clearly beyond the scope of any single volume. While I abhor prefaces that begin with apologies, it is nevertheless the case that this study could have been written several times over, with a different set of writers and texts each time. Despite the immense corpus of work my initial research produced, I knew that I did not want my discussion to turn into a sweeping overview in which it would be impossible to do more than gloss a list of titles. I also knew that I wanted to cover as wide a range of contemporary women's rewriting of myth as I could, encompassing canonical figures and less well-known writers, the so-called literary novel alongside more popular works, as well as a broad band of fictional genres. Consequently I have chosen to include writing that might in other contexts come under the category of science fiction, romance, lesbian fiction, horror, erotic writing, crime fiction, comedy. One's choices nevertheless begin with oneself, and I am aware of the extent to which my previous work on French as well as English women's fiction has shaped the decisions I have made. The rich seam of women's postcolonial rewritings in English of myth and cultural traditions is not considered here, nor are fictions which I am only able to read in translation. While the texts I discuss cover a large spectrum of mythical antecedents from Egyptian, Greek, Christian, literary and contemporary cultural sources, their compass is not complete. When Anne Sexton, in her opening poem to her collection of radically altered fairy tales, has her narrator identify herself, she is locating a starting-point feminism has since revealed to be crucial.[1] Choices, then, are never neutral, but neither is reading. My work over the past twenty years has involved an ongoing engagement with literary theory and particularly French feminist preoccupations with the constitution of the self and the role of language and writing in that formation. This theoretical material has provided me

with a rich basis from which to read contemporary women's rewritings of myth, which I have preferred to the historical interests of feminist mythographers.

In the opening chapter, I survey past and current thinking on myth
in order to consider myth's nature and function, as well as recent literary theory to examine the issue of feminist rewriting. Chapter 2
begins with Apuleius' tale of Psyche and pursues its twin themes of
beauty and monstrosity in relation to stories by A. S. Byatt and Fay
Weldon's *The Life and Loves of a She Devil*. Since both authors employ
comic techniques, my reading draws on theories of comedy as well as
feminist material. Chapter 3 focuses on Hélène Cixous's *The Book of
Promethea* and Christine Crow's *Miss X or the Wolf Woman*, both of
which foreground love as a crucial arena for myth-making and myth-
breaking. Religious and particularly Christian myth is the concern of
Chapter 4, which explores the issue of women's relation to God in the
context of Michèle Roberts's fiction and the theoretical writings of
Luce Irigaray. Chapter 5 examines the rewriting of literary myths,
concentrating on horror stories by Anne Rice and Emma Tennant.
Julia Kristeva's work provides the theoretical framework for the discussion here. Female beauty is once again the starting-point for
Chapter 6, in which Marina Warner's retelling of the legend of the
Queen of Sheba, Emma Donoghue's feminist fairy tales, Sheri
Tepper's ecological fantasy and Alice Thompson's spoof detective
novel are read in connection with Judith Butler's concept of perfor-
mativity. The final chapter continues this investigation into the nature
of perception and reflection through the fiction of Angela Carter.
Carter's view of myth as 'consolatory nonsense' is linked to her portrayal of the maternal, and to Nicole Ward Jouve's notion of literature
as a powerful aid in the ongoing task of separation from the mother
and accomplishment of selfhood. Underlying the entire sequence of
readings is my thesis that myth's form and collaborative gestation
offers empowering paradigms for our collective and individual presen-
tations, analyses and transformations.

Acknowledgements

Many people have contributed to the completion of this book. In particular, I should like to thank Jill Gamble, in the School of English at the University of St Andrews, for her diligent help in preparing the final typescript, and Margaret Bartley, my editor at Palgrave, for her unswerving encouragement and advice. This book was researched and written following the birth of my son, Benjamin, and could only have been done so with the aid of family, friends, colleagues and neighbours: I am sincerely grateful to them all.

Finally, I would like to thank Jeremy Thurlow for the many, many ways he contributed to the project: it could not have been accomplished without his unstinting support.

For Jeremy, with love

1
Contexts
Theories of Myth

What is myth?

Dictionaries are always a useful place to start, even if only to provide a jumping-off point for disagreement and quibble. *The Oxford English Dictionary* gives a surprisingly short definition of the word 'myth'. It states it is 'a purely fictitious narrative usually involving supernatural persons, actions, or events, and embodying some popular idea concerning natural or historical phenomena'. It points out that as a consequence it can mean 'a fictitious or imaginary person or object', and that there is the subsidiary meaning in standard usage of 'an untrue or popular tale, a rumour'. In this instance, the dictionary definition does not advance us very far, since its insistence on the 'purely fictitious' appears to override the complex interactions between life and story that seem the generating force of myth even while its inclusion of the 'popular' returns it to the common domain. Perhaps mythographers will provide us with more fruitful descriptions.

A myth, writes Lewis Spence in what appears to be an expanded gloss of the *OED*, is the account of the deeds of a god or supernatural being, often devised in order to explain our relation to the universe, the environment or a social programme.[1] Michael Bell, hedging his bets on the dictionary options, defines it as 'both a supremely significant foundational story and a falsehood'.[2] For Eric Dardell, myth is a 'typical' story with immediate and exemplary impact, whereas for Riane Eisler it concerns 'larger-than-life' people and events that are passed down from generation to generation.[3] R. G. Stone stresses myth's moral dimension, whereas what is important for John J. White is the fact that myth is so continually repeated that it gradually creates

1

its own resonant force.[4] For Sigmund Freud myth is the projection of psychology onto the external world; for Jean-François Lyotard it is a form of fantasy; for Albert Cook it is a 'technique for handling the unknown'.[5] Robert Graves suggests that myth has two main functions: the first is to answer the type of 'awkward' questions children ask, such as 'who made the world?', the second is to justify the existing social system and to account for rites and customs. Myth, according to his view, offers a 'dramatic shorthand record' of historical, geographical and social changes.[6] W. R. Halliday agrees with Graves that the origins of myth lie in the human endeavour to understand the universe, and he sees the commonality of the problems of existence as the reason for the striking similarity of myths around the world.[7] F. Max Müller calls myth 'a disease of language', while Nor Hall describes it as 'the original mother tongue'.[8] For Mircea Eliade myth is timeless and eternal; for Eric Dardell, what is striking about myth is that it actualises everything in a constantly repeated 'now'.[9] Lauri Honko identifies twelve different ways of perceiving myth, ranging from myth as explanation for enigmatic phenomena, to myth as unconscious projection, myth as art form symbolically structuring the world, myth as religious genre, myth as a charter for behaviour, and myth as a legitimation of social institutions.[10] For T. S. Eliot myth's usefulness lies in the order its designs impose on the flux and anarchy of modern life; for Marina Warner, it is the openness of myth, allowing for the weaving of new meanings and patterns, that creates its ongoing potency.[11]

A common view of myth, particularly among nineteenth- and early twentieth-century mythographers, is that it is the means by which so-called 'primitive' peoples understood the world. J. G. Frazer, for instance, in his pioneering twelve-volume study *The Golden Bough*, sees human evolution as progressing through cycles characterised by magic, then religion and culminating in the rationalism of science.[12] Raffaele Pettazzoni, to cite just one critique of Frazer's approach, refutes the idea of successive cycles, on the grounds that magic and religion are inextricable and that human thought is both 'mythical and logical at the same time'.[13] Pettazzoni's first point parallels the concerns of Jessie L. Weston's influential study *From Ritual to Romance*, in which she shows the links between fertility rites that involve a dying and reviving god and the Christian Jesus.[14] Margaret Dalziel argues that myth originated in the incantation accompanying a ritual act, while G. R. Manton shows how this spoken component was freshly elaborated at each performance, depending on the occasion and the nature of the audience.[15] Implicit in Manton's view is the notion that myths were gradually embellished and honed over time through audience participation and the invention of the tellers until they achieved the maximum effect.[16] Bronislaw Malinowski believes that although myths depict the origins of phenomena and customs, they serve to perpetuate rather than elucidate these. Myths posit an ideal precedent which warrants the validity of things as they are. In some instances, he writes, in an interesting twist on the stigma of falsehood that appears woven into the very etymology of myth, their function may even be one of deception; he details, as an example, how a myth of rebirth does not explain death but on the contrary explains it away, by diminishing or denying it.[17]

This traditional view of myth as a 'primitive' people's equivalent of science has continued to hold sway among more recent mythographers – though with some interesting new twists. An example is the work of Hans Blumenberg, who sees myth as a means of dealing with the anxiety generated by our first ancestors' transition to an upright, bipedal position. He argues that their subsequent exodus from the sheltering forest left them vulnerable in open savanna where there was rarely a direct threat, and where the 'fight or flee' mechanism was consequently inappropriate. Myth, he suggests, evolved as a way of rationalising anxiety by subdividing it into specific agencies which could be addressed and dealt with. It compensates for our biological non-adaptation by reducing the absolutism of reality, a fact which explains its continuing power since it assuages where rational explanation cannot.[18] While there are evidently many problems with Blumenberg's position – his crude analysis of the evolution of the human brain and his narrow definition of myth among them – I cite his argument here as an illustration of the ongoing endeavour to connect mythology to human origins.

Sigmund Freud's infamous account of an 'Oedipus' complex at the core of psychic life is itself an example of how myth can frame the way we understand and interpret our experience. What is perhaps less well known is his study of myth in terms of human individuation. In an interesting reworking of Frazer's *The Golden Bough*, Freud equates myth with the blissful ignorance of early infancy, religion with the developing awareness of childhood, and science with the fully mature adult who has come to terms with reality. According to this view, myth-making belongs to the infant period of fusion with the world, before the differences between self and m/other and the laws that govern the social order are assimilated – a point to which I shall return.[19] For Freud, myths function in the mature adult in the same way as individual fantasy by offering concocted solutions to intolerable situations, and he suggests that they operate according to the processes of condensation and substitution, dramatisation and symbolisation that structure dreams.[20] Freud's correlation between the origins of myth and individual human development has continued to resonate in the assessments of more recent critics, such as Colin Falck, who argues that myth is a universal stage that precedes and accompanies the acquisition of language. He links the emergence of myth to a child's gradual discovery of its bodily capacities and limitations, and he sees the attribution of 'gods' as satisfying the need to give form and comprehension to powers that cannot yet be fully conceptualised. Falck rejects the view that myths are proto-science or 'primitive' endeavours to explain the world, stressing that at this stage the disjunction between fact and reason has not occurred. Myth, in his account, is thus a mode of perception rather than an attempt at elucidation, and he insists that 'mythic consciousness' continues to shape our vision of the world.[21] Nicole Ward Jouve, taking up psychoanalyst D. W. Winnicott's notion of the function of a 'transitional object' in easing the child's passage from the early, illusory state of connectedness and omnipotence to acceptance of the world of others, sees literature (and myth as a crucial part of it) as effecting such a role. She endorses Winnicott's view that this process of 'reality-acceptance' is never complete to argue for the continuing importance of narrative and symbol, with the reminder that – like the child's thumb, cuddleblanket or floppy toy – such an 'object' is in itself gender-neutral.[22] Joseph Campbell also sees myth's significance in its capacity to deal with what he identifies as the two major transition points of human life: the passage from immaturity to autonomous adult and the ultimate relinquishing of responsibility and preparation for death. His assessment prompts him to describe this function of myth as a 'second womb'.[23]

The work of Carl Jung underpins so much current thinking about myth that it is worth outlining his position in some detail. The key to his theory of myth lies in his idea of a collective unconscious common to all, comprised of 'archetypes'.[24] These he defines as typical forms of behaviour which manifest themselves as ideas and images to the conscious mind. He argues that archetypes generate and shape all our most powerful thinking, initiating science and philosophy as well as mythology and religion. Drawing on the writings of Schopenhauer, Jung posits the idea of the ultimate unity of existence, which he considers stands outside space and time: such categories, he believes, are imposed on reality by the limitations of human thought and language. Archetypes derive from this transcendental unity, and even though they may be shaped by consciousness into opposing concepts they remain facets of the same reality. For Jung, the continuing influence of archetypes explains why identical motifs reoccur throughout world mythology and even appear in the thoughts and dreams of individuals today who have no knowledge of mythical tradition. If his theory is correct, then it would also shed light on why myth continues to exert such a compelling hold, since the motifs it employs derive from our most basic motivating instincts. Jung describes the archetypes as 'deposits of the constantly repeated experiences of humanity', thereby leaving open the possibility that as our experiences alter so will the archetypes that instigate our myths.[25] Jung also believes that myths have an organising function since they 'behave empirically like agents that tend towards the repetition of these same experiences'.[26] Given that we are no longer, thankfully, living at the time of Homer when – as anyone who has read his *The Iliad* and *The Odyssey* can testify – war dominated and women figured as prizes to be possessed and exchanged by men, Jung's theories offer a compelling manifesto for feminist myth-makers despite the many objections, ranging from mysticism to a tendency to universalise on the basis of Western sources, that can be laid against them.[27]

Jung argues that the archetypes are not determined in terms of their content but in terms of their form, and this only to a very limited degree. They provide an 'empty' structure, the content of which is filled with the material of conscious experience and which consequently changes in each new manifestation:[28]

the archetype is essentially an unconscious content that is altered by becoming conscious and by being perceived, and it takes its colour from the individual consciousness in which it happens to appear.[29]

For Jung, myths are much more than an allegorical expression of natural phenomena: they are the symbols of inner, unconscious drama which only become accessible through projection and telling. As such they offer crucial messages, providing insights into unrealised or neglected aspects of personality and issuing warnings of imbalance or wrong action. Jung insists that it is the structure rather than the content of myth which constitutes its power, since the structure is transhistorical while the content is relevant only within a specific time and place. The myths and folk tales we have inherited are consequently expressions of the archetype which have received a specific time stamp and been handed down.

One way of distinguishing between nineteenth- and early twentieth-century studies of myth and more recent analyses is to see the former as endeavouring in the main to establish origins and the latter as more concerned with structure and functions. Claude Lévi-Strauss, in a series of ground-breaking investigations conducted from the 1940s to the 1970s, worked on thousands of myths from around the world in an attempt to articulate their common format. He categorically rejects the idea of myth's origin in a 'primitive' mind as itself a myth, arguing that the level of thinking myth displays is as rigorous as that to be found in modern science. Similarly he discredits the idea that myths are devised to express common feelings or to explain phenomena since such a notion does not answer the question of why, if it is the case, this should be done in such elaborate or circuitous ways. Lévi-Strauss draws on structural linguistics to examine the composition of myth. He argues that myth, unlike poetry, is infinitely translatable, and he analyses its presentation of events as apparently timeless to suggest that its substance is contained not in its style or syntax but in the story it tells: in the way its constituent components or 'mythemes' combine together to create meaning. He proceeds from this to see the structure of myth as a progression from the awareness of opposites to their resolution, stressing that it is this that gives energy to a myth as it burgeons and mutates through its various tellings, until the impulse from which it sprang is exhausted and the myth dies.[30]

Roland Barthes, another influential French thinker of the 1950s to 1970s, also draws on structural linguistics in his analysis of myth. For Barthes, myth is best thought of as a type of speech, characterised not by its message or purpose but by the way the form in which its message is couched is elaborated. He describes myth as a 'second-order semiological system', a definition he explains with reference to the linguist Ferdinand de Saussure's model of language as a tripartite structure, encompassing the concept to be expressed, an acoustic or graphic form representing the concept, and the relation between the two.[31] Barthes suggests that this pattern is found in myth, but with the crucial difference that it is built upon an already established linguistic conjunction. In other words, myth arises from an existing association between concept and form, on which it then builds its own supplementary system of signification. It is this 'language-robbery', Barthes writes, which gives myth its richness and makes it appear natural, since its oppressive exhortations are disguised while the primary signification is overlaid with new directives.[32] The imperative, 'button-holing' character of myth is nevertheless neither constant nor inevitable.[33] Barthes insists that 'there is no fixity in mythical concepts: they can come into being, alter, disintegrate, disappear completely', and that around the meaning of every myth 'there is a halo of virtualities where other possible meanings are floating'.[34] Another equally crucial conclusion of Barthes' work in the light of feminist rewriting is his insistence that anything can be turned into a myth, as his colourful essays on a variety of social phenomena – from a plate of steak and chips to a boxing contest – show. As the readings in this volume demonstrate, feminist critique necessarily spans the broad spectrum of classical, religious, literary, psychoanalytic, media and other myths that have chronicled women's existence.

Marina Warner endorses Roland Barthes' view that myth's 'secret cunning' is its pretence to present things as they are and must always be, and, like him, she disputes the idea that this means that they are therefore immutable.[35] She believes that myths can operate as a lens onto human culture in its historical and social context, binding the reader in stock reactions or else providing the starting point for new tellings. Even the most immediate and intense personal experience, she suggests, passes through the common net of images and tales that comprise our understanding of the world. Myths offer ways of making sense of our experience and give crucial insights into the ideologies that underlie our understandings. By scrutinising myth we can work to loosen its negative strangleholds, sew new variations into its weave, and jettison those myths that cannot be satisfactorily altered. Warner insists that any new tellings are at least as authentic as those of antiquity which themselves derive from a long tradition of borrowings and mendings, and that this tailoring is an activity we should all engage in.

My own view, and the one I shall present in this book, is that Warner is right to stress the careful examination, reworking and fresh creation of myths as a valuable and communal enterprise. Even the most cursory survey of the history of myth supports her insistence that there is no ur-version, and the continuing popularity of monster-slaying and 'Cinderella' variants, the current fascination for stories of Princess Diana, and the circulation of such new tales as that of the wife who sells a brand new Mercedes to spite her divorcing husband testify to the continuing vitality and invention of myth.[36] Though I reject the notion of an original, I do believe that the communal process of telling and retelling a myth until it contains the input of

many in a pared-down form has the paradoxical effect of reflecting our
experiences more powerfully than if it were to retain a profusion of
personal details. I see practising and creative story-tellers and writers
as playing a vital but not unique role in this process. While I agree
with Warner that some myths must be reworked and others rehabili-
tated (and that some should be simply deleted from our repertoire), I
would also place emphasis on the importance of myth's ability to resist
change. Warner, in my view, grants the individual with too much self-
knowledge. My own experience of reading myth is that its knack of
surviving all but the most sustained attacks can challenge us to confront issues we would rather avoid, force us to examine our prejudices,
or perceive things in a new way. Myth's finely honed symbolism and
form contribute to this process by lodging in the mind to re-emerge
at unexpected, apposite, or occasionally unwelcome moments. Alix
Pirani, in her account of her use of myth in psychotherapeutic work-
shops, gives a poignant illustration of this, as she describes how the
inexorability of a mythical figure's actions forces the follower to
encounter difficult situations and perhaps discover new insights.[37] I
am not arguing here for a return to the misogynies or staggering and
apparently gratuitous violence of the *Mahabharata* or *The Iliad*, far
from it; but I am suggesting that the different voices that contribute
to the creation of a myth may be instructive and prevent us from
automatically rejecting tales which do not flatter our individual view.

Myth versus Fairy Tale

If myths are stories which distil aspects of common experience in a
concentrated and therefore highly potent form, what then are fairy
tales? Even the term 'fairy tale' appears open to question, as Italo
Calvino's use of the label 'folk tales' for his collection of Italian stories
or Marina Warner's decision to adopt 'wonder tales' for her edition of
the fantastical *contes* told by aristocratic French women during the
reign of Louis XIV illustrates: as Angela Carter so pertinently points
out, fairy tales rarely have fairies in them.[38] Jack Zipes argues that the
pervasive English coinage is a misnomer, since it derives from the
translation of the published literary tales of the Paris salons in the
seventeenth century and is then transferred to all subsequent stories,
including the oral folk tales collected in the Grimms' *Die Kinder und
Hausmärchen* (Children's and Household Tales).[39]

Critics and analysts of the genre once again provide an Aladdin's cave of interpretations. G. S. Kirk, for instance, insists that myth has a serious underlying purpose whereas folk tales (his preferred term) reflect simple social situations that play on ordinary fears and aspirations and pander to our wish for neat and ingenious solutions.[40] Alan Dundes draws on 'sacred' and 'secular' to designate the differences between the genres; in this he follows Mircea Eliade for whom folk tales are a profane and even rebellious alternative to the sanctity of myth.[41] Marie-Louise Von Franz, by contrast, refuses to distinguish between myth and fairy tale on the grounds that both deal with 'archetypal figures'; her view is shared by Jack Zipes, who argues that any initial distinctions have disappeared in their long history of oral and printed retellings.[42] Zipes endorses Roland Barthes' view of myth's transformation of what is cultural and contingent into what appears to be natural and inevitable to suggest that this is now also the purpose of fairy tale. Margaret Dalziel perceives subtle distinctions between a range of genres that includes myth, folk and fairy tale but stresses that what they have in common is a refusal of verisimilitude, a notion Angela Carter shares.[43] Maria M. Tatar, studying the Grimms' tales, argues that a crucial identifying feature is the way fairy tale reverses all the conditions outlined at the beginning of the story.[44] It is, she writes, a radically unstable genre which violates all narrative norms and confounds immutability. Tatar argues that it nevertheless betrays misogynist and inflexible attitudes to gender: the hero's rewards of power, wealth and wedded bliss are presented as consequences of his innate qualities, whereas the heroine must endure a process of humiliation for an ending that signals loss of pride and an abdication of power. She points out that the protagonists of the tales are often schematised or reduced to their function within the plot, and she cites, as examples, the way adjectives such as 'innocent' or 'foolish' are applied again and again to characters or the way the prince-rescuer rarely has a name or history.[45] G. S. Kirk sees this tendency to employ generic characters as a distinguishing feature from myth where, he suggests, the character's background is fleshed out.[46] While this is laboriously true of Homer, where even the frequent battle scenes are interrupted to document the (usually patrilineal) history of competing warriors, Kirk's distinction holds less sway if we consider contemporary urban myths such as the one detailed in the previous section. Vladimir Propp, an influential figure in the field, takes this point a stage further to suggest that what the protagonists of fairy tale do is more important than who they are, and that what they do follows remarkably similar lines. He believes that it is this that gives the genre its characteristic and paradoxical quality of variation and uniformity.[47] For Cronan Rose, fairy tales are 'embryonic stories of development'; in this she shares Bruno Bettelheim's position that they symbolically present the path to independent existence by reducing the complicated and difficult process of socialisation to its constituent paradigms.[48] For Maureen Duffy, myths and fairy tales enable us to experience vicariously states and desires we are unable to live out.[49] She connects them to dreams and suggests that their generic conventions supply a framework in which anything can happen and the rules that govern existence are transgressed. Since the unconscious continually struggles with censorship and guilt she believes that this ambivalence between conformity and rebellion continues in the tales. She too follows Bettelheim in seeing the tales as particularly potent for children since they enable children to participate emotionally in situations they are still too immature to understand, and she perceives a continuing vitality in the emergence of such new fairies as UFOs. Italo Calvino describes the tales he collects as the stories of the vicissitudes of ordinary folk; he, too, points to their concern with the first stages of life: the trials of growing up, the departure from home, and the attainment and proving of maturity. For Calvino, the spells that dominate the tales represent the way existence is predetermined by complex and mysterious forces, while the manifold shape-shifting indicates both possibility and the commonality of life.[50] Marxist critic Frederic Jameson sees fairy tales as 'the irrepressible voice and expression of the underclasses of the great systems of domination'; for Michel Butor, fairyland is an inverted or exemplary world criticising 'ossified reality'.[51] Alison Lurie attributes the survival of fairy tale to its vividly symbolic presentation of common experience; Ernst Bloch highlights the importance of magical wish-fulfilment in expressing collective fantasy.[52] Rosemary Jackson argues that the distinguishing feature of fairy tale is the absolute authority of its omniscient narrative voice. The formulaic 'once upon a time' and 'happily ever after' that frame the story transpose it into a remote past, with the effect that the reader becomes a passive receiver of events that follow an unalterable pattern. For Jackson, the power of fairy tale rests in the vicarious wish-fulfilment it provides through its figurations of incest, rape, murder, parricide and rebellion, a function that works to sustain the social order by providing compensation for its privations. Jackson's analysis offers persuasive arguments for feminist rewriting of the genre, despite her indication that such an enterprise is impossible: her insistence that replicating the

genre's format buttresses the very ideology feminism seeks to undermine, while introducing differences disqualifies it as fairy tale, are points
to which I shall return.[53]

Three prospectors in the land of fairy tale have been of particular
significance in shaping my own point of view, and I will therefore
delineate their positions briefly here. For Bruno Bettelheim, the
importance of the genre lies in its role in human socialisation.[54] He
argues that fairy tales teach children about basic predicaments and
suggest the correct solutions according to the rules of their society in
ways that children can understand. Bettelheim points to the simplicity
of the genre, to its refusal of abstract concepts and minimum of detail,
to its clear-cut presentation of a dilemma and depiction of fears or
hopes by vivid images and actions, to demonstrate how the tales offer
children a framework through which to externalise and control their
powerful but imperfectly understood inner processes. He believes it is
vital that fairy tale characters are either wholly good or wholly bad
rather than combinations as in real life, since this makes it easier for
children to identify with the good and condemn the bad; ambiguity,
he suggests, can only operate against a secure sense of self established
on the basis of such identifications. Once again, Bettelheim's view
raises interesting questions for feminist rewritings which reveal that
the wicked witch was good, or was wicked only because she had been
unfairly treated. His prescriptions imply that any tampering with the
genre will destroy it.

Bettelheim outlines a number of distinguishing features between
fairy tale and myth. He stresses that whereas the mythical hero is often
presented as a divinity or semi-divinity for the hearer to emulate, in
fairy tale the figures make no such demands: their function is to per-
sonify and illustrate inner conflicts and suggest how these may be
solved. Their message is reassuring, indicating that a happy life is possible providing 'one does not shy away from the hazardous struggles
without which one can never achieve true identity'.[55] Bettelheim sees
a further difference in myth's portrayal of events as beyond ordinary
mortal experience and fairy tale's signal that even its most fantastic
strokes of fortune could happen to us. Both genres address the questions that continually preoccupy humankind, but whereas myth gives
answers that are definite, those of fairy tale are suggestive. Myth most
frequently ends in tragedy, Bettelheim concludes, while fairy tales end
happily.

For Bettelheim, the truth of fairy tale is the truth of the imagination and not that of ordinary causality. He sees this as intrinsic to its

socialising function, stressing that for the developing boy it is crucial that it is a dragon as stand-in for his father and not his father that he slays in his bid to secure his princess/mother, since the image is acceptable and hence reassuring at the same time as it promises autonomy as a positive accomplishment. Bettelheim defends the undeveloped 'happily ever after' ending so frequently criticised by feminist and other commentators as an essential component of the genre, on the grounds that it holds out a pledge that present difficulties will be resolved.

There have been numerous critiques of Bettelheim's position, ranging from the charge that his analyses derive from misreadings of Freud, to condemnation of his refusal to take into account the gender bias of the genre, the differences between children, or the historical origins and evolution of the tales.[56] While I acknowledge the problems with his work, I cite it here as an influential study of the way fairy tale shapes our experience and understanding from our childhood years. Although I do not agree with Bettelheim that fairy tales speak primarily to children, I do believe that they can impact on adult life with all the resonance and force childhood memories produce – whether the emotions stirred by the tales are ones of terror, grandiose dreams of achievement, or puerile satisfaction in justice being dispensed.

For Jack Zipes, a prolific and important writer on the genre, folk and fairy tale share common roots with myth in their endeavour to explain natural occurrences and social customs.[57] He argues that it is this that gives the stories their generic quality, and he demonstrates how early tales deriving from a matriarchal world-view underwent successive stages of 'patriarchalization' to reflect the conditions of feudal society so that, by the Middle Ages, the goddess had been recast as evil witch, bad fairy or malevolent stepmother, and the emphasis on maturation and integration had become subordinate to the exploits of a male protagonist intent on domination and wealth. Zipes documents how matrilinear marriage and family ties were subsumed under the new patriarchal economic order, with the result that the ancient matriarchal symbols were altered or rendered benign.[58] Zipes goes on to analyse the impact of literacy and the invention of the printing press in the fifteenth century on the form, themes and circulation of the tales as they became the province of a different class, and suggests how their rewriting in the Paris salons of the seventeenth century involved new emphases based on notions of *civilité* derived from the French court. He sees the choice of the term fairy tale (*contes de fées*) during this period as a blatant attempt to distinguish the genre from the *contes populaires* (folk tales). Zipes points out that many of the *contes de fées* were written by aristocratic women, and he shows how they often contained a subversive element as alternatives to the imposed male norms were conceived and elaborated. He suggests that, in a similar manner, the Grimm brothers imposed their own ideal of 'benevolent patriarchal rule' on the stories they collected a century and a half later.[59] Zipes then unravels the trajectory of subsequent tales through the nineteenth century to show how they were used to critique social mores and as a vehicle for moral instruction.[60] He argues that this dual role continued in the twentieth century, when fairy tales were co-opted by the Nazis, for example, to legitimise their regime through an appeal to a shared Teutonic heritage, or became rich pickings for commercial corporations such as Disney whose exploitation of their escapist elements lulled consumers into accepting the status quo, as well as the instruments for dissident attack.

For Zipes, then, the fairy tales we have come to regard as classics are neither ageless nor universal but the products of a particular historical and economic conjunction.[61] As his survey shows, the stories have been continually rearranged and transformed to reflect changing values and tastes, and he suggests that they assume mythic status only when they resonate with the dominant ideology: a constellation that has been predominantly male for thousands of years. Zipes quotes as an example 'Rumpelstiltskin' which, he argues, began as a tale concerning the female activity of spinning.[62] In the early tale, Zipes writes, there was no father, the name was discovered by a female servant, and the original 'Rumpelstiltskin' flies away at the end on a cooking ladle – a kitchen utensil. In the later Grimms' version the story is framed by men – from the boasting father to the megalomaniac king – and spinning is itself devalued since what counts is its transformation into gold. Zipes contextualises the Grimms' retelling in terms of nineteenth-century industrialisation and the concomitant transfer of power into male hands.

Zipes' distinction between fairy tales which aim to instruct and those which seek to propel their readers to criticise social control leads him to distinguish between two kinds of revisioning. The first involves the transfiguration of a well-known tale in which the author depicts its familiar ingredients in an unfamiliar manner, so that the reader is forced to consider their negative aspects and perhaps reject them. This typically entails the breaking, shifting, debunking or rearranging of traditional components in order to liberate the reader from their programmed response. Zipes locates a second type of reworking in the fusion of 'classic' configurations with contemporary settings and alternative plotlines. He argues that such revisions do not reassemble the tales into new wholes, but expose instead the artifice of the stories and present the reader with different options and points of view.

At the opposite pole to such liberatory rewritings, Zipes believes that fairy tales today fulfill a conservative function, compensating the individual for the restrictions imposed by repressive administrative and bureaucratic regimes.[63] Unlike the original folk and fairy tales, which were communal, told by gifted tellers responding to the needs and wishes of their listeners, and embodied general problems in an accessible form, Zipes suggests that the mass-mediatised versions that currently circulate are mere make-believe, with little relevance to the lives of their audience. They are 'a technologically produced universal voice and image' which stultifies a general public with escapist fantasy.[64]

Zipes' detailed work into the history of fairy tale and his insistence that stories are continually being rewritten to respond to the prevailing ideology seem to me crucial starting points for a feminist reading of the genre. His work on liberatory retellings also appears to me important, though I would weight the emphasis differently to argue for a balance between the retaining of familiar elements and the introduction of the new. One of the problems with the type of postmodern variant Zipes cites is that its continual efforts to break open or debunk traditional modes can leave the reader disoriented to the point of paralysis. One of the strengths of reworking fairy tale, I would suggest, is precisely the interplay between the known and the new: like the good fairy, the presence of customary elements reassures and underpins our daring to defy prohibition and go to the ball.

Like Jack Zipes, feminist critic Marina Warner stresses the importance of historical context when considering the meanings of the tales. She maintains, for example, that critique of the formulaic happy ending is based on a misunderstanding of its origins, since for the Parisian women tellers of the seventeenth century companionate marriage, involving the right to choose one's partner on the basis of love, was a feminist objective.[65] In her monumental study *From the Beast to the Blonde: On Fairy Tales and their Tellers*, Warner unpicks the accusations of misogyny that are levelled against such figures as the malevolent stepmother to reveal the accusers' ignorance of the situation in which the tales evolved.[66] For Warner, the vital connection with the web of tensions in which the women of the stories were enmeshed has been lost, with the result that every poisonous female is taken as an archetype, representing all women in all circumstances and at all times.

To demonstrate her thesis, Warner shows how absent mothers were a frequent feature of family life at a time when death in childbirth was the most common cause of female mortality. Surviving orphans were often raised by their mother's successor, and Warner suggests that the inclusion of the harmful stepmother may have started as a warning: as she points out, history is full of examples of heirs and heiresses murdered by a new spouse, ambitious for their own offspring. The enmity of stepmothers towards children from earlier unions that marks so many tales from around the world is, Warner stresses, the product of patrilineal systems that arrange women's exogamous marriage and prevent their autonomy. The wrong that women do in such stories should not be extended to all women, since it arises from their vulnerability within a social and legal framework which continues to change.

For Marina Warner, fairy tale is an inherently feminist genre. She notes how the reading of fairy tale is popularly regarded as a 'girly' activity, and recalls how as a child the genre's characteristic shape-shifting appeared to her to hold out the possibility of change: its wonders, she writes, disrupted 'the apprehensible world in order to open spaces for dreaming alternatives'.[67] For Warner, the tales are optative rather than prescriptive. Though they have the purpose of teaching us where boundaries lie, it is their paradoxical refusal of limits that achieves this. She argues that the genre has a double function, on the one hand charting perennial drives and terrors, while on the other mapping actual, volatile experience. It is this, she stresses, that gives the stories their ongoing fascination and power to satisfy. They imagine what might lie ahead and suggest ways of proceeding: their happy endings are promises or prophecies rather than accomplished conclusions. For Warner, the enchantments of the tales act as camouflage, wrapping brilliantly seductive images round the harsh truths or daring utterances they speak. Thus she links the role of fairy tale to its etymological history, tracing the close correlations between the words for fairy and speech.[68]

Warner shows how the majority of the fairy tellers were women and contends that the downgraded status of the genre enabled women to speak when they were otherwise deterred from doing so.[69] Her book is full of shocking details of the exhortations on women to be silent, including a sixteenth-century engraving of the paragon 'Wise Woman' whose lips are pierced and sealed with a padlock to which, presumably, only her father or husband holds the key.[70]

For the purposes of this study, I have opted to keep the label 'fairy tale' despite its problems, since it is more widely used than its alternatives such as 'wonder' or even 'folk' tale. I draw no distinction between myth and fairy tale as the terms seem currently synonymous, even though I recognise important differences in their historical evolution and I continue to see a happy ending as the peculiar province of fairy tale. I am also aware of the ongoing tendency to 'gender' the two, and the hierarchy which the equation of myth with masculinity and fairy with femininity produces. I agree with Maureen Duffy that our definition of a fairy cannot be restricted to saccharine and largely nineteenth-century images of figures dressed in white tulle: I consider that fairies can just as easily be alien space craft or even an accommodating bank manager. I also believe that the simplifications of the genre are important, presenting general shapes onto which the reader can paste the necessarily more complex and idiosyncratic details of their experience. Even though such formulaic devices as the customary 'once upon a time' are late additions, I see the way they encapsulate fairy tale's ability to transport us beyond the confusions of our lives into a realm where destiny is clear, and where we benefit by example, as intrinsic to the genre's power. For me the tensions between the 'anything can happen' promise of the magic that we will transgress all the rules and the inexorability of the story as its sequence of events is played out are enabling, because they echo the complicated patterns of our own desire to dare and to need to conform. I find Bettelheim's work helpful in identifying fairy tale's connections with the powerful motivations and emotions that drive childhood; I am convinced that these connections continue to resonate in adults and that this explains the genre's enduring appeal as it fuels, shapes, alleviates and alters our fears and dreams. Jack Zipes' and Marina Warner's careful investigations into the specific historical and economic geneses of the tales seem to me necessary to bear in mind, while Warner's positive insistence that the tales can change and change again offers a rallying cry to feminist writers. As Angela Carter puts it, fairy tales are rather like potato soup. No one knows who first invented it, there are a million subtly different recipes, and all we can do is tell our own version.[71]

The Mother Goddess

Feminist critic Mary Daly argues in her book *Gyn/Ecology* that the patriarchal myths we have inherited derive their potency from '*stolen mythic power*'.[72] Daly's insistence that mythologies around the world originated in the worship of the mother goddess as the source and destination of all life draws on the scholarship of a number of leading mythographers. In order to present this view, I have chosen to concentrate here on the work of Monica Sjöö and Barbara Mor, and Riane Eisler.

In their richly researched and passionate account, Monica Sjöö and Barbara Mor present a wealth of biological, anthropological and archaeological evidence to conclude that religion originally centred on worship of the cosmic mother.[73] They show how archaeology and anthropology have consistently downplayed any contrary evidence, overlooking, for example, the fact that among hunting-and-gathering peoples between 75 and 80 per cent of a group's subsistence derives from women's food-gathering activities, in order to argue for the primacy of the male role in human evolution. Similarly, they query the way science has sidelined such discoveries as the fact that maleness in mammals is a derivation from the otherwise female embryo so as to uphold the view that women are inferior to men.[74]

Sjöö and Mor study the surviving images from the earliest periods of human civilisation to demonstrate how the earth was originally perceived as the female source of cyclic birth, life, death and rebirth – a belief, they argue, which underpinned all mythological and religious thinking for at least the first 200,000 years of human existence. They document how in all the oldest creation myths the female goddess creates the earth from her own body, how the earliest human images known to us are the pregnant guardian 'Venuses' found in Upper Paleolithic remains (from approximately 35,000 to 10,000 BCE), and how burial arrangements from around 200,000 BCE vividly illustrate the connection between death, rebirth and a universal mother.[75] Sjöö and Mor draw on Marija Gimbutas' extensive study of pictographs found in Old Europe between 6500 and 3500 BCE to show how life was viewed as a continuum deriving from and destined for a cosmic goddess, whose associated motifs of horns, the lunar crescent and a cross symbolised the waxing and waning moon.[76] They speculate on the impact a woman's capacity to give birth must have had on peoples unaware of the connection between intercourse and pregnancy: while men may well have been seen as 'opening' the womb, pregnancy and childbirth must have been thought of as involving a magical connection between women and the fertile earth, or else as an act of parthenogenesis with the woman as autonomous creator. Sjöö and Mor argue that such analogies fed into a celebration of the female for a substantial period of human history; an emphasis that was gradually

co-opted by male groups devising their own imitations of menstruation and childbirth, as in the Australian Aboriginal initiation ceremony
where cuts are made on the penis and the initiate passes between the
legs of his elders, or in the circumcision of the foreskin and reverence
for the magical wounds of Christ that mark the Jewish and Christian
religions: in both cases, Sjöö and Mor write, the imitation is deemed
sacred while actual menstruation and childbirth are debased or
considered dirty or sinful.[77]

Most of the famous goddesses of Greek myth, Sjöö and Mor suggest, entail the dismembering of the earlier figure of a universal goddess into her constituent aspects: Aphrodite as goddess of love,
Athene goddess of wisdom, Demeter the mother, Persephone the
daughter, Artemis the virgin huntress, and so on. Sjöö and Mor show
how in these guises the goddesses are often presented in conflict with
one another.[78] They document the introduction of Zeus, the sky-
father, into Mycenaean–Greek myth by nomadic invaders, and trace
the gradual transformation of the goddess's son or lover into a war
god and increasingly dominant patriarch, usurping her functions and
powers and served by a male priesthood actively remaking the old
mythologies.[79] Sjöö and Mor suggest that the advancement of food-
management techniques and the decrease in the need for hunting during the Neolithic period altered men's role. They speculate that their
new task of guarding food supplies from marauding thieves coupled
with substantial developments in the use of metals during the Bronze
Age generated an interest in warfare. Women, who had played a primary role in Neolithic society, were ousted with this shift to male, military power: they became, along with children, animals, land and
resources, the prizes in a new regime of raid and conquest. Sjöö and
Mor argue that this is why patriarchy's inaugural myths, from the
Indian *Mahabharata* to the Greek *Iliad*, revel in the glorification of
war. They are warrior tales describing the feats of a battle-loving elite
bent on victory and theft. Sjöö and Mor delineate how their patriarchal sun or sky god was everywhere imposed on the formerly earth-
and-moon worshipping communities by invasion or internal revolt:
where the vision of a universal mother goddess was not entirely obliterated she was turned into a harmless consort with limited or negative
powers.[80]

Sjöö and Mor suggest that when a mother goddess was the origin
of the universe all creation was perceived as being of her substance,
just as a child is thought to be of the same flesh as its mother. With
the introduction of a male god, however, this vital link could not be

maintained since the male body can neither produce offspring nor itself feed them, with the result that the notion of an originary oneness became dualised and the universe, including god, was dislocated from the self and objectified. Sjöö and Mor connect this development to the emergence of the rigid class system of royal masters and slave labourers that coalesced around the new patriarchal elite, overturning the preceding 300,000 to 500,000 years of communal Stone Age living. They stress how such a regime required punitive ideologies which justified the privileges of the few and the exploitation of the many in order to sustain itself; they study the writings of the Bronze Age to demonstrate how creation was newly paraded as evil while the creator alone was revered as good. The concept of original sin consequently supersedes a belief that we all share in the divine substance to persuade us of our corruption and need for leadership and salvation. Sjöö and Mor argue that all patriarchal religions emphasise the Father's separateness and absoluteness; he is pure spirit divorced from matter, perfection knowable only through abstraction, the Logos. As a corollary, they write, it is the corrupt mother who becomes responsible for the existence of death, illness, pain and decay in conjunction with her evil lover or devil. This is the antithesis of the mother goddess who was neither consummate nor motionless but figured the ceaseless renewal of life in parallel with the waxing and waning moon; she thereby reconciled the opposites that have subsequently determined our thinking, since within her being diminishing and dying are as integral to continuation as birth and becoming.

In two influential studies, Riane Eisler supports Sjöö and Mor's account of the transition from a matriarchal to a patriarchal worldview although with a different emphasis.[81] Eisler charts her discovery that the culture she grew up in, where either the only or the most powerful deities were male, was the product of a societal shift during Western prehistory from what she terms a 'partnership' to a 'dominator' model. She studies the 30,000-year-old images found in caves in the Dordogne region of France of the female vulva which, she argues, was revered as the magic 'portal' of life, possessing the power of physical regeneration as well as spiritual illumination and transformation.[82] Eisler traces the proliferation of such female images through the Palaeolithic and Neolithic periods into the Bronze Age, and argues that until the Bronze Age the extant art suggests a mythology based on the interconnectedness of all life rather than a sense that nature, woman, darkness or evil are forces to be conquered and controlled.[83] Eisler draws on a number of archaeological studies to speculate that the societies which developed in more fertile areas where nature could be viewed as a life-giving and sustaining mother and where agriculture gradually replaced hunting-gathering oriented towards a partnership model, involving a celebration of the feminine and rites concerned to align the community to beneficent nature. This did not preclude the destructiveness of periodic storms, droughts, floods, sickness or accidents which, she suggests, could be explained as part of a cyclical process rather than as opposing and hostile forces. In contrast, Eisler argues, in less hospitable areas the powers governing the universe would have appeared malign. Rituals were consequently less a celebration of propitious nature and more an endeavour to placate and control its unreliable, apparently angry and harmful powers. Eisler suggests that in this climate hierarchies based on fear and force were common, particularly during times of scarcity. She documents how these patterns were gradually institutionalised and inscribed in mythological and religious precepts. Eisler points out that Homer's *Iliad*, which is commonly considered as the repository of much that is noble and valuable in Western heritage, takes place several thousand years after the invasions that sealed the transition to the dominator model, and is itself about the exploits of war. The qualities its mythical gods and heroes portray are those of consummate killers, and she cites the opening quarrel between Achilles and Agamemnon about their rights to a young girl Achilles claims as a trophy of war as an instance of its heinous attitude to women.[84]

Eisler sees in the surviving documents from Sumer a pattern for what happened elsewhere. Sumer is the oldest Western civilisation from which there are extensive deciphered written records, and Eisler studies these in conjunction with the hymns to and about the goddess Inanna, the Sumerian queen of earth and heaven, to show how an early mythology dating as far back as the Paleolithic period which celebrates the sexual union of female and male partners as a life-sustaining rite is superseded by tales of battle, conquest and domination. Eisler links this transition to the establishment of a military hierarchy under the threat of invasion by the formerly free Sumerian city-states where power rested with the citizens. She observes the disbanding of a partnership in favour of a dominator model throughout world mythology, and details, as an example, how in Indian iconography the infinity sign represented by two circles initially indicated equal sexual union between female and male before its meaning was altered, so that the symbol is now understood to refer to two male deities.

This view of a shift from communities which valued and celebrated the female to societies which depended on violence and a commanding father has also been expressed by a number of male mythographers. In *The White Goddess*, Robert Graves studies the language of myth in northern Europe and the Mediterranean which, he argues, was a magical language connected with popular religious ceremonies in honour of the moon goddess, some of which date back to the old Stone Age.[85] Graves suggests that the underlying theme of this mythology was the birth, life, death and resurrection of the god of the waxing year, and that a pivotal moment concerned his defeat by the god of the waning year for love of the all-powerful, triple goddess: their mother, bride and layer-out. He shows how this 'language' was converted during late Minoan times as invaders from central Asia substituted patrilineal for matrilineal beliefs and practices and altered or falsified the existing mythology to reinforce their changes. Graves sees the Greeks' rejection of myth and institution of a rational poetic language which became the model for classical enlightenment in this context, since worship of the moon goddess required men to pay spiritual and sexual homage to women. Despite numerous problems with Graves's study, his relegation of women to a position of muse rather than creator among them, his analysis of the transformation and continuing presence of an early matriarchal mythology has had a widespread impact.[86] Joseph Campbell shares Graves's view of an originary goddess, arguing that her demise came under the influence of marauding invaders for whom an organic, non-heroic relationship to nature was at odds with their reverence for battle and an inaccessible, patriarchal god.[87] Campbell outlines how the earlier, goddess-oriented mythology celebrated the equality of female and male and gave women status within the community, in contrast to the invaders' notions of opposition and domination. Like Graves, Campbell discerns the enduring influence of the goddess in mythologies around the world, interpreting the biblical story of Eve in the garden of Eden, for example, as a reworking of a more ancient tale in which the goddess gives fruit from the tree of life to a male visitor.[88]

Reading through the evidence, of which the work presented here is only a small selection, the argument that an early mythology based on a cosmic and maternal power was supplanted by invaders whose aggression and competitive hierarchies were presided over by a remote 'Father' appears convincing. Equally accurate, it seems to me, is the suggestion that traces of this early mythology still resonate, since it explains why myths continue to exert such a hold. According to this view, rewriting myth is not only a matter of weaving in new images and situations but also involves the task of excavation, sifting through the layerings of adverse patriarchal renderings from which women were excluded, marginalised or depicted negatively to salvage and reinterpret as well as discard. It means looking at the petrifying figure of Medusa and perceiving the vitality of the ancient snake goddess beneath the veneer of loathing she has been condemned to wear. As Riane Eisler points out, our cultural landscape, in which the average US child will watch over 20,000 screen murders and witness more than 200,000 acts of violence by the time they are eligible to vote, must be reconstructed as well as deconstructed if we are to establish an alternative to a system driven by punishment and fear.[89] As Sjöö and Mor contend, changing economic and social conditions is only one step: repressive behaviours, sadistic power relations and competitive greed have been wired-in to our nervous systems, and it is this sanction to exploit and dominate that we must counteract through a *total* revolution.[90] We must ply the persisting power of myth to this end while shearing away the misconstructions of destructive regimes: we must jettison myth's lies while simultaneously reinvigorating its truths.

Mythos and *Logos*

In an influential essay published in the 1970s, feminist critic and writer Hélène Cixous argues that man's endeavour to place himself at the origin in the guise of a transcendental Father has reverberated through history, determining our society and culture to the extent that it is now virtually impossible to conceive of the world in any other way.[91] Structures of binary opposition, in which one term is defined against what is deemed as its other, have organised our thinking and decreed that woman shall operate as the negative of man. This pattern is transmitted in our culture and language as they create the world for each new generation. For Cixous, women are no longer magnificent and powerful goddesses: they appear in our myths and legends only as passive victims, ruinous sirens or unheeded Cassandras. Her strategy for circumventing this repressive scheme involves reading those writers such as William Shakespeare and Heinrich von Kleist who, in their renderings of the stories of Antony and Cleopatra or Achilles and Penthesileia, bring into being modes of relating that are not dependent on opposition, as well as employing literature's rich potential to inscribe alternative accounts.

Cixous's essay draws on the work of contemporary critics, including the French philosopher Jacques Derrida.[92] For Derrida, Western thought is founded on the mistaken notion of an originary 'logos', a term borrowed from the Greek which Derrida variously glosses as truth, reason, meaning, thought and speech. Since this foundation is an illusion it is inherently unstable, as whatever it refuses or devalues continually threatens to destroy it. Derrida coins the term 'phallogocentrism' to indicate the indissociable link between phallus and logos. Since it is man who constitutes the origin, and since its institution and reproduction can only be achieved through the reduction or effacement of what is different, woman serves as its site of alterity: she is the sacrificial victim of a system within which she exists only as a void.

An eloquent illustration of this endeavour to appropriate the origin can be found in the problematic transfer of power from father to son that founds Western mythology.[93] In Hesiod's *Theogeny*, Gaia, the primordial goddess of the earth, bears Uranos, the sky, and takes him as her lover. Their progeny are feared by Uranos, who forces them back into Gaia's body until the overwhelming pain causes her to turn to her other sons for assistance. Cronus castrates and disposes of his father, but then worries that he in turn will be overthrown by his children and so swallows them as soon as they are born. In this he is finally outwitted by his wife Rhea, who when her youngest son Zeus is born fools Cronus by wrapping a stone in swaddling. Zeus calls on his uncles for support, and a ten-year battle ensues following which Zeus is ensconced as the supreme Father.[94] This pattern is repeated in the story of Danae, imprisoned by her father Acrisius because of a prophecy that her son will destroy him, as well as in the tale of Oedipus.

The concept of *mythos* as distinct from *logos* has an interesting history. G. R. Manton outlines the transition in the classical Greek period from an attitude that regarded myth as true to its subsequent relegation to the category of 'story'.[95] He delineates how truth gradually came to be understood as what can be empirically tested, and he compares, as an example, the histories of Herodotus, which include portents and supernatural explanations, with those of his successor Thucydides, whose accounts are based on research and evidence. John Creed charts how *mythoi* began to be considered as unreal or fantastical stories, demonstrating how by the time of Plato's *Republic* the term was synonymous with falsehood.[96] *Logos*, on the other hand, as Albert Cook points out, indicated both the narrative and its explanation: in contradistinction to the fictions of myth it derived from the apparently superior realm of reason.[97]

The Enlightenment's return to the precepts of classical Greece initiated a fresh attack on myth, as Joseph Addison's publication of a
mock-edict forbidding any poet to invoke a god or goddess illustrates.[98]
The contemporary historian Michel Foucault suggests in his study
Words and Things how the renewed emphasis on reason that emerged
during the seventeenth century altered our world-view from recogni-
tions of resemblance and interconnection to a system of rigid demarcations.[99] *Mythos*, according to this view, conveys a less partisan mode
of perception and organisation to the code of abstract representations
that separates words from things and the speaker from the subject he
strives to master. *Mythos* here comprises the playful possibilities of language to create a plurality of meanings that will exceed all rational
binary orders, including the foundation of the *logos* itself.[100]

The conjunction of *mythos* and *logos* presents some challenging
questions. If woman only exists within the current order as the negative other of man, how might it be possible for women to rewrite the
myths that have scripted their demise? Is it the case, as feminist
philosopher Luce Irigaray suggests, that women can have no voice at
all within the present scheme, or can speak only as the mimics of
men?[101] Can women's writings inscribe alternative modes of being
and relating to those dictated by the *logos*, as Hélène Cixous believes,
or will they, as critic Elisabeth Bronfen fears, hover on the difficult
border between terrorism and collusion?[102] If it is true, as linguist and
psychoanalyst Julia Kristeva maintains, that we can only operate from
inside the system of representations within which we are immersed,
does it follow that women's writing will repeat the way we have been
taught to see?[103] Can the different trajectories of *mythos* exceed and
undermine the totalising forces of *logos*, or are they merely a safety-
valve for dissidence? It is to these and other problems as to how myth
might be plied for feminist ends that I now turn.

Is Feminist Rewriting Possible?

In the two 'princess' tales that frame a collection of stories by Jenny
Diski, a princess placed alone in a tower at birth spends her life reading books.[104] In the final story, towards the end of the princess's life,
it begins to dawn on the princess that the books she has been given to
read might be wrong, and that despite their insistence that what
princesses in towers do is to wait, she might not be rescued after all.
One of the many interesting features of Diski's stories is that the

narration casts doubt on whether or not the princess is actually a pris-
oner. There is a door in the tower and the door has a keyhole and on
the other side a key hangs on a piece of string but neither we nor the
princess ever discover if the door is locked. The ending to the stories
is equally ambiguous. Although the princess is not rescued in the classic manner something does finally happen to her: her cat, her lifelong
companion Dinah, dies and is replaced by a kitten. This ending seems
to encapsulate the problems that beset the feminist rewriter. There is
undoubtedly a questioning in Diski's stories, an ironic revelation of
the perfidious effect of fairy tale on women's lives, there are even new
events, yet these appear insignificant when set against the multitude of
texts that continue to keep princesses in their towers. We are left as we
finish reading in exactly the same place: Dinah may have died but her
successor has already been installed. Princesses may periodically question the regime that promises rescue, but they are too firmly stuck
inside the story, Diski's tale implies, to even try the door. The pattern
is too entrenched for an insurgent princess to be anything other than
an exception which proves the rule.

Jenny Diski's stories return us to the *logos*, and to the notion that
the view it ordains is so deeply embedded in our culture and language
and hence in our conception of ourselves that it is impossible to see
beyond it. For Jacques Derrida, the *logos* functions through a destructive dialectic of opposition, a strategy which is doomed to fail since
the very process of demarcation and rejection means it is shaped by
whatever it designates as its other and struggles to deny. These traces
threaten its jurisdiction, and Derrida suggests a strategy of rebellion
which should inspire all weary princesses. He argues that writing in
particular retains the knowledge of its own creation, since the system
of differences whereby its meanings are produced allows other possibilities to come to the fore, disrupting every attempt by the writer to
control what is said.[105] This 'supplement' within writing constitutes
its radical potential, since a text can always be made to reveal its history, including its manipulations and suppressions. For Derrida, this
'feminine' excess entails the possibility of a plurality which deconstructs
our conceptual system. He consequently urges writers to employ a
multiplicity of styles and to work to keep the opportunities for meanings open, by attending to and incorporating the myriad other pathways that are generated as one writes. In contrast, therefore, to the
logocentric text which strives to establish and police its own weave,
what might be termed a 'feminine' text is an unguarded network that
continually unfolds outwards towards others.

Derrida's insistence that writing has the revolutionary potential to counter the phallogocentric system is a notion shared by Hélène Cixous.[106] Writing, she argues, presents an unbounded space in which the self that strives to constitute itself through mastery of the other is relinquished and in which the other can finally be received. Consequently, she suggests that the feminine writer's task is to actively inscribe the heterogeneous promptings that are thrown up by the process of writing, an endeavour that will bring into being an alternative mode of perception, relation and expression to that decreed by the prevailing schema.

The psychoanalyst and critic Julia Kristeva ties the process of language acquisition to the infant's developing sense of itself as distinct from its mother's body and surroundings, and the accompanying requirement for it to control its innate instincts to conform to social convention.[107] She argues that in order for writing to contravene the rules we have been taught it must return us to the metaphorical scene of castration, in other words to the point of separation between our unsocialised, drive-governed selves and our constitution within a 'symbolic' order of precepts, so that we can re-experience and perhaps redraft the premisses which currently organise this division.[108] The writer's task is to embrace in their writing the 'semiotic' or heterogeneous corporeal energies which reject, disrupt, supplement and alter the terms of one's relation to the cultural contract, a practice radically at odds with the monological procedures of the present patriarchal regime. Like Derrida and Cixous, Kristeva urges the writer to continually reflect on the processes of writing, to inscribe plural meanings into their work, and to draw on the unconscious for inspiration since this is where outlawed alternatives to the prescribing order are lodged. Significantly in relation to the rewriting of myth, she maintains that disruption can occur both through the inclusion of unanticipated meanings generated by a word or phrase in the course of writing and through references to other texts. This 'intertextuality', Kristeva maintains, can offer a potent strategy for dissidence.

Luce Irigaray stresses that the Law which organises Western culture is the patriarchal desire to distinguish, reproduce and exchange the *same* image. Woman under this regime exists only in relation to man: she is the other in an exclusively male scheme, with no value or attributes of her own apart from her reflective capacity. Irigaray contends that language is the mainstay and medium of this order, but argues that women can at present do little more than 'mimic' the discourse we have had no part in creating: any attempt to speak will merely

reproduce its repressive hierarchy. Despite the bleakness of her denunciation, Irigaray's writing indicates a possible subversive tactic as it
strives to disclose the mechanisms of the phallogocentric procedure
and identify alternatives.[109]

Feminist critic Judith Butler examines Irigaray's assessment to
pinpoint a number of difficulties which are relevant to feminist rewriting.[110] Butler suggests that Irigaray's strategy of mimicking Plato in
order to expose the assumptions and manipulations of his account
makes it hard to tell whether it is Irigaray or the philosophical father
who is speaking. If Irigaray is 'in' the father's voice, Butler asks, how can
she also be at the same time outside it? If she locates herself 'between'
the two positions, then doesn't this leave the system of binary oppositions she wishes to dismantle intact? How can Irigaray's different voice,
Butler goes on, be identifed as she retells Plato's story, and doesn't the
act of retelling reproduce the very story she wishes to undo? Butler
locates some possible solutions to these dilemmas in Irigaray's tactic of
mimicking the *excesses* in Plato's narration as well as in her mimes which
'reverse' Plato's intention, both of which reproduce the original so as
to highlight the prejudice and grandiosity that underlie Plato's claims.
As will be discussed below, these expedients can be seen at work in the
fictions of a number of contemporary women writers.

Irigaray's insistence that phallogocentrism is so all-pervasive that
mimicry is currently the only option available to women and Butler's
analysis of the difficulties involved in such a manoeuvre are echoed in
feminist critic Diane Purkiss's essay on women's rewriting of myth in
contemporary poetry.[111] Purkiss identifies three recurring modes of
rewriting which can also be traced in women's fiction: shifting the
focus from a male to a female character, as in Barbara Walker's stories
of 'Gorga and the Dragon' and 'Jill and the Beanroot'; transposing
the terms so that what was negative becomes positive, as in Angela
Carter's reinterpretation of the wolf from 'Little Red Riding Hood';
and allowing a minor character to tell their tale, as in Alison Fell's
novel of Mrs Gulliver.[112] There are problems contained in all three
modes, Purkiss argues, since they all tamper with internal patterns,
leaving the mythical discourse in which they are embedded intact. She
stresses that the endeavour to retrieve a buried or marginal voice has
the paradoxical function of endorsing the original myth. Postcolonial
critic Gayatri Chakravorty Spivak takes this argument a stage further
to suggest that it is *impossible* to restore a voice that has been dis-
possessed, since the very act serves to re-cover it; an assessment that
points to the more general dilemma of how to rewrite a text without

'mastering' its source and so reproducing the objectifying and annihilating procedures of binary law.[113] Derrida's notion of opening up the weave of writing to enable other meanings to come to the fore is a potentially empowering one for feminism, yet it leaves the question of what will happen to this tactic when confronted with the particular requirements of the genre unanswered. If the feminine writer adheres to Cixous's admonition that there can be no ordered beginnings and endings, no definitive characters, or events that follow a predetermined course, then isn't what she is writing the very antithesis of myth? If we adopt Kristeva's richly suggestive stance, how can our corporeal drives find expression in a mode of narration from which the personal has been successively erased? The difficulties confronting the feminist rewriter appear immense. Must we conclude, then, with Camille Paglia, that the feminist project of rewriting myth is both pointless and absurd?[114]

If Diane Purkiss is right, and altering internal patterns or attempting to express silenced or marginal voices leaves the central discourse inviolate, does it follow that feminists must begin again, from a place outside myth? Yet if we do this, we not only vacate the arena to allow myth's power to continue unimpeded, we also deprive ourselves of its undeniable force. I am also more optimistic than Irigaray or Purkiss about the potential impact of rewriting a myth. As Elisabeth Bronfen argues in a different context, the disruption caused leaves traces, so that the regained order contains a shift and is no longer the homogeneous realm from which difference is eradicated.[115] The work of feminist critic and myth-maker Mary Daly presents an example here. In a series of influential books, Daly works to dismantle the stranglehold of patriarchal myth and to create woman-focused words, images and tales.[116] For Daly, this metaphorical shape-shifting and gynocentric spinning opens up previously barred meanings and areas of experience, which have the capacity to unlock corresponding 'metamorphospheres' in us.[117] It is impossible, having once read Daly's etymological tracings and new glosses on words such as 'virgin', 'spinster' and 'hag', or laughed at her pun on 'phallosophy' and hilarious definition of patriarchy as 'Yahweh & Son: mythic paradigm for any corporation of cockocracy, for any all-male family business', to view their sources in the same light.[118] The problem, then, is not to avoid myth, but to find ways of rewriting it which do not return us to the negative prescriptions of the *logos*.

I see a first response to this dilemma in Derrida's insistence that the text will always slip away from us: just as the logocentric enterprise is never intact, so our own rewritings will always exceed and disrupt our intentions. We can actively encourage this process by leaving the web of the text open: as Derrida reminds us, 'to weave is first to make holes'.[119] Yet if we make too many holes we are in danger of writing something other than myth. Perhaps the answer lies in rethinking the conjunction between the old and the new – or the live and the dead, to borrow philosopher Paul Ricoeur's resonant phrase.[120] This would involve keeping and benefiting from those elements which are still potent for us, while discarding or revitalising those which are dead, deadly, or simply no longer appropriate. It would enable us to envisage rewritings not only as pleasurable reversals or ingenious tinkerings but as new embroideries, adding fresh images and colours to radically alter the picture. Feminist rewriting could thus include ironic mimicry and clever twists as well as a whole gamut of tactics that would open the myth from the inside as well as out, leaving in place enough of the known format to provide evocative points of reflection for its reader, but also encompassing different possibilities and other points of view. Marina Warner's rewriting of the tale of Susannah and the elders offers an illustration here, employing our knowledge of the original to complicate our relation to it through its invitation to identify with but also spy on Susannah. Warner reworks the existing template to prompt us to question our own roles as accomplices and voyeurs.[121]

My answer then is to try for the difficult and perhaps impossible balancing act. To follow the figure of Little Red Riding Hood and stick to enough of the path so as not to get lost completely, while taking in whatever flowers or strangers we encounter on the way. Critic Rosemary Jackson suggests that the fantastic nature of the genre can contribute to this: since it is free from many of the conventions that restrict our thinking it opens up spaces where unity and order are normally imposed.[122] She argues that its generic make-up disrupts the drive towards the institution of a single, reductive 'truth', introducing contradiction and polysemy. Jackson sees the movement of metamorphosis that is a persistent feature of myth as metonymic rather than metaphoric, since one object does not stand for another but rather slides into it, blurring the divisions and any concomitant hierarchy; she cites the psychoanalytic critic Jacques Lacan's contention that metonymy offers a means of eluding the repressive strictures of the social order to argue for its subversive power.[123] The honed quality of mythic symbolism also seems to me to provide rich potential since it encourages multiple interpretations, as the various configurations of the maze in Carol Shields' novel *Larry's Party* illustrates.[124] Some of Hélène Cixous's own feminine writings are notoriously difficult to read as they glide from word-play through dense allusion to disruption of all the 'rules' including those of grammar, punctuation and page layout, to the point where rebellion dissipates into chaos.[125] It is my contention that the rewriting of myth can circumvent some of these dangers, since the known forms operate as compass points around which we can weave new and different stories. Employing the existing weft and warp in this way replicates the psychoanalytic notion of holding, in which boundaries encourage the individual to progress. The double momentum of security and innovation similarly mirrors Kristeva's strategies for dissident writing, since it provides a context within which we can rend and renew our relation to the established order: prompting us to reject what unfairly binds us while reaffirming our allegiance to what is productive. As Kristeva points out, we must adopt the social-symbolic code in order to function, and our revolts will be fruitless unless they occur within it in ways that can be understood. Feminist rewriting can thus be thought of in two categories: as an act of demolition, exposing and detonating the stories that have hampered women, and as a task of construction – of bringing into being enabling alternatives. Having drawn up some initial guidelines, we must now consider in more detail how myth can contribute to such an undertaking.

Why Myth?

The causes of the Greek–Trojan war that provides the subject matter for Homer's *The Iliad* are a tangle of invasions and thefts of which the kidnapping of the famous Helen is only one example.[126] *The Odyssey*, Homer's second great epic, which charts the return journey of Odysseus 'the city-sacker' after the war, similarly commemorates deeds of extraordinary brutality culminating in the wholesale massacre of his wife's suitors and the serving-women who have loved them.[127] It is perhaps surprising, therefore, that the legacy of twentieth-century feminism should involve a return to tales in which violence is celebrated and where women are possessions to be won or disposed of. Do women writers retell these founding stories of Western myth in an attempt to set the record straight? Are they concerned to eradicate the distortions of patriarchy to reveal an anterior, matriarchal world-view and to create a more woman-centred account? Is it the case, as Camille Paglia would have it, that the savagery is a source of pleasure?[128] What is it that has prompted contemporary women fiction writers from

Margaret Atwood to Jeanette Winterson to rework these ancient narratives?

One answer to this conundrum is the dominant role of classics in Western education.[129] George Eliot, in *The Mill on the Floss*, gives a heart-rending account of young Tom Tulliver's struggles with the irregularities of Latin grammar because his father, the mill-owner, wants him 'to be a man who will make his way in the world'.[130] One of the many ironies in Eliot's novel is that Tom's sister Maggie is linguistically more gifted than her brother and learns the declensions easily, yet as a girl she is denied the education that is wasted on the practically-minded Tom. Virginia Woolf, who wrote a devastating essay on the fate of William Shakespeare's talented but female and therefore uneducated imaginary sister Judith, was refused the education automatically accorded her brothers (though she was given the run of her father's library): it is significant that when she could she chose to study Greek.[131]

A more important reason lies at the heart of the myth-making process itself. As Nicole Ward Jouve observes, drawing on the work of Paul Ricoeur, we make the otherwise alien world a 'habitable' place through the stories we tell ourselves about it.[132] The process works in two ways, since what we know of ourselves and can project onto the world is itself a product of the language and literature we have received. Story-telling shapes us as we use stories to shape the world.

Drawing on theories which refute the idea that the self is a single and consistent entity, Don Cupitt argues that the multiple layers on which myth operates accommodates individual complexity.[133] This, he suggests, is the contemporary function of myth: to enable us to compose from the vast range of possibilities enough coherence to perform. Cupitt supports his thesis by demonstrating how myth's multiplex structure corresponds to the circuitry of the brain. Each neuron, he writes, is wired to hundreds of other neurons creating countless strata of neural networks; a number of such networks must be stimulated for a response to occur, a condition that is satisfied by myth. For Cupitt, this link between physiology and myth has two further repercussions: it means we remember stories more easily than lists of data and that myths can open new neural pathways, equipping us to deal with situations we have not yet encountered. Like Ward Jouve, Cupitt believes that stories generate desires and models of behaviour. They offer a forum in which we can conduct imaginative experiments, distinguishing as well as providing an outlet for feelings and attributing value to them. Myth's highly symbolic form prevents a crude or mechanical reaction and induces a more considered and enhanced response.[134]

Cupitt's analysis provides a compelling manifesto for myth, and also indicates that we must be ethically responsible in our choice of what to write. Repeating Homer verbatim will only ensure that violent tales of warfare and rape are wired into the brains of each new generation.

A further reason for the continuing potency of myth is the way the tales have been refined over centuries of telling. As Nicole Ward Jouve suggests, there is still much truth in myth, despite its distortions and the unjust way it apportions roles.[135] What we write as individuals cannot so easily achieve this resonance. We need to deploy myth's power, weaving our own versions onto its potent templates to attain the maximum effect. Mary Shelley's *Frankenstein* may have acquired mythic status, but it began with the story of Prometheus.[136]

Roland Barthes' work on mythology similarly uncovers an answer. His view that myths function by attempting to restore what they have stolen for their effect is empowering for feminist rewriters since it highlights the constructed nature of myth as well as the disruption caused to the plundered order by the act of theft.[137] Barthes suggests that the way myth creates its meaning makes it difficult to refute its power: once we have received the myth its impact cannot be erased by explanation or qualification. Deconstruction or the reading of myth to expose its manipulations and suppressions is not enough, we must counter with our own mythopoeia; as Barthes writes, our best weapon against myth is to mythify in turn.

Don Cupitt contrasts the way myth operates with the functioning of philosophy, which, he contends, has concerned itself since Plato with contemplating what it postulates as the unchanging, unitary 'Truth'. Stories, on the other hand, have a temporal structure which echoes how we experience life.[138] Truth, Cupitt stresses, in a metaphor that evokes the combat and violence of Greek myth, is a battlefield, an endless struggle for domination between rival stories. While I am not persuaded by Cupitt's assessment of competing stories, which seems to me to return us to the *logos* he is elsewhere at pains to undermine, I do share his insistence on the greater veracity myths contain. A final response, then, to the question 'why myth?' might be that its procedures enable the expression of more individually resonant, less easily co-optable, multifarious truths.

Reading Myth

In her essay 'Sorties', Hélène Cixous describes how as a child she read Homer and Virgil, trying out the positions of the different male heroes.[139] Her insistence that as readers we identify with characters irrespective of sex complicates feminist critiques of myth and fairy tale on the grounds that they portray gender misogynistically.[140] Kay F. Stone, for instance, argues that feminist rewriting which attempts to offer women positive role models by turning fairy tale heroines into dragon-slayers ignores the way we actually read.[141] It is, she stresses, a tactic which responds to the story's surface meaning overlooking other levels, such as the fact that the prince might symbolise inner strength or that Cinderella's glass slipper might stand for her vagina.[142] Alison Lurie similarly suggests that what we receive from myth and fairy tale depends on how we connect them to our life experience.[143]

For Hélène Cixous, a feminine practice of writing must be accompanied by an equivalent style of reading.[144] She believes that like the feminine writer the feminine reader must remain open to the myriad meanings of a text, without imposing their own prejudices and predilections and selecting only those elements which corroborate their view. Cixous stresses that this has implications for the type of texts we read, which should deal in an open and questioning way with the fundamental issues of human experience and contain the capacity to alter our perspective, motivating us to reconsider the manner in which we live.

Julia Kristeva argues for a mode of reading that involves the reader's active participation in the multifarious movements of the text, which, she contends, bring into play the drive-governed terrain of sexuality and the unconscious and consequently return us to the unordered realm of the pre-Oedipal before the divisions and requirements of social-symbolic law.[145] Like Cixous, Kristeva believes that this should influence our choice of reading, which should continually call us into question rather than assist the desire for mastery.[146] We must reject those texts which flatter our position and work with those which, through their pluralising and disruptive tactics, force us to consider our constructions and tenets. Kristeva describes such a text as whisking the reader through a process of dissolution by the exploding force of its rhythms, linguistic and syntactic transgressions and semantic possibilities. The reader, she insists, must work to follow this trajectory and refuse the demands of the super-ego for dominion, seeking, once the reading is over, to restore the relation to the cultural contract but with a new awareness of what is at stake.

In the introduction to their collection *Forbidden Journeys: Fairy Tales and Fantasies by Victorian Women Writers*, Nina Auerbach and U. C. Knoepflmacher suggest that Victorian women turned to fairy tales partly because they were considered to be primarily for children which consequently made them more acceptable for women to write, and partly because their generic composition allowed the expression of otherwise forbidden truths.[147] Auerbach and Knoepflmacher argue that the ingredients which, in the early years of the century, were employed by the didacticists who dominated juvenile literature for moral instruction, gave rise in the middle and later years to tales that voiced women's frustrations and yearnings for autonomy. Since women were still expected to comply with rigid conventions, fairy tales offered strategies of indirection and disguise which produced a new generation of deviant, satirical, angry and even violent writers and readers.[148]

Auerbach and Knoepflmacher's contention that the magic and metamorphoses characteristic of the genre can be read 'contrapuntally', to borrow Edward Said's word, is one shared by numerous commentators of myth and fairy tale.[149] For Lévi-Strauss, to quote just one example, the units of myth only make sense if they are read in conjunction with other 'mythemes'.[150] He argues that we must read myth as we would a musical score, since we can only understand its components if we consider their relation to what is happening at other levels.[151] The fact that myth and fairy tale derive from countless generations of oral telling mean that we cannot canonise their diversity into standard versions and authorised interpretations; it is even possible that the disruptions to this variety caused by printing will be altered by a future of electronic publishing with its facilities for audience interaction and rapid updating. Certainly the plethora of rewritings of individual tales, of which this book presents a small selection, indicates that their form allows for very different readings. There are, however, critics who qualify or dispute this openness. Angela Carter represents a strong school of argument which insists that the context in which one reads shapes what one reads, and she cites, as illustrations, how the struggle towards German unification affected the version the Grimms chose to print as well as the way nineteenth-century prudery effaced the more salacious points from the tales.[152] Jack Zipes is one of a line of detractors for whom the stories have been standardised so that reading them reinforces the status quo.[153] Perhaps, then, the reading attitude we should adopt is Ricoeur's one of a 'post-critical naiveté', the difficult conjunction of critical alertness while remaining open to the wonders of the tales themselves.[154] It is this attitude that I have endeavoured to adopt in what follows.

2

The Double-Voice of Laughter

Metamorphosing Monsters
and Rescripting Female Desire in
A. S. Byatt's 'The Djinn in the
Nightingale's Eye' and Fay Weldon's
The Life and Loves of a She Devil

> You only have to look at the Medusa straight on to see her. And
> she's not deadly. She's beautiful and she's laughing.
> Hélène Cixous. 'The Laugh of the Medusa'[1]

> The joke then represents a rebellion against that authority, a libera-
> tion from its pressure.
> Sigmund Freud. *Jokes and their Relation to the Unconscious*[2]

In Apuleius' comedy *The Golden Ass or Metamorphoses*, written in the
second century CE, the love-stricken Pamphile employs magic to
transform herself into a bird in order to procure her man.[3] The narrator Lucius is fascinated by her art and begs Pamphile's servant to steal
some of her ointment so that he may try the metamorphosis himself.
Unfortunately the servant mistakes the jar and Lucius is changed into
an ass, giving rise to a series of savagely comic social satires. 'The
Story of Cupid and Psyche' which *The Golden Ass* contains reiterates
the themes of female desire and bodily representation in forms that
have become familiar to us as fairy tales.[4] In Apuleius' version, Psyche

is the youngest daughter of a king and queen, whose beauty is so great it arouses the envy of Venus. The goddess accordingly commands her son Cupid to strike Psyche with one of his arrows so that she will instantly fall in love with a 'degraded' creature.[5] Venus' plan is foiled by Cupid himself who wounds his own body with the arrow and becomes Psyche's lover. Ignorant of these divine schemes, Psyche is conducted to a mysterious and beautiful palace where her every need is attended to and where each night Cupid makes love to her. Psyche, we are told, gradually adjusts to her new situation, which in time 'became pleasurable to her by force of habit'.[6] This stasis is broken by Psyche's sisters, whose jealousy of her beauty is inflamed by the extraordinary opulence of her palace and the manifest luxury of her life. Though the sisters are by no means condoned in the narrative, their comic bleatings about the miseries of their own arranged marriages to ailing and miserly husbands sheds an interesting light on women's lives at the time. The sisters persuade Psyche to do what she has been forbidden to do and look directly at her husband's face. The justification they give is that a monstrous serpent has been seen in the region which they fear may be masquerading as Psyche's husband. The twin motifs of beauty and monstrosity are pursued as Cupid, burnt by a drop of oil from the lamp Psyche holds up to his face, accuses Psyche of seeing him as a monster and abandons her to Venus, whose punishments include a journey to the Underworld to obtain a fresh source of beauty. Tempted by the thought that she might thus entice Cupid back to her, Psyche resolves to steal a little of the beauty for herself and opens the box the queen of the Underworld has given her – only to discover that it is empty.

    In A. S. Byatt's 'The Djinn in the Nightingale's Eye', the central character, Gillian Perholt, is told the story of the gifted and clever Zefir, married at fourteen to a rich merchant to be part of his harem.[7] Zefir is tormented by her unused powers and wonders if she might be a witch, but then reflects that if she were a man her talents would be considered normal. Like the magnificent pictures Zefir sews, her tale is part of a complex embroidery of narratives in which men have power and women do not. Gillian herself tells Chaucer's 'Patient Griselda' at an international conference of narratology, the theme of which is 'Stories of Women's Lives'. In Chaucer's tale Griselda is chosen by the local lord to be his wife because she is beautiful and virtuous. Before he marries her, however, the lord makes Griselda swear that she will consent to his every desire without protest or hesitation, an oath he tests by taking the children she bears and telling her he intends to kill them. In a further trial of her submission, he orders Griselda to leave him and prepare a wedding feast for a new bride which he finally reveals to be her daughter. The story as retold by Gillian focuses not only on Griselda's unswerving obedience but also on the lull in the narrative while her children are growing up. Gillian fills in this gap by pointing out the link to Shakespeare's Hermione in *A Winter's Tale*, whose adult life is similarly atrophied by the caprices of her husband and master, and by reflecting on the 'stopped energies' that more generally characterise women's lives in fiction.[8] The wide applicability of Gillian's narration is underscored not only by other literary examples and her reminder that Chaucer's tale derives from Plutarch which is itself a reworking of Boccaccio, but also through her story of the Ethiopian woman recorded in a television interview who believes she can do nothing to end the famine that threatens her family because she is a woman. Gillian's conference is in Ankara and among her audience are three young women whose headscarves proclaim their allegiance to Islam. When one of the women is asked why she wears a scarf she replies that her father and fiancé believe it is right and that she agrees with them. This intricate weave of past and present stories in which women are subordinate to men prompts Gillian to suggest that the answer to the Queen of Sheba's famous riddle is that what women most desire is not to be women.

In another of A. S. Byatt's fairy stories, 'The Eldest Princess', the princess in question is sent on a Quest.[9] Since she is a 'reading' princess she recognises the story she is in, and wonders how she might avert the pattern which will lose her precious years of her life. She toys with the idea of simply walking out, but worries that she will be punished for this and that it will not stop the next princess from being sent in her place. Through the agency of a number of intelligent animals who have all been wounded by men's stories she resists the temptation to be rescued, and arrives at last at the Old Woman's cottage. Here the animals are healed through the telling of their hurts and the princess too discovers the pleasures of narration. She has escaped, the Old Woman tells her, because she realised that she was stuck inside a story and had the sense to alter its course.

The Old Woman's insistence that stories are not history and can change is set against her account of the youngest princess who has no tale and consequently feels sickly giddy from the empty space around her. The youngest princess's decision to ask for the thread of a story to follow instead of the vision of true love she is offered is endorsed in the Old Woman's account as the right choice. Thus, while it corroborates Gillian Perholt's exposition of women trapped within narratives that hinder them, 'The Story of the Eldest Princess' also displays the equally unsatisfactory alternative of not having or being outside the story. This Gillian believes to be her own case, since she is a woman in her fifties whose children are adults and whose husband has deserted her for his mistress. She is, in the modern sense of the word, 'redundant', though when the word occurs to her it is in the context of Milton's gorgeous serpent who tempts Eve in the garden of paradise.[10] The serpent's crested head and jewel-like eyes, its golden neck and spiralling coils that 'floated redundant' on the grass are in sharp contrast to Gillian's own body, which has lost its youthful allure and is consequently a reminder of her inevitable mortality. Significantly, Gillian's awareness of her declining body first transmutes into an image of her death during her lecture on Chaucer. As she analyses Griselda's reaction to her children's restoration, Gillian is petrified by the sight of 'a huge, female form' whose blank awfulness is the antithesis of Milton's magnificent and potent snake.[11] The connection between Gillian's lecture and the monstrous apparition is reinforced through her insistence on the terrible greyness of the figure and her description of Griselda and Hermione's wasted lives turned by their husbands' plotting into 'a grey void of forced inactivity'.[12]

The pointed contrast between the resplendent serpent that is the driving force of Milton's poem and the ageing body of the story-less Gillian is given an exuberantly comic twist in A. S. Byatt's 'Medusa's Ankles'.[13] Unlike the Medusa of Homeric myth, in this tale the protagonist Susannah is only partial temptress as she hopes that her self-absorbed hairdresser will disguise her thinning hair so that she will not appear ridiculous in a forthcoming television interview. The monstrous female form that so terrifies Gillian is here tempered to a depiction of Susannah's own greying and sag. Even the moral of the tale, announced at the outset as Susannah is enticed into the salon by a Matisse nude whose contours offer Milton-like 'reflections on flesh and its fall', has a flippant codicil as the hairdresser confides that he only bought it to complement his decor.[14] In a final hilarious parody of the Medusa myth, Susannah's piled coils of hair reflect in the salon mirrors as she listens to the hairdresser attempt to justify his decision to leave his ageing wife because of her swollen ankles, provoking her to destroy the 'great glass cage' and 'petrify' the staff with the available arsenal of jars, hairpins and 'hissing' trolleys.[15]

Gillian Perholt's exposition of women's entrapment within stories that are not of their making is the paradoxical theme of Fay Weldon's comic novel *The Life and Loves of a She Devil*.[16] Like Chaucer's 'Patient Griselda', its protagonist Ruth learns 'The Litany of the Good Wife', only to be abandoned by her husband Bobbo for his petite, blonde mistress Mary Fisher.[17] The fact that Mary is a writer of romantic fiction and hence responsible for perpetuating the myth that the pretty 'princess' will live happily ever after with her man is instrumental in Ruth's desire for revenge, since its promise is one Ruth is excluded from: as she later confesses, she could forgive Mary everything except her novels.[18] Like the brilliant and frustrated Zefir, Ruth's six feet two inches, dark hair, hooked nose and jutting jaw would be acceptable in a man, but as a woman they deny her the only power she can hope to wield in the planned suburban paradise of the ironically named Eden Grove where she and Bobbo live.[19] Recalling Psyche's sisters, Ruth's jealousy is sparked as much by her realisation that Mary's looks have made her fairy tale come true as by her own more difficult path.[20] Like Pamphile and Psyche before her, Ruth determines to transform herself in order to retain her man, though she does so in terms of the story that has hitherto excluded her. As she puts it at one point: 'since I cannot change the world, I will change myself'.[21] Ruth's answer to the question 'what do women most desire?' is consequently double-edged: she wants power and vengeance, yet in order to achieve this will submit herself to extensive and agonising surgery that will leave her, like Hans Christian Andersen's mermaid, feeling as if every step she takes is on knives.[22] The result, to borrow Finuala Dowling's phrase, is 'an uproarious feminist revenge comedy' which pursues the logic of the myth whereby beauty and fragility equal power to its bitter end.[23] As Ruth pointedly tells the doctor she employs to bring about her metamorphosis: 'I want to look up to men.'[24] She will turn herself into the she devil her husband pronounces her to be, but her most effective strategy for attaining her desire is to become the fairy tale cliché.[25]

In an essay entitled 'The Laugh of the Medusa', Hélène Cixous provides a theoretical underpinning for the argument that women are constrained within hostile tales that illuminates both Byatt and Weldon's fictions.[26] Woman, Cixous writes, functions within discourse as the other that enables man to be, with the result that it is drained as a signifier of any distinct meanings of its own. She cites as an example of this process the way the Medusa myth has become encoded within our culture so that it is now petrifying to both sexes, forcing men to master and women to believe they are monsters to be mastered. Cixous argues that it is essential to re-examine such mythopoeia, peeling away the constructions that have been laid upon its figures and considering them anew. This, she believes, in a formulation that evokes Gillian Perholt's lecture, will reveal that what has been perceived as women's monstrosity is often the insurgent force of their energies which patriachy has sought to contain. Significantly in terms of the comic modes employed in 'Medusa's Ankles' and *The Life and Loves of a She Devil*, Cixous suggests that laughter will play a vital role in this deconstructive task.

Critical reaction to Weldon's *The Life and Loves of a She Devil* has included hostile commentaries from reviewers who have interpreted the extremes of Ruth's behaviour as indicative of the excesses of 'women's lib'.[27] Such responses, as Dowling points out, fail to grasp the grim humour at the heart of the novel which, as Hélène Cixous's essay indicates, presents Ruth's savage self-tailoring as an indictment of the mechanisms that turn women into monsters rather than as a call to follow suit. By parodying the system in which, as Janet Todd has noted, it is female desirability, not desire, that gains women power, Weldon's novel exposes the deadly narratives women are subject to in order to lessen their hold.[28] As an early Weldon character cannily proclaims: 'myths are not true. Myths simply answer a need'.[29]

Cixous's essay similarly sheds light on a further aspect of the novel that has caused its readers problems. Despite initiating events through his desertion of Ruth, Bobbo's role in the narrative is increasingly subordinate to Ruth's jealousy and intense hatred of Mary. The various character transformations Ruth undergoes includes joining a feminist collective, derogatorily heralded in the text by the spelling 'Wimmin'.[30] Ruth's reason for enlisting in the commune is that she needs to lose three stone in order to begin her programme of cosmetic surgery and calculates, correctly, that the regime of physical labour and health food will enable her to achieve this. Before she leaves the collective, Ruth strips naked in order to survey for the last time the body she will now relinquish to the surgeon's scalpel. One of the women sees and admires her strong, capable body and Ruth is momentarily tempted to align herself with the commune's alternative mirroring. Her decision to reject their offer and remake herself in the image that will guarantee success is the logical consequence of a system that has taught women self-loathing. As Cixous argues, the power of the Medusa as she is currently invested is not only that she offers a rallying point for men's fears, but that she mobilises women against themselves.[31]

Ann Marie Hebert, in an article on Weldon's fiction, offers a further illuminating explanation for the strategy Ruth adopts.[32] Drawing on John Austen's notion of 'performative utterance', Hebert argues that scripts can be prescriptive as well as descriptive when they carry the weight of the dominant ideology with them.[33] According to this theory, Ruth's decision to remodel herself derives from her internalising the scripts that venerate a certain type of female beauty. As Mrs Black, wife of one of the doctors responsible for Ruth's transformation realises, what Ruth has accomplished in her metamorphosis is 'an impossible male fantasy made flesh'.[34] The power of such narratives is highlighted in the novel through the numerous allusions to their mythical, fairy tale and other widely known inscriptions. These include the myths of Pygmalion, Venus and Lilith, as well as a sequence of comic references to Mary Shelley's *Frankenstein* such as Mrs Black's fear that Ruth will be a female version of the popularised cinema image complete 'with the plates of her scalp pinned together with iron bolts', the escape of the polar bear borrowed by Mrs Black to support her charitable appeal, and the electrical storms that threaten and then stimulate Ruth at crucial moments of her surgery.[35] These allusions reinforce the weight of the scripts that drive Ruth's actions, and provide the necessary conditions for comedy. As Henri Bergson demonstrates, laughter occurs when something different from what we have anticipated happens, a situation the well-known trajectories of myth and fairy tale enable Weldon to supply.[36]

In a more recent Weldon novel, *The Cloning of Joanna May*, the impact of her husband's performative pronouncements on Joanna are explicitly signalled in the text.[37] Discovered by Joanna to be having an affair with his secretary, Carl May counters his wife's accusations with a series of self-justifications that draw on the full weight of the prevailing orthodoxy to annihilate her:

> Because I am Lord of the Dance, he says, and I am man and you are only woman, and I am something indeed and you are nothing at all ... .
>
> I am so something, she wept, I am, I am ... but already she felt herself vanishing.[38]

Like Ruth and Gillian Perholt, Joanna's 'redundancy' as an abandoned and childless woman is exacerbated by her physique, a theme humorously introduced at the beginning of the narrative as Joanna battles her ageing reflection with moisturisers and make-up.[39] This coupling of the themes of subjectivity and appearance is underscored in the novel through the story of the woman in Holloway gaol who plucks out her eye, which gives rise to a sequence of disquisitions on the relation between 'eye' and 'I'.[40]

Although A. S. Byatt's 'The Djinn in the Nightingale's Eye' is not
in the same comic register as Weldon's more schematic fiction, its protagonist is not exempt from the narratives that legislate for women
despite her superior knowledge, as Gillian's decision to use one of the
wishes the djinn grants her to rejuvenate her body demonstrates.[41]
Gillian's sense of release when she first receives her husband's fax
informing her that he intends to leave echoes Ruth's feelings of newly
unleashed power as she embarks on her devilish campaign. That the
djinn incarnates Gillian's emancipation is explicitly signalled, as his
jocular uncramping in her hotel bathroom after a century and a half of
captivity reiterates her description of herself as 'a gas confined in a
bottle, that found an opening, and rushed out.'[42] Despite its more
subtle humour, therefore, Gillian's tale offers an equally witty parody
of women's containment within an extensive tradition of prescribing
stories.

This use of parody to expose the mechanisms of narration can be
further explained with reference to Mikhail Bakhtin's theory of the
'double-voice' that inheres in particularly mocking or ironic
discourse.[43] For Bakhtin, consciousness is a product of the incessant
dialogue between our internal experience of the world and the shaping of that experience in language. Recalling Ruth's metamorphosis to
fit the prevailing story, Bakhtin argues that a sense of self can only
occur in language, our use of which is predetermined by the dominant
ideology of the society in which we live. This situation, Bakhtin suggests, inevitably results in a double-voice, since there is a split between
those utterances which accord with the dictates of our community and
which are consequently official, and those which it censors or omits.
Significantly, in terms of the strategy Ruth adopts, Bakhtin stresses
that this official discourse encompasses both our inner and external
speech acts, and that even those which the dominant order excludes
are at least partly governed by its rule. Equally significantly, especially
when considering the extra-linguistic elements of Weldon and Byatt's
tales such as the figure of Gillian Perholt's djinn, Bakhtin also maintains that these unofficial cognitions cannot be fully expressed within
the language prescribed by the ruling regime, though he does believe
such perceptions often constitute a lively counter-force, exposing contradictions within its legislation that cumulatively have the power to
challenge its control.

Bakhtin's notion of a 'double-voice' is also contained in his theory
of the 'dialogic'. For Bakhtin, each speech act is a response to all previous relevant utterances and is shaped by the responses it in turn

anticipates. Bakhtin contends that this double-orientation is positive, since it blocks any endeavours by the presiding hegemony to monologise meaning. As Gillian Perholt's witty unravellings of the etymologies of 'redundant', 'hag' and 'prestigious' illustrate, a word answers forwards as well as backwards and can always be reaccentuated.[44] Bakhtin develops the idea of the dialogic to embrace his view of self, which, he contends, is formed in an ongoing polemic with the voices that initially determine it. Our early, inevitably mimetic internalisation of these authoritative pronouncements subsequently leads to a double-voice, as we gradually realise their errors and re-evaluate them. This process of achieving what Bakhtin describes as active, independent and responsible speech involves the classic comic components of contradiction, parody and irony, and he suggests that the laughter these discourses produce comprises an important source for new creation.

For Bakhtin, there is a centripetal force at work within language which serves to centralise and unify meaning. He argues that this force is necessary in creating a shared basis for communication, though the danger is that it can be co-opted by a dominant power group and used to impose their version of the truth. Pulling against this force, however, Bakhtin suggests that there is also a centrifugal pressure, which disrupts any homogenising procedure and ensures that ideology remains open to different views. Bakhtin contends that this centrifugal dynamic is behind what he terms 'heteroglossia' or the presence of multiple narratives, a process that enables the mapping of discourses as their contours are outlined in relation to each other, and which thus relativises any claim to a monopoly. This notion can be fruitfully applied to the numerous mythical and other allusions that are woven into the fabric of Weldon's *The Life and Loves of a She Devil* and Byatt's 'The Djinn in the Nightingale's Eye'.

Bakhtin's analysis of the phenomenon of carnival is similarly instructive when considering Weldon and Byatt's fictions. Bakhtin focuses on the role of carnival in the Middle Ages, and notably its double movement as it simultaneously celebrates and ridicules, crowns and dethrones. Of particular significance for *The Life and Loves of a She Devil*, he examines the often grotesque comedy of the body that carnival includes, suggesting that its inflated role is symptomatic of the fact that it represents the body of the people rather than an individual per se. In this light, Ruth's excessive surgery can be viewed as a parable of the female body within the jurisdiction of romance fiction: the preposterous six inch 'tucks' she has taken in her legs parodying the monstrous mouldings women undergo to fit themselves to its prescribing myth.[45] Critiques of Bakhtin's work on carnival have noted its function as cathartic release for those energies which the prevailing order cannot contain, an ultimately conservative mechanism that is arguably challenged in *The Life and Loves of a She Devil* through its unsatisfactory climax: not only is Mary dead and Bobbo reduced to the position of confused servant, but Ruth's triumph has a distinctly hollow ring.[46] The effect, as Hebert has noted, is an overwhelming sense of disease: there will be no return to rule at the end of the she devil's carnival but neither has misrule won any significant victories.[47] Patriarchy's fairy tale may well have been discredited by Ruth's exorbitant campaign, but Weldon is too shrewd a novelist to advocate any single solution in its place.

Sigmund Freud's work on jokes provides a further illuminating perspective from which to read Byatt and Weldon's narratives.[48] Freud studies jokes in the context of the way individual desire is subjugated according to the dictates of the social order, a process that involves the repression of whatever that order does not allow into the unconscious. Like Cixous and Bakhtin, Freud is interested in how this order is reconstituted in the individual, and he suggests that the importance of jokes lies in their ability to circumvent the internalised inhibitions necessary for the individual to conform. Jokes, Freud writes, function to pleasurably satisfy desires that are outlawed by the social code, through conceptual and verbal arrangements which escape the mechanisms of self-government. This 'joke-work', Freud goes on, is crucial in preventing the scrutiny of our internal censors, and he argues that this is especially significant for those jokes which stem from dissatisfaction with the dominant order.[49] Authority, he writes, is protected as much by our own inhibitions as by any external measures it constructs, and the joke-work creates a 'façade' that allows the expression of forbidden dissent. In this light, it is tempting to interpret Weldon's fiction as an exposition of women's internalisation of the social code played out to its bitter end. By placing Ruth within the precepts of the legislating story, the narrative side-steps critical judgement long enough to cast its own luring spell. The extraordinary metamorphoses that occur in both Weldon and Byatt's stories can equally be seen as lulling devices which evade condemnation. Freud argues that the laughter a joke produces acts to stave off reproof, since it creates a disposition in which it is difficult for the censor to operate. Evoking Bakhtin's notion of a double-voice, Freud contends that the dual propensity of jokes to produce pleasure by impeding castigation is made possible by the ambiguity of language itself.[50]

For Freud, a joke's capacity to circumvent internal inhibitions returns us to the freedoms of early childhood before the intervention of social law. He suggests that through their disguises jokes reopen the arena of play in which language can be reviewed and reinvested.[51] As was discussed in the previous section, this is an idea that has been developed by a number of contemporary theorists, including Julia Kristeva for whom the return to a pre-verbal domain offers a unique opportunity to recast our relation to the social contract.[52]

The fact that jokes are told to another person is, for Freud, one of their essential characteristics. He argues that since the pleasure the joke produces occurs most fully in the hearer, it can shatter respect for institutions and truths in which they may have believed by circumventing their system of internal regulations, thus increasing the joke's subversive potential. Freud's analysis here can be applied to the disease Hebert has identified at the conclusion to *The Life and Loves of a She Devil*, indicating that the onus for responding to the final outcome rests with the text's recipient.[53]

Freud's argument that it is impossible for us to laugh if we empathise with the object of the joke offers a further explanation for the format Weldon adopts, since the numerous metamorphoses Ruth undergoes – from her initial guise as suburban housewife, via her roles as successful entrepreneur, housekeeper and masochistic sexual partner to Judge Bissop, to her final apparition as Mary – prevent our close involvement. Similarly, while the repeated insertions of Ruth's stringent 'I' into the otherwise third-person narration are important in endorsing her newly-discovered power as she devil, the changes of point of view impede our investment in her as a character.[54] This switching relativises Ruth's claims as well as those of the narrator and prevents any single perspective from dominating the text. Even Ruths's first-person confessions are frequently undercut by statements which qualify or discredit her meaning, as in her ambiguous reply to the doctors that what she wants is to look up to men. Earlier in the novel she attempts to count her blessings: 'it is a good life. Bobbo tells me so. He comes home less often, so does not say so as often as he did'.[55] Such utterances reiterate Bakhtin's notion of a double-voice and reveal the contours of the different discourses that motivate Ruth. By juxtaposing them Weldon is able to disclose the slippages and contradictions between the different constituents of the feminine script, with the result that we begin to question both its construction and its hegemony. Whether or not such indirect methods circumvent the censor that oversees the internal legislation of this script, Weldon's tactics avoid the danger of assimilation contained in a head-on collision by adopting what Roland Barthes has termed a more 'eccentric' form of subversion.[56] As Barthes argues, laughter is a primary weapon in such a strategy.

For Freud, it is crucial if the joke is to work for any allusions it involves to be immediately obvious. This explains the occasionally laboured references in *The Life and Loves of a She Devil*, such as those to the she devil as the new Christ.[57] Freud suggests that an important technique in joke-telling is the heightening of tension in order to enhance the pleasures of release, an observation that sheds light on the careful, step-by-step concoction of Ruth's demonic campaign, even though the final outcome in Weldon's case is an increase of frustration rather than cathartic laughter. Surprise is another common component of jokes identified by Freud, an ingredient paradoxically provided in *The Life and Loves of a She Devil* by Ruth's determination to pursue her vendetta to its bitter end.[58] Freud's account of the joke-work's overriding of internal censorship can similarly be compared to the various means Weldon adopts to prevent us from abandoning her narrative. These include its furious pace, its subdivision into short chapters and paragraphs, and the easy prose-style liberally seasoned with phrases that have a distinctly catchy ring.[59] All of these elements function to rush us headlong through the text, so that we have little time to pause and reflect. On its own, break-neck speed can have the adverse effect of alienating us from a tale, a problem circumvented here by the host of detailed and comic touches Weldon includes, such as Ruth's admission that being a she devil is exhausting.[60] These tactics, Freud stresses, increase our attention while arresting the regulatory mechanisms that would prohibit the joke. Freud ends his investigation into jokes with a short essay in which he highlights disguise, caricature, exaggeration and parody as among the most important components of comedy.[61] He contends that of these exaggeration is the most productive, since it causes a superfluity of energy as we follow a character which can be released as laughter. This suggests why Ruth's exorbitant efforts to exact her revenge are funny in a way that other, more modest love-vendettas – such as the story of the foresaken fiancée in Stella Duffy's novel *Singling the Couples* – are not.[62]

Freud's analysis of jokes nevertheless highlights a number of problems with Weldon's text. As has been argued, by having Ruth pursue her programme to its shocking climax and by disclosing the pathetic figures of Mary, dying alone of cancer, and Bobbo scared and confused in prison, Weldon stalls the laugh we might otherwise have had. While the unease we feel at the novel's conclusion may well prompt our own rebellious warfare, it will be an offensive deprived of laughter's ability to disarm the commanding scripts. As Ruth expresses it so pertinently in the last line of the narrative, she is a comic turn that has turned serious. Despite its swift pace, and the revelation of some of patriarchy's more monstrous and absurd precepts, there are discrepancies in the narrative that cannot be explained as transgressively expository. While it is both funny and a devastating critique of male power that Bobbo wants Mary to be his sexy mistress *and* his mothering wife, Ruth's contradictory assertions that all women are she devils under the skin and that Mary will win because she is a woman, not a she devil, are more difficult to square with a subversive feminist campaign.[63] Perhaps, as Jaye Berman argues, we must be careful not to idealise women's humour, which may well be a tactic for coping rather than a rallying call to arms.[64]

Freud's work on jokes also throws light on Byatt's 'The Djinn in the Nightingale's Eye', where the extraordinary figure of the djinn can be productively considered in the context of Freud's remarks on arrangements of disguise which inhibit prohibition, and Gillian's first sighting of the djinn's enormous, yellowing toenails illustrates Freud's emphasis on exaggeration as a primary comic tool. It is Freud's investigation into dreams, however, the procedures and purposes of which he sees as closely comparable to jokes, that is most instructive when analysing Byatt's text. Freud contends that the task of the dream-work, like the joke-work, is to prevent the operation of self-censorship. He suggests that dreams achieve this through transformations which camouflage the true nature of their motivating desire by turning them into images that are acceptable to the social order. For Freud, the movement of dreams is from the optative to the present indicative, transposing the wish of 'if only' into an 'hallucinatory representation' of 'it is'.[65] Whereas jokes are an extended form of play, dreams are endeavours to fulfill our forbidden desires. This proclivity can be seen in Ruth's manifesto of hate against Mary Fisher as she uses her fantastical stock market and surgical successes to turn herself into her rival. It more exactly fits the contours of Byatt's novella, as Gillian's desires for a rejuvenated body and for the djinn to love her magically come true. The second purpose of jokes – to return us to the arena of childhood plenitude before socialisation is accomplished – is similarly effected by dreams, which, Freud contends, involve similar 'plunges' into the anarchic and desiring unconscious. One way of reading the djinn in Byatt's text, with his childlike curiosity, playfulness and capacity for wonder exemplified in his transportation of the miniature tennis star Boris Becker from the television screen into Gillian's hotel bedroom, is as a manifestation of the unconscious. The longevity of the djinn also accords with Freud's description of the unconscious as 'the ancient dwelling-place' of our ability to play with words.[66]

Although Freud argues that dreams, like jokes, employ devices which ward off censorship, such as the representation of an object by its opposite and the use of nonsense, he nevertheless perceives differences in the tactics they adopt. In dreams, for instance, he suggests that disguise is most often accomplished through displacement or the selection of images which, while they have a relation to the motivating idea, are sufficiently distinct from it to escape condemnation. These include diversionary or indirect representations but most particularly the replacement of an element that would be objectionable to sanctioned thinking with one which, while alluding to the originating impetus, is not. This explanation presents an interesting commentary on the metamorphoses which are a pre-eminent feature of both *The Life and Loves of a She Devil* and 'The Djinn in the Nightingale's Eye', since whereas Ruth's incarnations are realistically depicted down to precise details of her surgery, Gillian's are entrancingly unreal.

For Freud, the difference between jokes and dreams also hinges on the fact that while jokes are intended to communicate to an audience, dreams concern the individual. This distinction points to a further contrast between the two fictions, since where Weldon's she devil acts as a cipher for the joke, Byatt's narrative explores a personalised dilemma. While Weldon's bequest of stalled laughter incites our own questioning and revolt, Gillian – djilyan's – incarnation of her djinn enables her to recover a self-image she is happy with and retain her childish faith in the power of art. In this sense, it may be Weldon's unresolved and simpler fiction that is the more radical of the two.

In Apuleius' *The Golden Ass*, Lucius' metamorphosis into an ass is presented as the manipulation of a blind and cruel Fate from which only his prayers to Isis, 'mother of the universe, mistress of all the elements ... representing in one shape all gods and goddesses', can release him.[67] In Weldon's *The Life and Loves of a She Devil*, Ruth endeavours to control her fate by attempting to succeed where Lucifer failed. Though she realises through her successive transformations the goal she has set herself, the novel closes on the hollowness of her achievement. While Ruth obtains beauty, wealth, Mary Fisher's tower home, power over men and the devotion of her husband – she even writes a plausible romance of the kind that so monstrously legislates for women – we are left in no doubt of her ultimate dissatisfaction.[68] She may hold back the waves by paying a team of construction engineers to alter the configuration of the harbour in which Mary's tower is set, neuter her dobermans and tame her garden with artificial copses, but these can provide only temporary and plagiarised triumphs and will do nothing to alter patriarchy's inexorable course.

The hideous apparition Gillian sees during her conference lecture is the petrifying figure of her death.[69] Though her desire parallels Ruth's as she asks for a more agreeable body and for the djinn to love her, unlike Weldon's protagonist she is aware that any wishes granted her will be fleeting.[70] Like the myth of Gilgamesh, in which his impossible search for the restoration of youth is brought to an end by a serpent, Gillian argues that tales are vital in preventing our denial of mortality.[71] Her decision to give her third wish to the djinn indicates both her acceptance of this and her faith in the power he does represent: that of art, through which human beings may briefly transcend their fate. The rediscovery of this power enables Gillian to transmute her ghastly apparition into the magic conjuring of the djinn. This capacity, already signalled in the narrative through her reaction to Milton's snake, is linked to her figuration of the djinn in an extension of the serpentine imagery, culminating in the description of the djinn's temptingly coiled sex.[72] Releasing her djinn is the means of safeguarding its metamorphosing potential, a transference that is encapsulated in the glass paperweights the djinn gives Gillian.[73] The first of these paperweights the djinn himself heralds as 'full of forever possibilities' and the antithesis to her deathly Medusa, since in contrast to the awful greyness of the earlier image the paperweight is an exuberant medley of serpentine colours that will remain unfaded inside the glass.[74] The second of the gifts endorses the first, since the new paperweights perfectly preserve the flower and serpent that symbolise Gilgamesh's failed quest, and are presented to Gillian some years after she has liberated the djinn. While a happy-ever-after ending can only take place in art, the novella concludes (unlike Weldon's) with an accent on Gillian's present happiness, since she has transformed the negative of her 'floating redundant' into the ability she had as a child to reincarnate herself through dreams and stories.[75]

Gillian's faith in stories – the echo of Perrault in Perholt is hardly incidental – recalls Hélène Cixous's view of the transformative potential of women's mythopoeia in her essay on the Medusa.[76] The tales Gillian hears and relates during the course of the narrative not only indicate her personal release from the 'stopp[er]ed energies' that typically constitute women's situation, but also respond, in Bakhtin's terms, to a vital history of women raconteurs.[77] In a more positive sense than the rescriptings of Weldon's she devil – and it is not insignificant that the main mythical references in *The Life and Loves of a She Devil* are ones of creative *failure* – Gillian's story is also a fore-telling.[78] Unlike women tellers of the past, whose fictions, as Gillian's colleague Orhan points out, were created from positions of powerlessness, Gillian is not redundant as a narratologist but 'on the contrary, in demand everywhere'.[79] As she is herself aware, her position is unprecedented, and may denote a future in which women will tell their tales from a standpoint of equal power. While Weldon's comedy exposes the monstrosity of the patriarchal Medusa, Byatt's more measured narration looks back to a tradition in which women's energies as exhibited in their myth-making were highly prized, as well as forwards to an epoch in which women's desire will contribute to metamorphosing the shared coil of mortality through the telling of their own potent splendour.[80]

3
Re-Creation in Other Love
Myth-Breaking and Myth-Making in Christine Crow's *Miss X or the Wolf Woman* and Hélène Cixous's *The Book of Promethea*

Sometimes I feel I know things but I cannot prove that I know them
or that what I know is true and when I doubt my knowledge it dis-
integrates into a senseless jumble of possibilities, a puzzle that will
not be reassembled, the spider web in which I live, immobile, and
truth paralysed.

> Timberlake Wertenbaker, 'The Love of the Nightingale'[1]

We *are* the stories we tell.

> Christine Crow, *Miss X or the Wolf Woman*[2]

Other-Love is writing's first name.

> Hélène Cixous, 'Sorties'[3]

In Timberlake Wertenbaker's play 'The Love of the Nightingale', the
myth of Philomela, raped by her brother-in-law Tereus and then pre-
vented from revealing what has happened by the violent removal of
her tongue, is restaged to depict the difficulties but also the necessity
of endeavouring to tell the truth. In Ovid's version of the myth,
Philomela finally communicates her story by weaving her experience
into an intricate cloth which her sister deciphers.[4] The obstacles to
speech figured in the mythical Philomela's mutilation are compounded

51

in Wertenbaker's play by a recognition of the inadequacies of language itself. As the female chorus argues, words can only grope towards answers when confronted with such brutalities as the eagle's daily devouring of Prometheus' liver or the rape of young girls in city car parks. Yet despite the problems, what Wertenbaker's reworking eluci- dates is that if the questions remain unasked then the future is lost, as inexorably as the mythical Tereus' son Itys – explicitly identified by the chorus as the future – is murdered and eaten by his father as punishment for his crime. In the play, the questions have been silenced for the sake of order. As Philomel's sister Procne says to her husband: 'I obeyed all the rules'.[5] Adherence to the rules, coupled with the apparent impossibility of determining alternative paths, is equally shown to be Tereus' predicament, since he has 'loved' Philomel according to the codes of violence and domination he has been taught. Wertenbaker's drama ends, like Ovid's tale, with the metamorphosis of all three characters into birds, a mythic allusion that here signals the possibility of hope since it prompts the still living Itys to ask a question.[6]

In Christine Crow's *Miss X or the Wolf Woman*, the difficulties of speaking are compounded by the fact that the tongue in our mouth may not be our own.[7] The text encompasses many of the classical, biblical, literary and even psychoanalytic myths that have constituted Western culture, unravelling and representing these to demonstrate the ways they obliterate or falsely report women's experience. Thus the myth of Danae's impregnation by Zeus as a golden shower and its reiteration in the biblical Mary's 'heavenly insemination' are shown through interjection and the setting in new contexts to derive from men's fear of women's bodies.[8] One of the central myths in the novel is that of the ancient Egyptian goddess Isis, who searches the world for the pieces of her brother-husband Osiris' dismembered body. According to Plutarch, Isis retrieves all but Osiris' phallus which has been eaten by a Nile crab, and magically reassembles the body despite the missing piece.[9] The myth is evoked in the structural layout of Crow's narrative which is divided into fourteen 'pieces', as well as the treasure hunt the protagonist Mary Wolfe devises as a schoolgirl and which continues to reverberate in her ongoing quest for identity.[10] The missing 'piece' in the novel – wittily signalled in the name of Mary's religious studies teacher Miss *Prick* – appropriately turns out to be Monique Wittig's text *The Lesbian Body*.[11] The crucial premiss of psychoanalytic theory that perceives woman as lacking in relation to the phallus is therefore revealed to be erroneous, since, as Mary discovers, women are perfectly able to love each other without it.[12] Woman's relegation to the role of Other depends on false notions of inferiority as well as women's acquiescence.[13] The novel's resurrection of the mother-goddess Isis as a potent alternative to the later myth of Oedipus offers her search and magical recreation as clues for the reader to follow in the composition of her own story. The only castration women need fear, the refiguring implies, is Philomela's loss of speech. Crow's novel begins while Mary is still at school, where her impressionable nature and hunger for knowledge are fed by the literary preferences of her headmistress, Miss X. These are exclusively male and almost exclusively French, and skew Mary's development to the extent that she misrecognises her feelings for Miss X on two counts: she comes to believe she is in love with Miss X because this is what Miss X desires, while failing to understand her homosexuality. Thus the novel also deconstructs the lesbian 'coming-out' story, endorsing the need for labels while at the same time exposing the distortions they impose.[14] Had Mary not been subject to Miss X's pronouncements she might have identified herself as a lesbian and been able to assume her emotions, despite her ultimately rejecting such procedures as destructive of the multifaceted nature of individuality.[15]

   In both Timberlake Wertenbaker's reworking of the myth of Philomela and *Miss X or the Wolf Woman*, the contradictory role of language in thwarting understanding while providing the essential means of communication is highlighted in the arena of love. Tereus laments the fact that he has not been taught how to love while Mary Wolfe's feelings are subsumed by Miss X's belief that Mary is in love with her.[16] As the mature Mary comes to realise, 'the fatal little spondee "I love you"' generates its own reality.[17] Such distortions are compounded in the novel by Miss X's own mythical, literary and biblical assumptions which she requires Mary to share. Her frequent admonitions to Mary to record what she says in her notebook recur as a parenthetical refrain that underscores her dictatorship. The schoolgirl Mary cannot but obey, her own development atrophied to the point that she forsakes even her name to play lamb to her lover's wolf.[18] Only through the alternative input of her Oxford tutor and Annabel is Mary able to release herself from Miss X's castrating mythology. In this, Crow's protagonist evolves beyond the doomed Ruth of Fay Weldon's *The Life and Loves of a She Devil* considered in the preceding chapter.

   Mary's chief defence against Miss X is to write. By inscribing her own story, she is able like Philomela to identify her executioner, and

paradoxically becomes the 'executioner' of Miss X by defying her prohibition and 'outing' her.[19] As in 'The Love of the Nightingale', the
reversal is not a straightforward one, however, since woven into the
intricate cloth of Mary's narration are the strands of Miss X's own
tragic tale. Born at a time when an admission of homosexuality would
have cost her standing, Miss X's strategy has been to bind herself like
Odysseus to the mast of the ship of state in order to prevent herself
from responding to the sirens' calls. A number of objects associated
with Miss X play a prominent role in Mary's telling of her story, such as
the stone paperweight nicknamed 'Petrus Borel' and the toy sheep and
goat she and Miss X exchange. These appear in a variety of lights, the
sheep and goat for instance figuring both love's tryst and the over-
throwal of its tyrannies in the sacrifice Mary conducts. While this
releases Mary from the mythic paradigm that has hindered her, the ritual is more than an act of destruction: it also presents the possibility of
recreation, a myth-making as well as a myth-breaking. Miss X follows
her hypocritical dismissal of a colleague for a lesbian affair with a pupil
with a reading during school assembly of the passage in Leviticus in
which a scapegoat is selected and sent into the wilderness.[20] Mary's
own act of sacrifice indicates her recognition of the ubiquity of
the myth apotheosised in Western culture in Christ's crucifixion, her
switching of roles from that of scapegoat to sacrificer, and above all her
acknowledgement of her capacity to occupy both positions.[21] The
stone paperweight, retrieved by Mary from the dustbin of the dead
Miss X, is similarly both a lifeless object and a catalyst to empowering
discoveries. Like myth, it is a source of potent revelations Mary only
gradually comes to see.[22] It is this paradoxical nature that is signalled by
the letter X, capitalised throughout the text as a mark of the silencing
of women's love but also an indication of language's potential to disclose the not-yet-known.[23] Challenging Annabel's feminist expedient of
usurping 'the plane of patriarchy' since this is shown to crash, the X signifies the rejection of the annihilating either/or in favour of connection.[24] The X thus heralds the process of 'creative change and refleXive,
self-eXculpating liberation from the petrified myths of enmity, domi-
nance and self-fearing homophobic aggression' that has been set in
motion in Mary's case '**by the self-devouring criss-X of WRITING**'.[25]
Mary's novel, as Nicki Hastie has noted, is consequently 'the coming
out story of writing itself', since its procedures offer a means of navigating the personal odyssey of understanding on which we are all necessarily embarked, while preserving our myths from the co-optive
monovision that has hereto hampered Western culture.[26]

In a school essay, Mary grandly announces the purpose of myth as a way to 'transcend the merely personal' and 'elevate us on its golden horns to the heights of Universal Man'.[27] The irony of her designated destination, coupled with the fact that the essay is written for Miss *Twee*, signals that there are problems with her proclamation: what the writing of her story subsequently reveals is precisely myth's ability to correlate paradigms that transcend the self with the personal quest for meaning.[28] Thus from the myth-breaking figured in the fourteen pieces of Osiris' body comes the possibility of creation. While the woman writer – also denoted by the X – may dispense with the universally imposed phallus, what she does require is Isis' magical power of resewing whereby she resurrects the potency of the myth.[29] Rejecting the male bias of psychoanalysis, Mary's self-prescribed 'cure' is thus the metamorphic potential of the imagination, discovered through her writing and represented in her transposition from Miss X's 'lamb' to the assumption of her own Wo(o)lf(e)ian surname.[30] In contradistinction to Miss X's warnings against the dangers of her imagination, Mary now realises that she did not have nearly enough. What Mary terms 'the self-devouring criss-X' of writing is its role in furthering this metamorphic potential, shifting the writer from one position to the other and preventing her final, stultifying identification with either/or.[31] Thus the X is ultimately imagination itself, 'queen of moral faculties', enabling us to metamorphose into all possible positions so that identity becomes a matter of choice, and love no longer depends on subjection but on recognising the other as a 'living anomaly' like ourselves.[32]

In her essay 'Sorties', Hélène Cixous reiterates the vital necessity of myth-making as well as myth-breaking expounded in Christine Crow's novel.[33] The myths we have inherited, Cixous stresses, record phallocentrism and its schema of opposition and concomitant destruction. Like Crow, Cixous sees writing as an arena in which an alternative might be produced, since the multiple and heterogeneous possibilities writing generates exceed phallocentrism's rule. Despite the immense obstacles to telling the truth and the ever-present dangers of co-option, Cixous delineates writing as a potentially boundless space in which the dominion of relational hierarchy and mono-meaning can be overturned. Echoing Crow's insistence that daring to imagine is the first step, Cixous similarly proposes that what becomes thinkable through this means has the potential to become real. For Cixous, love is the medium whereby such changes can occur, since love has the capacity to undo the deadly mechanism of the other's appropriation, freeing

both lovers to become autonomous and equal. Her work thus continues Mary Wolfe's odyssey of the self by contending that this other-
love is at once the crucial source of writing and what writing can
engender. For Cixous it is the other-who-is-loved who figures the
unknown Mary has above all located in myth, challenging our pre-
conceptions and opening us to new visions which have then to be
inscribed. This opening to/by the other does not, however, preclude
self-knowledge, which Cixous identifies as a necessary prerequisite to
equality, since without it one would merely repeat the paradigm and
become the object of the other's desire. Cixous believes that such a
relation subverts the current hegemony, and suggests a new mode of
perception and expression founded on mutual respect. Writing will be
essential in the institution of this alternative because of the way it too
works on the self, rescinding imposed demarcations and propelling the
self ceaselessly to exchange with others through its multiple, trans-
forming opportunities. While Cixous too is suspicious of the labels
that are the restrictive products of the present regime, like Crow she
recognises the political importance of naming given the existing climate. She consequently opts to call the new approach 'feminine',
arguing that women's marginalisation makes it easier for women
to adopt and that the female body contains a capacity for otherness
that defies the universalising phallus. Instead of the author's seeking
through writing to res-erect his 'castrated' penis, feminine writing,
like Isis' sewing, works to preserve the other's mystery. The fetishisa-
tion of identity that has all but paralysed Western culture gives place,
as in Wertenbaker's drama, to interrogative recreations that promise a
different future.

Cixous's notion of a feminine writing grounded in love for the
other is enacted in her novel *The Book of Promethea*.[34] According to
Hesiod, Prometheus defies Zeus' prohibition against the gift of fire to
mortals by transporting it to earth in the slow-burning pith of a fennel
stalk.[35] In Cixous's reworking, the gift of fire symbolises the female
Promethea's love for the narrator as well as the positive conflagrations
her love inflames. Unlike the gift that leaves its recipient in debt,
Promethea obtains the narrator's love by 'giving herself bound-
lessly'.[36] The fire is the passion her love kindles in the narrator, which
begins by setting alight all her previous conceptions humorously
imaged in the descriptions of her former way of life. These range from
her 'well-ordered intellectual drawers' to the numerous personal items
she has used to keep others at a distance.[37] Although the narrator now
acknowledges her various constructions to have been 'no more than

hypothesis and illusion', they have nonetheless provided her with a means of anchoring herself in the world.[38] Ignited by love, she realises that she too must pass through the ring of fire and begin her life anew. This 'burning of her boats' is beneficial, since it opens her to the myriad new experiences the love relation sparks.[39] The fire is risk, the unknown, the possibility of metamorphosis, reigniting through the text in a CiXousian parallel to Christine Crow's finally untranslatable X.[40] Like the X, the fire in *The Book of Promethea* is also the blaze of creation, complicated here by the fact that it may engulf the narrator if she fails to give it her full attention.[41] Thus the fire is simultaneously the ignition and combustible material of writing, the flame of the present, its burning truth, which – unlike Moses' burning bush – can never be resurrected into the stasis of law, but only experienced in all the illuminating radiance of its momentary flash.

In an essay on *The Book of Promethea*, Emma Wilson takes issue with those critics who have failed to engage with the text as a lesbian love story.[42] While Wilson is right to insist on a reading which encompasses the many powerful descriptions of women's love-making in the novel, to view it exclusively in this light is to misrepresent it. There are a number of places in the text where the narrator stresses the importance of identifying herself as a woman. The first of these occurs in the opening pages, with the narrator arguing that because of the present climate of 'gynocide' she has a duty to the variously 'veiled' women of the world to proclaim her sex.[43] This connects to the narrator's telling of her own life-story of narrowly surviving the holocaust, since the testimony of her existence brings with it traces of those who did not escape.[44] In this context, her writing becomes a Philomela-weaving of memories that would otherwise be obliterated. As Cixous suggests in 'Sorties', it is equally crucial to inscribe women's sex-specific experiences in writing, since she believes these present an alternative to the deadly mode of self/other relations currently ordained. This is achieved in *The Book of Promethea* in the recurring image of the positive maternal as well as in the various delineations of the writing arising from Promethea's woman's body: affirmations and ecstasies which 'breach...the hide of the old tongue's hard blare'.[45] At the same time, however, the narrator reiterates the desire of *Miss X* to be rid of all such labellings, as products of a phallocentric regime and ultimately destructive of the incessantly changing nature of the individual.

The problem confronting the narrator of *The Book of Promethea* is that of creating a writing capable of conveying the potent conflagrations enkindled by love. Just as the narrator has had to relinquish all her previous constructions in order to love, so she must resist using writing as a shield or allowing words to distort Promethea's blaze by imposing their own configurations. Her difficulties are variously portrayed in the text, contained, for example, in her doubts about her abilities as a writer and her fears that her words put to death rather than bring to life, as well as in the comical account of her struggle to convey 'the ...'.[46] Since *The Book* is to be *of Promethea*, the narrator must endeavour to find a way of representing Promethea that does not 'make her up' with words or appropriate her otherness for her own self-serving ends.[47] The narrator's decision to split her appearance in the text – figured by the indicators 'I' and 'H' – is a mark of her struggle to avoid the usual co-options of authorship.[48] The determination to render the 'truth' of Promethea involves the narrator in the adoption of new literary forms, such as the resolution to refrain from reworking the rough drafts of her notebooks or resorting to the customary order of a beginning, middle and end.[49] As in *Miss X*, these decisions have implications for the future reader: *The Book of Promethea* is to be given as a necklace which 'everyone can try on' and to which 'you can add all the things you would really like to receive'.[50] The absence of a chronology does not mean, however, that there is to be no progress through the writing: on the contrary, one of the book's possible titles, noted in the aptly named 'Notebook of Metamorphoses', is 'the book of changes'.[51] Thus, like *Miss X*, the narration highlights the positive nature of transposition, which the operations of writing can help to produce. A horse metaphor, for example, employed early on to describe the satisfied pasturings 'on symbolic fields' of the narrator's 'theories', turns in a dream into Promethea 'the great magical mare' and then signals the 'marvellous ride' writing gives her.[52] Writing, in this sense, is a means of defying castration, through the inscription of what has been sparked by love. The narrator's task is to facilitate these births, by inventing the means to deliver them 'wet and twitching, onto the paper'.[53]

The punishment Zeus devises for Prometheus' theft of fire is to have him chained to a pillar and for an eagle to tear out his liver.[54] Since the liver grows back overnight the torture is repeated daily. There are various echoes of this component of the myth in *The Book of Promethea*, such as the narrator's account of love's merciless arrow ripping into the lover's flesh.[55] Prometheus' agony is also evoked in the painful self-destructions the narrator must undergo in order to love, signalled in her plea to Promethea to 'be the eagle'.[56] The dismantling of oppositions between self and other can propel the narrator into the place of 'eagle', as is indicated in her description of her plunging into Promethea's breast in order to approach her 'heart'.[57] The cruelty of Zeus' penalty highlights the negative emotions love can induce, illustrated here in the narrator's desire to hurt Promethea for what she perceives to have been her wrong-doing.[58] This portrayal of the way love can turn into its opposite and release contrary feelings of hate and rage connects to its overarching depiction as a paradise which can be a torturous hell for the fallible human beings who inhabit it.[59] To maintain love's paradise – to love without its sliding into hate – requires the lovers' constant attention. Like Prometheus' torment, love must be recommenced daily.[60]

The difficulties of paradise are those of maintaining a love relationship in which self and other co-exist as equals.[61] The narrator must find a way of receiving Promethea's gift which is open to its blaze but which does not result in her own annihilation.[62] It is, as she stresses, 'a matter of delicate balance'.[63] Since we are different each day, this equilibrium must be constantly readjusted. Love is the necessary condition for this reinvention, since its flames fuel the desire incessantly to resume the work.

Despite the many parallels between *The Book of Promethea* and *Miss X or the Wolf Woman*, there are, nevertheless, a number of significant differences. For Mary Wolfe, writing is a means of releasing herself from the destructive bonds of love, while in *The Book of Promethea* it is love that sets the narrator free. *Miss X* is written from memory as the mature Mary looks back at what has happened, whereas the challenge of Promethea's narrator is to inscribe her present before memory distorts it.[64] This suggests a vital distinction in the perspectives of the two 'authors', since where for Mary writing is a means to ponder motivations and the conundrums of language, the narrator of *The Book of Promethea* insists: 'I am not writing: I am exposing myself to impressions as faithfully as I can.'[65] This points to a further discrepancy between the two texts: in *Miss X* the power of myth is to be reclaimed, while for *The Book of Promethea* it must be continually created afresh. As I argue below, this difference is an important one in contemporary women fiction writers' approach to myth.

The stone paperweight, whose nickname 'Petrus Borel' prompts the narrator of *Miss X* to a number of illuminating discoveries, only reveals a last, vital clue towards the end of her quest. Despite her study of French literature enforced by Miss X, Mary fails to notice that Petrus Borel is the other name of Champavert, a nineteenth-century French poet who periodically imagined himself to be a wolf.

Her realisation of the connection accompanies her rejection of her role as Miss X's 'lamb' and her assumption of herself as Mary Wolf(e). This is symbolised in her 'crying wolf', which is both her howling denouncement of the tyrannies of others and the proclamation of her 'own unique self-identity': her 'giv[ing] tongue at last'.[66] Her response to her Philomela-like 'castration' is not, however, a straight-forward adoption of prevailing rubrics, but the conducting of herself in a vocabulary which, while it borrows from and can be inspired by existing constructions, comprises her own 'feminist' reworkings. One of the threads of *Miss X* concerns the pervasive influence of Freud, whose case-study of a patient he labels 'the wolf man' is already over-turned in the novel's subtitle: *or the Wolf Woman*. Mary's alternative mythopoeia involves the exposure of the numerous biases and errors of Freud's prescriptions, as well as the extraordinary inscription of her-self as the 'great She-Wolf'.[67] This metamorphosis also signals her rejection of the either/or categories figured in the biblical distinction between the sheep and the goats that has been insisted upon through-out her schooling, and images her simultaneous acknowledgement that hunter and hunted are never opposites but facets of the self.[68] The transposition, effected in her writing, is thus finally an affirmation of the ongoing potency of myth, which can be dismembered and imagi-natively reassembled in the vital personal process of 'giving tongue'.

In an essay translated into English as 'Love of the Wolf', Hélène Cixous explores various connotations of the mythic animal, echoing its figuration in *Miss X or the Wolf Woman*.[69] The starting-point for Cixous's discussion is Marina Tsvetaeva's confession of her secret childhood passion for a Pushkin character she names 'the wolf'.[70] Tsvetaeva's love propels her towards this 'other' despite its extreme differences from herself and her consequent fear, since, as Cixous argues, when we love we admit the other inside us so that it becomes impossible to flee. This amalgam of love and fear, indicated in our attachment to what also threatens, offers, Cixous contends, a return to childhood – 'the age of myths' – the realm prior to the separation of our experience into the categories of good and evil.[71] For the child, Cixous suggests, the 'truth' of love is 'both-at-once', imaged in the tale of 'Little Red Riding Hood' in the beloved grandmother we take food to who is also the terrifying, devouring wolf.[72] Unlike the child who can experience 'both-at-once', the adult is subject to 'either/or': we see either our 'candy' grandmother or the ferocious wolf.[73] Either we believe in the danger, or else, as in Timberlake Wertenbaker's play, Little Red Riding Hood's questioning 'what big teeth you have,

grandmother' loses its force.[74] Cixous's insistence on the importance of such 'paleolithic' returns connects to the presentation of
Promethea's 'savagery' as a positive force for change in *The Book of
Promethea* as well as to Mary Wolfe's realisation that: 'only when
you've once more confused the word and the thing, can you ... start
to live and die in your own separate skin'.[75] For Tsvetaeva reading
Pushkin, love, Cixous argues, is not directed towards a person but
passes through the word she gives to one of his creations, the word
'wolf'. Like Mary Wolfe's 'X', this 'scintillating Signifier' is a 'magic
word', a 'beacon beam' in Tsvetaeva's construction of her own genealogy.[76] To write, Cixous suggests, we must return to this 'other' world
of love for the 'wolf'.[77] At the same time, the 'wolf', the 'X', indicates
the role of writing in readmitting us to this world, by bridging the
divisions that have been cut into our experience and by lighting our
(re)creations. Like 'Petrus Borel', they signal an array of possibilities
that eXceed the prevailing rules.[78] Writing, in this sense, is the god-
dess-worker of our miracles, our Isis-magician conjuring the means for
what we dare to say.

The return to childhood is variously indicated in *The Book of
Promethea*. In an echo of Cixous's delineation of the devouring wolf,
for example, there is an insistence on love's rekindling of primal
desires figured in the numerous images of cannibalism that are
employed to describe the lovers' relationship.[79] One of the narrator's
wishes for the book is that it should be 'a Children's book' for adults,
offering a means of re-entering:

> our first world, the new world, eternally new, resounding with ener-
> gies and sympathies; the wondering world filling us with wonder;
> the world a child again and again and again ... the world abound-
> ing ... in powerful and maternal gestures, in possible unions ... the
> world teeming with chances, large, full, patient, always there and
> ready to play with us.[80]

It is by re-accessing this mythical realm, in which our bodies communicate directly, that we can reinvent our relation to the world of
others.[81] Writing, which as Cixous argues in 'Sorties' is itself a body
function, is our aid in this process, since its rhythms and articulations
inscribe these experiences that are otherwise silenced. The narrator's
creation of *The Book of Promethea* challenges the erasures of cultural
authority, as in her struggle to present the configurations of their love
she endeavours to reconstitute 'the cord binding words to her body'.[82]

At one point in *The Book of Promethea*, the narrator confesses that the only stories she knows are love stories which end in tragedy.[83] She declares her intention to tell her own love story with Promethea which will be, on the contrary, a story of 'Luck'.[84] This does not mean that she will ignore the death that has terminated the stories she knows, but – like Gillian Perholt in A. S. Byatt's 'The Djinn in the Nightingale's Eye', discussed in the previous section – that she will write affirmatively despite – and even *because* of – its presence.[85] In 'Love of the Wolf', Cixous offers her own disquisition on 'crying wolf' in connection with the childhood game of being lost and found. Loss, she suggests, is the precursor to living, since it is what motivates us to create.[86] In *The Book of Promethea*, the narrator links this specifically to writing, which she describes as a means of covering over the abyss opened up by loss and death.[87] This underlies her determination to record the present, which can only ever be apprehended in terms of human mortality.[88] It is this endeavour not to lie that constitutes the only god the narrator will acknowledge.[89] What she regards as the 'divine spark in humans' is our capacity to 'live … in complete mortality as if all the labor, every work, constructions worthy of gods, were not destined to vanish behind crimson funeral curtains'.[90] It is this 'Promethean ambition' that she endeavours to write, the myth of the second paradise which is no longer that of the child, but the efforts of the adult for whom loss and death are the avowed conditions of existence.[91] It is consequently a paradise that must be continually remade, since the means of inhabiting it have to be reinvented daily.[92] This 'magic' writing can help to conjure, by proffering stories 'endowed with the power to put things back together and bring them back to life'.[93] This does not mean reinstituting Osiris' phallus as the universal marker of 'Truth', but rather, in the manner of Tsvetaeva's beacon 'wolf', Promethea's 'fire' or Mary's illuminating 'X', the creation of 'living phrases' that 'cast enough of a glow to light our separate ways'.[94] Love provides the ignition for this work, by offering paradigms of communication that enable us to transcend the existing scheme. Writing is our witness to this other-love, presenting a space in which we can assemble and record the god-like infinity of our recreations.[95]

4
Becoming Gods and Umbilical Wordbows
The New Hagiography of Michèle Roberts

We women, sexed according to our gender, lack a God to share, a word to share and to become. Defined as the often dark, even occult mother-substance of the word of men, we are in need of our *subject*, our *substantive*, our *word*, our *predicates*: our elementary sentence, our basic rhythm, our morphological identity, our generic incarnation, our genealogy.

Luce Irigaray, 'Divine Women'[1]

Do not be dismayed, daughters, at the number of things which you have to consider before setting out on this Divine journey.

St Teresa, *The Complete Works of Saint Teresa of Jesus*[2]

In Michèle Roberts's *Impossible Saints*, the central character Josephine is taken as a child to a festival at which she sees a fat lady attempting to walk across a wire she has hung between two parked wagons.[3] The fat lady is a ridiculous figure in her gaudy costume and the crowd for the most part ignore her, but Josephine is entranced as she watches the fat lady delicately launch herself into the dangerous space ahead, twirling her wand for balance. Josephine cries at the fat lady's daring to be more than herself as she progresses across the wire, and she realises, as she recalls the incident some thirty years later, that her own life by contrast has been circumscribed by fear and that her religious vocation is a lie. The terror the Church has induced her to feel is graphically illustrated, as Josephine remembers how a few hours after seeing the fat lady she watched the heretics sentenced to death by the Inquisition being tied to their stakes. The wood for the heretics' fires came from the wagons the fat lady used to secure her wire, and as the flames kindle it seems to Josephine that they consume her intrepid, pirouetting figure.

Josephine witnesses the heretics' plight from the vantage-point of her father's shoulders. The detail is significant and connects to an earlier point in the narrative where Josephine recites the Lord's Prayer in an effort to please her father. At the end of the first line Josephine stops, confused, for 'our father' is not 'in heaven' but in front of her, seated on a chair as ornate as the bishop's throne in church. Her father's angry frown as she pauses forces her to continue, and she hurries through the remainder of the lines she has learned by rote to receive her reward of a place on her father's knee. The link between God and Josephine's own father is carried forward through the text: it is underscored in the lives of the women saints that interleave Josephine's story and plays a major role in her decision to become a nun.[4] Caught by her father enacting an adolescent fantasy of the first night of marriage with her cousin Magdalena, Josephine is sent away to a convent to be educated. She internalises the pain of being separated from her family, believing that for her wickedness she will burn eternally in the flames of hell. The only escape she can foresee is to dedicate her life to God. Strikingly, the metaphor used to describe Josephine's sense that by entering the convent she can 'annihilate her evil self' images even the natural activity of her breathing as corrupt.

> To guard her soul from the waiting fiery pit she would have to spend her entire life in penance and mortification. It would be a kind of holding her breath, lest even by breathing she did something wicked. Damaged the air, stole goodness from it and gave back only poison.[5]

Josephine performs her convent duties as diligently as she has learned the 'Our Father' until the day her own father dies.

In an essay entitled 'Divine Women', Luce Irigaray offers an analysis of the predicament confronting women in relation to God that provides an illuminating frame from which to read Michèle Roberts's novel.[6] For Irigaray, our task as human beings is to become, by fulfilling the whole of ourselves and by refusing to allow to shrivel and die whatever has the potential to grow. Irigaray argues that in order to *become* we need a God, as we can only orient our finite selves in relation to an infinity which incarnates our goal of becoming; it is this divinity which ensures our freedom as autonomous and sovereign subjects. Irigaray contends that since we are sexual beings we can only become in relation to a similarly gendered divine: man, she suggests, is able to be in the world *because* God is male. As woman has no corresponding divinity she can neither establish her subjectivity nor achieve a goal of her own; the ideal other imposed on her is man and the most divine goal she can imagine is to become a man. Woman, Irigaray maintains, in a formulation that recalls Gillian Perholt's lecture on the 'stopp[er]ed energies' of women's lives in A. S. Byatt's 'The Djinn in the Nightingale's Eye', is consequently paralysed in her becoming as the term of the other since there is no figure for the perfection of *her* subjectivity. As a result, Irigaray believes that women are the weak, formless, insecure or aggressive supports of a system in which we function only as the idols, fetishes or symbols of men. She argues that if we are to escape this slavery we must do more than simply destroy the master: we need to establish a divine image of our own to glorify our becoming as complete and sexual beings. Like the fat lady launching herself across the wire, Irigaray stresses that women can only achieve this autonomy if we posit a God, place or path to inspire us forward.

Irigaray reasons that one of the problems women face is that we lack a space for self-contemplation in which we can limit our exposure to the defining gaze of the other. We need, she insists, a 'margin' in which we can repossess ourselves and establish our vision. Figured by a God in the feminine gender, such a space would guarantee woman's present and future, motivating individual women to become and to remain fully themselves.

After the death of her father, Josephine can no longer adhere to the restrictions of the convent and begins to dream of a different life. She tells Lucian, the priest responsible for hearing her confessions, that her twenty years as a nun have been governed by fear and dissembling. When he tries to reassure her she points out the inequality in their positions: he has freedom and authority whereas her role is to obey. Lucian had previously encouraged Josephine to write her 'Life' in order to avoid the scrutiny of the Inquisition, a task she had undertaken with zeal. She now realises that what she had considered her cleverness in fooling the Inspectors merely fulfilled their expectations of her: she has bowed and scraped and curried favour, using the prescribed gestures and words, like Ruth in Fay Weldon's *The Life and Loves of a She Devil*, to turn herself into the male Inspectors' epitome of what a woman should be. It is one of the many ironies of Roberts's novel that the submissive figure Josephine creates in her 'Life' is the one she will be remembered by.

As a girl Josephine reads to her mother from a store of books kept in a chest in her mother's room. The books are covered in different coloured silk cloths and Josephine is allowed to read any wrapped in blue. After her mother's death she finds the key to the chest and redis-covers the books, and although most of them are burned by her father a few are rescued by Magdalena and returned to Josephine during her stay at Magdalena's house. Josephine now realises that the texts her mother had kept hidden at the bottom of her chest are the treatises of an ancient religion banned by the Catholic Church. She reads her mother's annotations of the incomprehensible scripts and then dreams that she is drawn back inside the earth's body. This 'rebirth' relaunches her faith:

> Now she could see that the earth was alive, teeming with life, hold-ing everything in a continuous dance, it was a vast memory swarm-ing with past, present and future life, this was what God was, this profound understanding, in this untranslatable speech, that we were all made the same, part of each other, rocks and stones and trees and people all whirling about together living and dying and being transformed into each other and so reborn, and so, dying, held so lightly in that connectedness.[7]

In line with Church doctrine, Josephine has hitherto blamed herself for Christ's crucifixion. As a result of her dream she realises that she is not wicked but good, part of the vast goodness of creation it is her task to express. Her second 'Life' is consequently written in a very different way to her first, dictated by the rapture she now apprehends as God.

Josephine's rejection of the Catholic Father and the self-denying regimen of his Church initially leaves her with a sense of loss. In Iri-garay's terms, she has relinquished the impositions that have disabled her but has not yet found a form of her own. Josephine's search for an alternative is figured in the novel by her attempt to establish a new kind of house. During her stay at Magdalena's, Josephine revisits the cathedral she attended as a child: its darkness and calm, the strong smell of incense, the memory of organ music and singing transport her back to her mother's side. She perceives that while she can no longer worship a distant, punitive Father, she must preserve this inspiring, maternal aspect of the divine in her plans for a new foundation.

Through the image of Christ on the cross, through the Church's teaching and her detailed knowledge of the instruments of torture used by the Inquisition, Josephine learns to devalue and deny her body.[8] As a nun she renounces physical freedom, sex, and even the pleasure of good food. Under Magdalena's influence, Josephine gradually recovers this side of herself: she walks wherever she wishes, becomes a passionate gardener, makes love, and relishes preparing and eating delicious meals.[9] As with her relationship to her father, the physical deprivations Josephine struggles to undergo are elaborated in the 'lives' of the women saints that punctuate her story. In 'The Life of Saint Paula', for example, St Jerome's insistence that pain and evil enter the world through the medium of the body and that virginity and discipline offer women's only hope of salvation causes Paula's daughter to starve herself to death. Her triumph is a hollow one: 'the woman she'd been', we are told, 'had completely vanished'.[10] In 'The Life of Saint Marin', the monks' Rule teaches that the beauty of the world, like the beauty of women, is a trap constructed by the devil to lure them to hell.

For Irigaray, there is an irony in women's attempt to redeem ourselves through chastity and suffering since the body is what we have been traditionally allocated: woman is flesh, nature, earth, carnality, in contradistinction to man's intellect and spirit.[11] Recalling Josephine's vision of the continuity of life, Irigaray demonstrates the falsity of such a division which ignores the fact that we are all constituted from the same matter. She queries men's need to postulate their God as an inaccessible transcendence, asking why the divine cannot be realised in the here and now *through* the agency of the body.[12]

In a series of short essays collected under the title *Food, Sex and God*, Michèle Roberts sets out her own views on religion, many of which echo Irigaray's analysis.[13] Roberts endorses Irigaray's argument that while men have been named guardians of the spirit women have been designated keepers of the flesh, to suggest that it is virtually impossible for women to believe that we are created in God's image. As daughters of Eve we inherit her guilt for introducing sin into the world, and so are doubly barred from God's powerful phallus. The only way for women to identify with this incarnation, Roberts maintains, is for us to deny our bodies and our sex. She sees recent attempts to resurrect the figure of Mary Magdalene as indicative of a yearning to undo this either/or split between spirituality and sensuality, and to locate in the desires of the body a new source of religious joy.[14] Despite Christianity's campaign, Roberts believes that any endeavour to repress the body will only lead to its return, as the extended play on Josephine's body in *Impossible Saints* – from the thefts and inexplicable reappearances of parts of her corpse to the final mingling of her bones among the eleven thousand skeletons that ornament the chapel – demonstrates. Roberts contends that there is a supreme irony in the Church's struggle to suppress the carnal, since God is worshipped *through* the physical images we create; we are our bodies, Roberts writes, and what is sacred is our capacity to make symbols of our material life. She believes that this is accomplished not only by looking outwards, but also by celebrating our corporeal selves. For Roberts, Irigaray's notion of *becoming* crucially includes the sexual experience of coming, a viewpoint that aligns her work with that of Hélène Cixous.

Josephine's dream of a new foundation, of an alternative space for women, focuses on the model of a dual house that will accommodate both the spiritual and the sensual life. She imagines one side of the house as a convent without Catholicism in which each woman would have her own inviolate spaces for work and self-reflection, while on the other she would have access to social life, parties, conversation, dancing, sex.[15] This communal, carnal life would be an integral part of each woman's fulfilment and celebration of God. Echoing Irigaray's insistence that becoming is never complete but is always in gestation, Josephine foresees that each inmate of the house will pass backwards and forwards between the two sides, as her needs and predilections dictate. Irigaray's account also suggests why the traditional Catholic convent could not work for Josephine. Without an infinite that will guarantee woman's accomplishment, Irigaray writes, there can be no sharing among women but only fusion/confusion or else hostile division as the inevitable consequence of our unbecoming. This is borne out by Josephine's experience as a nun, which deprives her of privacy and is marked by petty rivalries and suspicion among the Sisters. Irigaray maintains that because God's act of procreation takes the form of the Annunciation he cannot speak to us of the joyous consummation that can derive from a sexual alliance. It is this possibility that Josephine's alternative foundation offers, presenting women with an opportunity to establish a divinity in and for themselves, and so end the paralysis that its lack has caused both sexes.

In concordance with her vision, Josephine's new order includes the replacement of the mass with a meal. Her final message to her niece Isabel – that it is all a joke – hinges on this alteration. At the start of the novel Josephine has interpreted the liturgy literally, believing God to be her Father, the wine to be his blood, and the wafer his body. Her new vision undoes what she now understands to be a metaphor, positing an alternative to Christianity's transcendent and immaterial God through the preparing and consuming of food that is both a source of bodily nourishment and pleasure. Although Josephine is unable to implement her dream in the novel, it is worth noting that it is at least partially realised in the arrangement of Magdalena's house, which provides Josephine, Magdalena and Isabel with a space to play as well as to retreat. One way of reading the dissolution of Josephine's plans by the Catholic Church is as an indictment of a regime that cannot tolerate women becoming themselves.[16]

In 'The Life of Saint Barbara' that interleaves Josephine's story, Barbara's father is so terrified of his beloved daughter's burgeoning sexuality that he builds her a jewelled bath-house in which he imprisons her. To avoid the possibility of men seeing Barbara in her bath the only windows her father allows in the building are situated high up under the roof. In her despair at being thus incarcerated, Barbara thinks of her dead mother whom her father has endeavoured to forget, and in response the trees shoot up through the wooden floorboards. Two of the trees push so hard that they completely destroy one of the walls, and their branches arrange themselves to form a giant window. When Barbara's father asks his daughter what has happened, she replies that he has forgotten to include a window for the mother's holy ghost.

For Irigaray, the fact that there is no female component to the Trinity prevents women's becoming by fixing us in the role of mother. She argues that the Christian image of maternity cannot figure women's fulfilment since it is an incarnation through which the *son* of God is made flesh. Women need a divine horizon that will include the maternal in our own terms, she writes, and not as a space of procreation for the male. Irigaray sees motherhood as comprising twin states, comparable to the two sides of Josephine's dual house: on the one hand a closure of boundaries imaged by gestation and on the other the radical opening that occurs in giving birth.

Josephine's rediscovery of God involves a return to the mother that results from her reading of her mother's commentaries and visit to the cathedral of her childhood. The terms in which the cathedral is presented reconstruct it as a maternal space: it is 'a rounded interior in which you curled up', 'a great heart beating in darkness', an 'embrace in which you soared and leaped'.[17] This perception of the mother as a source of divinity connects to Josephine's dream of rebirth into the

body of the earth. Although this is nowhere made explicit, the fact
that her dream occurs immediately after reading the inscriptions of her
mother's faith makes it possible to surmise that this is a pre-patriarchal
religion celebrating the maternal as a powerful life-force. The descriptions of the cathedral also suggest the blissful symbiosis of mother and
child before separation and the imposition of external precepts, where
the mother's body guarantees survival and provides a secure, nurtur-
ing space for the child to grow. Through her mothering of Isabel as
well as herself Josephine appears in the novel as the model for such a
mother: if she is a saint then it is in this sense of a maternity that seeks
to develop the self while enabling others, rather than the Church's
appropriation of her 'as amongst the most humble and self-effacing of
her sex'.[18]

Despite the positive aspects of Josephine's mothering, Isabel's relation to her aunt is complicated. After Josephine's death Isabel realises
that she has taken on some of her aunt's characteristics, and she is
determined to discover and piece together the writings of Josephine's
second 'Life'. Yet Isabel also chafes against Josephine's power over
her and is critical of what she perceives as her aunt's selfishness in
abandoning her in order to fulfill herself. Isabel does not attend
Josephine's dying, and she later admits that the first account she gives
of this in which she lovingly embraces her aunt is a lie.

In an essay entitled 'Love of Self', Irigaray argues that women must
oppose the Christian tradition of a God–Father engendering a God–Son
through the medium of a virgin mother, with a corresponding divinity
of our own transmitted from mother to daughter.[19] At present, she
writes, the maternal serves the generation of men, with God figuring
the return to the mother that can never take place. This substitution
presents men with a bridge between past and present that is denied
women: since there is no transcendental made to our measure which
can effect a comparable return to childhood and the maternal, we are
paradoxically denied the potential for becoming. For Irigaray, a mutu-
ally enveloping love between mother and daughter in which each
would also remain open to difference is the vital first step towards
women's establishing a *female* divine.

Despite the difficulties Isabel experiences, there are signs in *Impossible Saints* of an enabling genealogy in the sense Irigaray intends.
Although all Josephine's later writings are destroyed and her final
message to Isabel is reinterpreted by Sister Maria in the hope of
endowing a convent of the kind Josephine rejected, Isabel's attempt
to piece together Josephine's second 'Life' and pass on her story to

her granddaughter can be seen as a template of hope. More emphatically, Josephine's message is transmitted to Isabel via a two-fold process that draws on Josephine's example but also requires Isabel to look inside herself. Appropriately, the transfer occurs immediately after Isabel's reflections on the nature of her aunt's saintliness, musings which take her back to memories of her own dead mother. As she ponders Sister Maria's contention that Josephine is a saint, she recalls her aunt's actual and often contradictory nature and tries to relate it to an image of sanctity. Echoing Irigaray, she gradually perceives that this is a figure of maternal absence, the longed-for body which relinquishes but also inspires. The nightmares of her mother's rotting corpse that haunted Isabel when she first arrived at the convent were quelled by her aunt taking her mother's place. Josephine's death undoes this substitution, and Isabel is forced to refigure her relation to her own mother. Following Josephine's example she meditates, and discovers an alternative Trinity:

> Here was the couple and the child, the three-in-one. Here was the woman in her golden dress, holding her girl on her hip, balanced against the crook of her arm, and the other wrapped about her man ... The woman was my golden mother.[20]

Recalling Irigaray, Isabel's vision extends beyond the self, providing a goal to aspire to – 'they floated in the air above me ... They were radiant with the gold light streaming from them' – yet at the same time emanates from within.[21] Developing Josephine's perception of the cathedral as a divine mother, Isabel relocates her Trinity in an image of her body as the mother's gift *and* a fecund space in its own right:

> Inside me, I found out now, there was a cathedral built of gold ... It was a golden flower that enclosed a pearl ... It was constructed with the precise engineering of love.[22]

Isabel's vision evokes the golden house where *Impossible Saints* begins and ends. A chapel is built into the side wall of the cathedral in order to house the remains of St Ursula and the eleven thousand virgins who are reported to have accompanied her – a discovery Sister Maria attributes to Josephine. The skeletons provide the Sisters who have followed Josephine with a livelihood, identifying and enshrining St Ursula and her chief lieutenants and using the bones that are left to decorate the chapel walls. Josephine's remains are mingled with those

of the vast, unnamed majority whose life-stories are lost as their bones
are sorted into piles to be used as the pieces in an intricate mosaic.
This outcome is echoed in the lives of the women saints that intersperse Josephine's story, all of which end in oblivion. It also connects
to a further point made by Irigaray, who suggests that because women
have no female divine we have no means of representing our death.[23]
Women, she contends, are the objects employed by a male imaginary
to deflect or mediate its own end: our sacrificial status ensures patriarchy's furtherance and leaves us with a corresponding blank for own
figurations. Irigaray's analysis suggests two possible readings of
Josephine's death. On the one hand, the fact that the stories of the
women saints included in the novel end in anonymity and Josephine's
mature writings are lost and her message co-opted by the Church
corroborates Irigaray's insistence that woman cannot exist within the
current order on her own terms. On the other, Isabel's continuation
of Josephine's divine vision reiterated in the descriptions of the chapel
inlaid with bones offers a powerful image of a female genealogy: as
readers we are taken inside the bodies of our foremothers. This is also
suggested in Josephine's irrepressibility after her death, played out in
the exuberant and slightly grotesque comedy of her physical and spiritual apparitions. While the fathers hack her perfectly preserved and
sweet-smelling corpse to pieces in order to determine if it is indeed
uncorrupted and hence miraculous, Sister Maria records Josephine's
new state:

> In the vision, so Maria said, Josephine explained these events in
> detail, while under her feet she busily trampled serpents and devils
> and pagan blackamoors. Maria knew this resplendent figure wearing
> a diamond crown and waving a silver sword was indeed Josephine,
> for her name was written in stars over her right breast.[24]

The fact that Maria inserts Josephine into the very pantheon she has
struggled to reject is equally double-edged, indicating, perhaps, that
women must continue to look for our mythology in the gaps and on
the margins of patriarchy, as Isabel is forced to piece together her
aunt's life from discarded remnants and the meanings hidden inside
the rosary, inventing wherever the lacunae appear too large. As a strategy this seems more limited than the mythic dismantlings, borrowings
and new creations of the texts discussed thus far, with the exception of
Fay Weldon's *The Life and Loves of a She Devil*, since women's visions
are subject to patriarchy's Inquisition and our alternatives in danger of
being appropriated by the very regime they seek to oppose.

Filling in the gaps and exploring the margins is also the starting-point for Roberts's *The Book of Mrs Noah*.[25] The novel opens with Noah's partner – the Mrs Noah of the title – inviting women to join her on board her imaginary ark. She has reached a turning-point in her relationship with Noah and issues the invitations in order to find out how other women have navigated their lives. The women who join her are an eclectic group of 'Sibyls' and the label indicates that the stories they tell will be prophetic rather than prescriptive. Their gathering attracts an unexpected intruder who presents himself as 'the speaker of the Word of God', and who gatecrashes the meeting in the hope that the Sibyls can kick-start him out of the writer's block he has had ever since he completed the Bible.[26] Nicknamed 'the Gaffer', his presence causes the Sibyls to note some of the Bible's distortions and makes a number of their own stories appear explicitly as attempts to fill its gaps. Thus the 'Forsaken Sibyl' argues that the Bible gives only a partial account in 'Genesis' and leaves out an accurate description of what the world was like before the Flood. These falsifications are partly rectified in a tale about the biblical Mrs Noah and the mythical world of Atlantis.

The interleaving of the story of the ark with the tales the Sibyls tell is structurally similar to the interspersing of Josephine's narrative with the 'lives' of women saints. There are striking parallels, too, in the thematic concerns of the two novels. One of the Sibyls' stories in *The Book of Mrs Noah* resembles Josephine's, since it concerns a young woman whose learnt terror of her body and the loss of her adored father's love goad her into becoming a nun and to starve and torture herself. The ark itself recalls Josephine's dream of an alternative foundation, offering women a quiet refuge as well as a place to work and play.[27]

As Irigaray argues, women's establishing of a female divine must not derive exclusively from our criticism of or opposition to the prevailing order but must involve the incarnation of new values.[28] She believes that there may be fruitful possibilities in reclaiming those elements which have been excised from patriarchy's austere and remote God, and she cites colour, music, movement and dancing as examples. Irigaray's suggestion sheds an interesting light on the dual nature of Josephine's alternative foundation as well as the social aspects of life on the ark. Irigaray's proposition is also evoked in Mrs Noah's retelling of the story of Daphne and Apollo.[29] In Ovid's *Metamorphoses*, the tale results from Cupid shooting the pair with two of his love-arrows because Apollo has scorned Cupid's prowess as an archer.[30] The arrow that hits Daphne is of the kind that repels love, and so Daphne flees from the love-stricken Apollo's advances. In desperation at his pursuit she prays for deliverance and is turned into a laurel tree.[31] This does not spare her, however, for Apollo continues to love her and adopts the laurel as his emblem. In the version Mrs Noah tells, the depiction of Daphne as a huntress is revealed to be a falsification and she is reinstated as a priestess of poetry. The laurel leaves with which she is associated are part of a menstrual rite in which women use their hallucinogenic effects to rediscover their potential and produce poems. The retelling resurrects physical intoxication, singing and dancing as a divine force, and suggests that Daphne's voice can still be heard inciting women to recover the power of poetry which men have usurped.

'In the beginning was the Word, and the Word was with God, and the Word was God.' Thus begins St John's Gospel. For Irigaray, such statements are an accurate description of patriarchy's functioning which, she maintains, has appropriated language for its own ends. She argues that unless woman can represent herself through the instating of a female divine in the realm of the symbolic, women will remain, like Daphne, immured within an exclusively male set of paradigms. In her essay 'The Place of Imagination', Roberts draws on Ferdinand de Saussure's account of language to highlight the dual nature of words which are at once actual signposts and totally arbitrary in their attribution.[32] Recalling Mary Wolfe's simultaneous rejection and rediscovery of language in Christine Crow's *Miss X or the Wolf Woman*, Roberts suggests that it is this paradox which gives words their mysterious, mythical power:

> Using them can seem like having some sort of religious or ecstatic experience, invoking those ancient gods who once dwelt in every aspect of nature and who I think still dwell in words; getting to the deep truth and reality of life, of things; and yet to be at the same time an artefact made by humans, a series of arbitrarily designed signs that can be swapped with one another ... piled up in layers of metaphor, whose meanings slip and change.[33]

In the story of the biblical Mrs Noah told by one of the Sibyls, the radical differences between the Gods which Noah and his wife worship are brought into conflict. Recalling Josephine's vision in *Impossible Saints*, for Noah's wife God is the result of self-reflection, of worshipping the daily miracles of the earth and participating in the ongoing process of creation. Her God is thus very different from her husband's remote, terrifying and destructive Father. In the new world that follows the Flood, it is her husband's religion that predominates, instituting a regime of mastery and sacrifice. Significantly, Mrs Noah's response is to invent words that will communicate her experience of God as connection, a language she incorporates in her new invention of writing.

In the retelling, Mrs Noah's divergent view of God means that she interprets the Flood not as the punitive act it is in the Bible, but as the breaking of the waters of the maternal body of the earth. Recalling Josephine's dream of rebirth and Isabel's vision of a maternal Trinity, this severance is perceived as the necessary condition for new life. As Mrs Noah's daughter-in-law asserts, in angry defiance of the prevailing mores that disparage women, she wants a daughter so that she can love her and then let her go. The rainbow that appears at the end of the Flood is consequently celebrated by Mrs Noah as a sign of the divinity of creation and as the umbilical cord that fastens us to it. It is wholly appropriate that her new language begins as the rainbow dissolves in the night sky, and that her first words should be 'God's bow' to symbolise the severed link.

In her essay on imagination, Roberts suggests that the impetus behind the fictional Mrs Noah's invention of writing to substitute for the maternal body is a general one. She argues that in a patriarchal world in which God is male and mothers are either sentimentalised or else despised and blamed, such a correlation is inadmissable. In reality we all have to grow up and leave the mother behind us, and art is one way in which we can re-make, re-member or at least search for her lost body. For Roberts, it is this re-creation that constitutes what she calls her 'myth of speaking and writing': language's ark-like function of piloting our 'birth into absence'.[34]

Roberts believes that the search for the mother can involve feelings of pain and rage at our abandonment as we try to summon back the life-giving presence without which we would die. It can include fears that we have killed the mother with our angry, hungry wanting, as the story of Angelina in *The Book of Mrs Noah* illustrates. In this tale, Barbara and her partner, who are lost, are lured by Angelina's gourmet cooking into spending New Year's Eve with her. The correlation between Angelina and the mother is highlighted as Barbara realises that the Angelina-like pin-up in her partner's porn magazine is the maternal body stapled finally into place. The beatings her partner requires her to give him are part of his inability to accept his mother's loss. Angelina's apparently ritual killing as part of the New Year festivities in which the old year must die in order for the new year to be born similarly emphasises the violence entailed.³⁵ Roberts argues that the desire to (re)create is the positive corollary of this emptiness and anguish:

> Out of this *chaos* of feeling, out of this overwhelming sadness at *absence*, we learn to create something beautiful: our words, later on our gifts, later still our works of art. We re-create the mother inside ourselves, over and over again.³⁶

The Gaffer's vision on the ark of the siren-like mermaids incites him to draft a new, unauthorised version in which everything begins and ends with an omnipotent, cosmic Mother. The writing dissolves into memories of his own mother and the Oedipal drama of realising that his father takes the prime place in her affections. His mother's mockery of his childish attempts to reverse this order and the birth of a new baby induce him to identify with his distant, punishing father in an endeavour to fill 'the space of loss inside him [which] has her shape'.³⁷ This space, Roberts suggests in her essay, exists inside each one of us and is at the heart of culture itself. Despite the Gaffer's struggles to deny the maternal relation and to ally himself with an image of paternal power, Roberts believes that, by returning us to our childhoods and the source of our connection to life, this loss can function as a productive matrix in which boundaries dissolve, certainties collapse, reductive either/or binaries give way and new perceptions emerge. Her view is exemplified by the 'Forsaken Sibyl' who longs to (re-)establish her relation to the world and who, in the absence of such a link, 'an umbilical cord' that can join her to the 'm/other', begins to write.³⁸ The parallels with Hélène Cixous's work are once again striking.

Mrs Noah's return to the lost city of Atlantis can be read as an embodiment of this space. In the 'room of metamorphoses', for instance, the divisions between human, animal and divine blur, and chaos and pleasure predominate. Underscoring the correlation between this world and the child's blissful symbiosis with the mother before the imposition of an external law, the narrative relates how God the Father brought this paradisal state to an end. Mrs Noah wanders freely through the labyrinthine rooms until, panic-stricken, she realises that she cannot find the way out. She associates the terror she feels at thus being trapped with the horror of the engulfing mother who will not let go. The incident corroborates Roberts's insistence that severance from the mother is necessary, as well as Irigaray's argument that women must figure a divine goal for our becoming which includes but also extends beyond our biology. It is appropriate that part of the panic Mrs Noah feels derives from her confusion about whether or not to become a mother herself, which caused the rupture with her partner. Her horror is bound up with all the negative images of motherhood that surround her and which constitute their own possessive and inhibiting maze.

During the voyage Mrs Noah refrains from going down to the hold of the ark, which she admits contains everything she has not been able to deal with and has attempted to repress. She now descends to the hold, which is guarded by a perversely maternal Snow White, hacking the feet off her 'babies' while she waits for her Prince to come.[39] With the help of the Sibyls, Mrs Noah's image of the hold turns into the library that has formed her perception of the ark – with the difference that here the books are in disorder and the authors have come to life. She realises that this is where her solution to the predicament that began her voyage has lain all along:

> All this time I have been searching. All this time I have been wandering around the earth, going out, out, to look for a solution. Now at last I've found what I've been needing. Here.
> Not Outsiders but Insiders.
> This is the house of language. The house of words. Here, inside the Ark, the body of the mother, I find words.[40]

Recalling *Impossible Saints*, Mrs Noah finally locates her Woolfian 'room of her own' in her own body, her own 'bone-house'.[41] Her voyage has initiated the process, furnishing her with the words to navigate the severance that is the foundation for her own becoming. The shimmering, dancing rainbow of stories that emanates from the ark symbolises the freshly (re)created cord, proffering an image of herself as mother *and* 'wanderer'.[42] In the essay 'The Flesh Made Word', Roberts suggests that the sharp division between the Virgin Mary and the carnal Mary Magdalene fractures the possibility of women's sanctity. By putting the two back together, Roberts offers us an incarnation of a wholly female divine.[43]

For Irigaray, women's instatement of a goal of becoming cannot be a fixed objective, since this would merely enshrine it as an immutable *logos*, but must serve as a 'bridge' that can assure the passage from past to future. In *The Book of Mrs Noah*, this bridge is figured in the rainbow, in the arc of stories that must be continually retold. For

Mrs Noah, this is the truth of genesis which the Bible has ignored: in contrast to its grandiose claim of forming the universe in seven days and nights, her own acts of creation will be 'as daily as dusting, or dreaming'.[44]

Roberts suggests that as patriarchy falls apart and the old certainty of God the Father crumbles, we have the opportunity to inaugurate a new and more enabling mythology.[45] Arguing that this cannot be located in a return to the ancient worship of a Mother Goddess, her answer is to celebrate the ongoing process of living. Born from the mother, and propelled by the need to compensate for her loss, we must all find a way to refigure the connection and so are all active participants in this incessant task of creation.[46] For Roberts, God is consequently an immanent reality, deriving from the maternal, and manifest in our endeavours to make and remake the world. Moving beyond the apparent impasse of *Impossible Saints*, what *The Book of Mrs Noah* indicates is that other women's stories – whether they are those of forgotten saints or sibylline visions – offer women inspiration and models for the becoming we have been denied. The continual telling of these stories ensures that their *mythos* will not replicate patriarchy's definitive and legislating account, but will instead forge pathways for the divine accomplishment of both sexes.

5
Unlimited Horror
Vampires, Sex-Slaves and Paragons of the Feminine in Anne Rice and Emma Tennant

It be all fool-talk, lock, stock, and barrel; that's what it be, an' nowt else. These bans an' wafts an' boh-ghosts an' bar-guests and bogles an' all anent them is only fit to see bairns an' dizzy women a-belderin. They be nowt but air-blebs! They, an' all grims an' signs an' warnin's, be all invented by parsons an' illsome beuk-bodies an' railway touters to skeer an' scunner hafflin's, an' to get folks to do somethin' that they don't other incline to.

> Bram Stoker, *Dracula*[1]

I hazard the guess that man will be ultimately known for a mere polity of multifarious, incongruous and independent denizens.

> Robert Louis Stephenson, *The Strange Case of Dr Jekyll and Mr Hyde*[2]

How can I be without border?

> Julia Kristeva, *Powers of Horror*[3]

When Mina Murray in Bram Stoker's *Dracula* meets the old sailor in the graveyard overlooking Whitby bay, he categorically rejects all instances of the supernatural as clever inventions designed to scare or coerce.[4] Despite the versimilitude of Stoker's narration, which intersperses eyewitness accounts with corroborating newspaper extracts and correspondence from estate and transport agencies, the return to order at the end of the novel tends to confirm the old sailor's assessment.

David Rogers, in an introduction to *Dracula*, suggests that while its author drew on an existing mythology of werewolves and nosferatu, Stoker's achievement in his tale of the villanous Count was to voice the anxieties of an age.[5] Rogers argues that the infecting, shape-shifting, evil menace of the Count incarnates the fears of late Victorian patriarchy, as the certainties of male privilege, class hierarchy, rationality and the Bible were increasingly called into doubt.[6] In *Dracula*, such apprehensions are effectively assuaged as Christianity and its self-appointed group of male protectors put an end to the Count's career. That this is the triumph of good over evil is made clear by Dr Van Helsing's description of the group as the 'ministers of God's own wish' and by the proliferation of hellish images employed to depict the Count.[7] The stirrings towards female emancipation that threatened Victorian society's placement of women as the guardians of virtue are similarly quelled, as Lucy Westenra's 'unholy' transformation to wanton temptress is reversed by Van Helsing killing her and her restoration to her former 'sweetness and purity'.[8] Even Mina, who after Dracula's attack has the closest link to him, is consistently excluded from direct participation, and though her emotional and secretarial services are praised Van Helsing stresses that her function is to represent their 'star and... hope'.[9] The vanishing of Dracula's mark from her forehead once he is dead and the final portrait of her as a loving mother underscore her resumption of traditional female values and roles. Despite Stoker's efforts at authenticity and the undeniable power of his creation, the unequivocal return to the status quo at the end of the narrative relegates Dracula to the comparative safety of nightmare fantasy.

In Anne Rice's rewriting of Stoker's mythic tale, the emphasis shifts from the vampire as that which threatens the established order to an exploration of the dichotomies and truths on which that order depends.[10] The first novel in Rice's 'The Vampire Chronicles', *Interview with the Vampire*, adopts and subverts Stoker's narrative method of first-person testimonies by presenting the exclusive story of the vampire himself.[11] The effect of this on the reader is to undermine the allegiances that are so strongly designated in the source-text, since the protagonist Louis's anguished responses to the vampiric imperative to kill engage our sympathy and make it impossible for us to dismiss his actions as purely evil. Immortality, which is regarded as an abhorrence in Stoker since it is linked to Dracula's diabolic plan, is similarly problematised in Rice. In his interview, Louis gives examples of the pain and difficulties being immortal involves, the most striking of which is his graphic account of the vampire Lestat's slow decay because 'his mind cannot accept' the changes of the present age.[12] Conversely, despite all Louis's warnings, the interviewer listening to Louis's story begs him at the conclusion of the interview to make him immortal. When Louis refuses, he determines to find Lestat and become a vampire with his help.[13] The contrast with the ending of Stoker's novel, in which Van Helsing's men kneel in a prayer of thanksgiving that the immortal Dracula is no more, could not be more marked. Rice's undercutting of the ultimately incontrovertible binaries that police *Dracula* is also apparent in her relocation of the interest away from a straightforward contest between vampires and humans to centre on the relationships between vampires. In *Interview with the Vampire*, Louis describes his early realisation that despite Lestat's powers the problems that beset him are 'human problems' such as money and keeping the truth about his vampiric nature from his ailing father.[14] As Louis's tale progresses, it becomes clear that his preoccupations as a vampire remain those of his mortal life: his interview charts his changing relationships with those he loves and his endeavours to attribute meaning to his existence. In the later 'Chronicle' *Queen of the Damned*, the threat the vampiric Queen Akasha poses to the future of humankind is resolved directly by the vampires.

This move away from a sharply demarcated struggle between good and evil is most clearly indicated in the very different attitude to Christianity in 'The Vampire Chronicles'. Early in *Interview with the Vampire*, Louis learns from Lestat that the tales about vampiric susceptibility to religious iconography are a fiction. Engaged in his own endeavour to determine meaning, Louis at one point takes refuge in a Catholic cathedral, and far from being damned by its precepts realises that it is a mere shell filled with 'dead forms'.[15] His furious disappointment is horrifically expressed in his vicious attack on the kindly priest who tries to help him. The intimation that good and evil are human constructs with no ultimate validity is confirmed in the second of the 'Chronicles', *The Vampire Lestat*, as Lestat's history of the vampires shows how human perception of them changed during the decline of the Roman Empire when the early Church relegated them to its invented category of the devil.[16] In *Queen of the Damned*, Christian belief is cynically exploited by Akasha in her attempt to implement her megalomaniac plan, while Lestat's rock concert is depicted as a Mass for those who have lost their faith.[17] Both representations are radically at odds with Stoker's institution of Christianity as the force for good on which Van Helsing and his men can depend. In Rice's reworkings, religion is itself the problem, since the superstitions and rituals it encourages prevent us from realising the fundamental meaninglessness of life. This truth – which is the same for both humans and vampires – is the first step towards the godless universe that Marius, Lestat's mentor, sees as the only hope of progress for humankind.[18] In this sense of recognising the absence of any transcendental purpose or law, Rice's fictions, like Stoker's before them, voice the anxieties of their time. The stripping away that Rice's 'Vampire Chronicles' advocate contrasts radically with the recreation drawing on existing paradigms propounded by Michèle Roberts's fiction.

While the vampiric act of sucking blood has an erotic component in Stoker's *Dracula*, in the depiction of Jonathan Harker's 'languorous ecstasy' as the lips of the vampire woman touch his throat, for instance, or Dracula's transformation of Lucy Westenra into a sensual temptress, any intimations of sexual pleasure are firmly occluded by the novel's ending.[19] In Rice's 'The Vampire Chronicles', the sexual nature of vampire killing is explored to the extent that it frequently obscures the fact that it is a murder that is taking place. Louis, when he is asked by his interviewer what it is like to drink blood, replies that it is as difficult to put into words as it is to describe having sex; he later tells the curious Claudia that human love-making is 'the pale shadow of killing'.[20] Where the mode of narration in Stoker, which gives all but Dracula's eye-witness account, means that the experience of sucking blood is omitted from the assembled testimonies, in Rice's reworkings it becomes a prominent feature of the fiction.[21] Louis's first kill as a vampire, for example, is presented in detail, and the depiction of his victim's warm, struggling body and the accelerating pace of their heartbeats as they pound together in unison before the final release clearly parallels sexual consummation. This explicit accentuating of the latent eroticism in *Dracula* further undermines the codifications on which its restoration of order depends.

The fact that Louis's first kill as a vampire is a young man similarly destabilises the gender certainties that circumscribe Stoker's novel. While it is possible to interpret a number of Dracula's distinguishing features as androgynous, his only victims during the course of the narrative are women. In Rice's tales, the pleasures of vampirism are homo- as well as heterosexual: Lestat's preferred kill, for instance, is a male on the verge of maturity.[22] Many of the most passionate relationships depicted in the 'Chronicles' are between vampires of the same sex, as the fierce emotions Armand arouses illustrate. Conventional gender roles are also subverted in Louis's mothering of the child vampire, Claudia, whom he cradles each night in his coffin and educates until Armand's stronger appeal prompts him to find a substitute mother for her.

A more controversial subverting of the gender binary that legislates in *Dracula* occurs in the revelation of the vampire Queen Akasha's plan for humankind in *The Queen of the Damned*. Arguing that the violence and war that have characterised millennia of male rule now threaten the survival of the earth, Akasha determines to institute a new ascendancy of women. The obvious links between this scheme and feminist programmes problematises the means Akashsa proposes for its establishment. Since men are perceived as the difficulty, all but one in a hundred must die until the world is sufficiently altered in its system of government for their increased presence not to matter. The diabolic nature of such a project is emphasised by the role Akasha envisages for herself in its execution and in the other vampires' reaction to it.[23] *The Queen of the Damned* includes a detailed history of the vampires that draws extensively on ancient Egyptian mythology to identify Akasha as their originating 'Mother'. According to this genealogy, an immortal and malevolent spirit enters Akasha's body through wounds made by conspirators against her, and in a reworking of the myth of Isis and Osiris Akasha then revives her similarly wounded husband and founds the race of vampires.[24] Rice's reconstruction here thus offers a striking contrast to Christine Crow's empowering retelling in *Miss X or the Wolf Woman*. Realising Akasha's reinvigorated capacity for evil, her vampirised minister persuades Mekare and Maharet – explicitly presented as the counterbalancing 'good mothers' – to allow themselves to be made immortal in order to curtail her power. *The Queen of the Damned* thus returns us to the terrain of *Dracula*, as the vampires join forces against Akasha.[25] Despite Mekare's ritual consuming of Akasha's heart and brain, with its implicit mixing of the polarities of good and evil, to ensure the vampires' survival, the overriding impression at the close of the narrative is that order has been restored. As in Stoker's *Dracula*, we are once again subject to an overarching and dichotomous law.

The presentation of a vampire genealogy in *The Queen of the Damned*, with its explicit reference to existing mythology, appears at odds with the ultimate meaninglessness Louis perceives to be the truth of his condition in *Interview with the Vampire*. When Louis is first made into a vampire by Lestat he determines to discover the origins and purpose of the vampires, a quest that leads him to Dracula's Transylvanian home as well as to reflect on the nature of existence, morality and religion. Far from uncovering an explanatory history, the only vampires Louis encounters in Transylvania are 'mindless corpses' who kill in order to survive, while his meditations and discussions confirm his worst fear that 'there is no meaning to any of this'.[26] The horror of Louis's realisation is graphically depicted in two incidents that occur early in the text. The first comes after Louis has been spurned as a creature of the devil by Babette whom he has tried to help, when looking into the night sky he begins to understand what it means to be immortal:

> It was as if this night were only one of thousands of nights, world without end, night curving into night to make a great arching line of which I couldn't see the end, a night in which I roamed alone under cold, mindless stars.[27]

This stark portrayal is echoed in the later account of Louis's bitter disillusion as he realises that he can henceforth only experience the blue waters of the Mediterranean as an endless vista of black under the cover of darkness.[28] These powerful images of emptiness appear to offer a more accurate and haunting myth for our time than the rather laboured and frequently derisory returns to the existing mythological corpus in *The Queen of the Damned*.[29]

Despite the striking illustration of the void Louis perceives at the heart of existence, the horror is to some extent undercut by the numerous endeavours to reinstitute an order depicted in the text.[30] When Louis at length finds the vampires who gravitate around Armand at the Théâtre des Vampires in Paris, he is disappointed to discover that in spite of their intelligence and artistry they have 'made of immortality a conformist's club'.[31] Their creation of a code of internal rules is reiterated in the more general vampire law Louis learns from them, according to which the killing of another vampire is a crime punishable by death.[32] Louis himself longs to discover a transcendent scheme for the universe, even if this means his eternal damnation.[33] Thus, while immortality teaches Louis that truths are illusions, since the certainties of one century are abolished by the beliefs of the next, he finds it difficult to do as Claudia instructs and relinquish himself to the pleasures of the flesh.[34] It is significant that, after Claudia's death and his abandoning of his final, fruitless search to find a purpose in art, Louis gives himself over to the sensuality of his vampire nature but tells Armand that it marks the death of any remaining vestige of humanness in him. By perpetrating what he knew as a human to be evil, and by removing himself from the possibility of any retribution for his actions, Louis loses his place in the world. As he tells the interviewer, any pleasure or knowledge he henceforth uncovers he must confine to himself.[35] Where Gillian Perholt, in A. S. Byatt's 'The Djinn in the Nightingale's Eye', releases her djinn in order to retain the power of art, Louis's refusal to recreate meaning entails his forfeiture of its corresponding compensations of connection and exchange.[36] Recalling the scenario of Hélène Cixous's 'The Love of the Wolf', his rejection incarnates the horrific flip-side of the absence of law. Outside the spectrum of good and evil humanity has devised for itself, beyond even the ultimate mortal limit of death, Louis the vampire is at the opposite pole to Michèle Roberts's Mrs Noah, whose endeavours to posit an alternative mythology serve to replenish and reshape the void.

This intimation that limits are what make us human is explored by Julia Kristeva in a series of essays collected under the title *Powers of Horror*.[37] Here Kristeva investigates the difficulties the developing infant has in comprehending its corporeal boundaries, as it endeavours to distinguish inside from outside and to realise itself as separate from others. Kristeva suggests that the infant's recognition of 'what is not me' is the foundation for its awareness of 'what is me', and that its need to represent 'what is not me' simultaneously opens the pathway to language and social interaction. For Kristeva, the infant's first efforts to delineate itself revolve almost exclusively around the mother's vitally sustaining but also overwhelming and sometimes menacing body. These first attempts at autonomy are often violent and always terrifying, since the infant does not yet possess the signifying resources that language will provide. Consequently, Kristeva argues that in these early struggles 'what is not me' is uncertain and threatening, even while it initiates the route the infant must follow: since the infant cannot speak, it cannot figure this other as a graspable object that can then aid it in its task of self-definition, and so this other remains, a compelling, rejected pre-object or 'abject', that tends to obstruct rather than enable the infant's constitution of itself as an independent subject.

Kristeva's analysis of the continuing influence of the abject on what she sees as the life-long process of separation sheds an interesting light on the vampire mythology.[38] The vampires' distinguishing characteristic of sucking human blood, for example, can be linked to her theory of the abject in a number of ways. Kristeva's argument that food items can operate as abjects, as the pre-verbal infant struggles against the parental desire for it to eat, can be connected to the revulsion the vampiric act provokes, while the transferal of blood this act entails disrupts the division between one's own and another's body.[39] This aberration is particularly striking in the account of how vampires are created in Rice's 'The Vampire Chronicles', where the human blood that is drunk must be replenished by vampire blood.[40] This paradoxical restoration positions the bestowing vampire in the place of the maternal, since its body is both vital for survival and that which must be repulsed. In this compelling, threatening guise, the vampire functions like an abject, as it simultaneously overwhelms and impels its subject.[41] Kristeva's suggestion that abjection returns us to our first, terrifying experiences of separation is given a further, significant twist in 'The Vampire Chronicles', as Louis compares sucking Lestat's vampire blood to his memory of suckling at his mother's breast.[42] This analogy is repeated in other depictions, such as Lestat's explanation of the vampiric imperative to kill as nostalgia for 'the perfect consummation of desire' that is contained in a mother's embrace.[43]

Kristeva argues that in order for the infant to become autonomous it must sever itself from the maternal body which it has experienced as coextensive, and convert the void that is opened up by this loss into a distinct, representable and non-encroaching space. The vampiric imperative to return to this moment suggests both the endeavour to heal the split that produces loss and its failure, as the other dies or is turned into a replica vampire. The void that Louis perceives as his consequent inheritance can thus be read as an extension of this inability to deal with separation, since it repeats the horror of loss without providing any of the compensations of signification and exchange which subject-formation offers.[44] Thus Louis tells his interviewer that despite the exciting, fleeting connection with another that killing presents, the crux of the act is 'again and again the experience of that loss of my own life, which I experienced when I sucked the blood from Lestat's wrist and felt his heart pound with my heart'.[45] For Kristeva, the father as representative of an external order of precepts and penalties plays a crucial role in the infant's becoming socialised, and this insistence sheds further light on Louis's motivation. Although Louis acknowledges that Lestat's powerful charisma had an effect on him, he outlines his main reasons for following Lestat as the devastating loss of his brother whom he believed he had killed and his subsequent 'desire to be thoroughly damned'.[46] Following Kristeva, we can interpret Louis's submission to the more powerful and knowledgeable Lestat in terms of his guise as symbolic father, since it is Lestat who will 'damn' him as he initiates him into the rules and practices of vampire existence.[47] Louis's disillusion with Lestat and his substitute Armand indicate, according to this reading, that his final abandon to the physical solaces of vampirism is as much a rejection of limitations as it is an attempt to contain the overwhelming abjection of unresolved loss.[48]

Kristeva's suggestion that a corpse can function as an abject similarly has resonance for the vampire myth. Unlike death, Kristeva writes, which is signified so that I can understand and react to it, the corpse performs the horror of the ultimate encroaching border, since it figures the annihilation that I must permanently thrust aside in order to be. This points to an interesting paradox within vampire immortality, as the vampires' compulsion to kill drives them to recreate what they cannot be. This is particularly striking in *Interview with the Vampire*, where Louis tells the priest who attempts to hear his confession that he is responsible for literally thousands of corpses. The fact that he cannot bring himself to kill anyone he knows and that vampires in general are unable to remain near the bodies of their victims serve to underscore the point. Kristeva's insistence on the *theatricality* of the corpse, as that which shows what I must not be, also illuminates the spectacle of the young woman's murder at the Théâtre des Vampires in Paris. Here, since the death takes place on stage, the audience's horror, desire and relief are incited as permissible responses to a work of art. As critic Elisabeth Bronfen has argued, the aesthetic representation releases us from death's menace because it occurs to another and as an image.[49]

Kristeva's study of abjection suggests that the ongoing potency of the vampire myth, particularly as it is figured in Anne Rice's 'The Vampire Chronicles', is its revelation of what we must permanently reject in order to be. The vampire demonstrates the fragility of identity and the social code, by unveiling its laws as a fabricated defence. As the old sailor tells Mina in Stoker's *Dracula*, these are inventions of the intellect devised to control fear and to impel us to do what we may not otherwise wish. The vampires' compulsive return to the loss that initiates these constructions displays this process, as well as the negative consequences of our inability to accept their limitations. Louis's realisation of the void to which he is condemned offers a powerful metaphor for an existence without signification and social interaction, a universe in which nothing is meaningful because nothing is taboo. In 'The Vampire Chronicles', our terror and relief as we empathise with the vampire predicament return us to our own foundational topology which is, as Kristeva points out, itself a myth.[50] The figure of the vampire may enable us to glimpse something of the horror and monstrosity that our failure to socialise would entail, but it can only do so through the secondary elaborations of our symbolising schema.

In her erotic fiction, which she writes under the pseudonym of A. N. Roquelaure, Anne Rice returns to mythology, this time borrowing her setting and characters from the story of 'Sleeping Beauty'.[51] Amalia Ziv, in an article on Rice's Beauty trilogy and Pauline Réage's *Story of O*, argues that this removal of the narrative from the real world to that of fairy tale enables Rice to construct the closed, rigid regime necessary for the staging of sadomasochism.[52] In the first of the novels, *The Claiming of Sleeping Beauty*, the slumbering castle is quickly violated by the invading Prince, whose rape of the spellbound Beauty awakens her into his slavery and an escalating ordeal of punishment and pain.[53] The Beauty trilogy, with its clear distinction between master and slave and the detailed descriptions of the penalties a refusal to submit to this order entails, is thus at the opposite pole to the lawless universe and the abortive search for purpose portrayed in 'The Vampire Chronicles'.[54] One way of approaching the debate as to whether pornography is cathartic or itself productive of perversion is to see it as a metaphor for the process of socialisation.[55] In the light of Riane Eisler's analysis, for example, discussed in chapter 1, the Beauty trilogy can be read as a parable of a dominator culture that relies on fear and pain to maintain itself, in which pain inevitably becomes eroticised. The texts themselves suggest reasons to view the trilogy as an allegory of the surrendering of our desires to external precepts so that we can become law-abiding subjects.[56] It is evident in *The Claiming of Sleeping Beauty*, for instance, that Beauty's parents have been through the same initiation, and their admonishment to Beauty to obey the Prince indicates their relinquishing the remainder of her education to him. The tortures Beauty undergoes are frequently referred to as 'training', which will result in her acquiring 'wisdom, patience, self-control, and all virtues'.[57] These theories of a metaphor for socialisation, while offering an illuminating frame from which to view the trilogy, do not, however, satisfactorily account for Beauty's willingness and pleasure in yielding to the Prince's terrifying, cruel and punitive programme.

The 'new strength' Beauty discovers in surrendering to the Prince can be explained more fruitfully in terms of Kristeva's notion of abjection.[58] Kristeva suggests that in some cases the body is not perceived as that which delimits the self, but as the property of the Other. This Other is not a productive source of identification, but rather takes the place of what might have been 'me' by preceding and possessing me.

In such instances, Kristeva writes, the Other's possession is vital, since it rescues the subject from the ever-present terror of non-being. Kristeva's analysis strikes chords with a number of features of Rice's portrayal, including the description of Beauty's non-being imaged in the spell of sleep prior to the Prince's arrival, the frequent depictions of Beauty's panic at being spurned by the Prince, and her own desire to be further enslaved.[59] Despite the clichés and inevitable monotony of the trilogy as it repeatedly replays the same scenario, its presentation of men as well as women in the passive role of slave challenges traditional views of gender.[60] Beauty's initiation is undergone by male princes, who are perceived as even more vulnerable than the female slaves because of the visibility of their arousal.[61] This liberality has incited critical attention, prompting Ziv, for instance, to describe the trilogy as 'a politically correct SM fantasy'.[62] Nevertheless, as Ziv herself points out, although such aspects as the occasional reversal of master/slave roles is emancipatory because it indicates that these positions are mainly constructs, the overall gender–power correlative is only superficially transformed.[63] The institution of a master, even if the person occupying that function alters, replicates the traditional hegemony and consequently renders the tale inadequate as a myth for our time. If in Rice's *Interview with the Vampire* we have the horror of limitlessness, here we have the lack of originality and creation that too overbearing a limit occasions.[64]

A short story by Pat Califia entitled 'The Vampire' combines the focus of Anne Rice's 'The Vampire Chronicles' with that of her erotic fiction to interesting effect.[65] Califia's story opens in a SM (sado-masochism) bar ironically called 'Purgatory', and the narrative is purposeful in its enumeration of the dominatrix Kerry's vampiric features, from the extreme pallor of her skin, to her prominent canine teeth, superhuman strength and, above all, fascination with the blood that her whipping of the submissive Bill produces. The violence of Kerry's treatment of Bill is in sharp contrast to the tame 'spankings' and 'paddlings' of the Beauty trilogy, where the code decrees that all punishments shall cease at the first sign of blood. Traditional gender distinctions are also far more radically subverted in Califia's story. Not only is the vampire a woman and her first 'victim' a male submissive, but the exchange with Iduna that concludes the narrative involves explicit details of lesbian sex.[66] The link between vampirism and maternal plenitude is highlighted in the story, as Iduna cuts a V-shaped slash between her breasts to tempt Kerry to feed, and Kerry's hands pump Iduna's breasts to increase the blood-flow as if they are 'nursing'.[67]

When Iduna faints from the force of the feeding, Kerry supports her 'the way a mother holds an infant'.[68] This interchange of positions from the one nursing to the one holding is repeated for Iduna as the narrative shifts to present her point of view, and the pleasure she experiences in satiating the other's hunger metamorphoses into the pleasure of 'being picked up, cradled'.[69] Thus, in contradistinction to Bill's apparently meaningless suffering, which sickens even the bar's regulars, Califia's story ends with an emphatically sexual delineation of vampirism as the longed-for return to mother–child symbiosis, in which it becomes possible to read the violence as an echo of primary separation. What is even more striking about Califia's ending, though, is the desire it manifests to play with that horror, by eroticising it, and by continually changing one's position. Here, however, the narrative halts, with a question, the suggestion of a possibility, rather than answers.[70] Perhaps, as Kristeva argues, the demarcations that comprise our symbolising code are too firmly implanted, so that the most we can hope for is to use its aesthetic possibilities to shatter the inertia of our own abjection.[71] If this is indeed the case, and myth-breaking cannot be followed by a new paradigm, then questions and suggestions may be as far as we can currently go towards articulating an alternative scheme.

Like *Dracula*, Robert Louis Stevenson's *The Strange Case of Dr Jekyll and Mr Hyde* is a nineteenth-century novel that has attained the currency of myth. In Stevenson's fiction, Jekyll, an eminent and respected physician, discovers a drug which enables him to incarnate the aspects of his personality that society obliges him to repress. The depiction of Jekyll's transmutations into the 'evil' Hyde can be productively viewed in the light of Kristeva's work on abjection. In his written confession at the end of the narrative, Jekyll outlines how he had always found it impossible to reconcile his 'pleasures' with the 'grave countenance' society required him to wear, an impossibility that had led to a 'profound duplicity'.[72] He recounts how, as Hyde, he at first revelled in the opportunity to indulge his more 'natural and human' side without incurring the penalties that would have jeopardised his standing as Jekyll.[73] The correlations between Hyde and an infantile, pre-social self are highlighted in a series of descriptions of the sensory and corporeal release Jekyll experiences as Hyde.[74] Jekyll's delight in his metamorphosis quickly turns to horror, however, as Hyde's inability to perceive beyond his own desires results in Carew's murder. Kristeva's study offers a number of illuminating insights into Stevenson's creation. According to Kristeva's analysis, the abject represents the infant's first efforts towards individuation, a movement of rejection which involves violent and negative emotions. These feelings – of revulsion, loathing, fear – are bound up with the infant's burgeoning sense of self and mark all his/her subsequent constructions. Unlike the object, which supports the signifying infant's attempts at self-definition, the emerging infant cannot yet delineate the space that is opened up by its repulsions: and so this abject persists in threatening its designations of meaning and identity, a familiar and abominable 'haunting'.[75] Kristeva's account is suggestive of Jekyll's reaction to Hyde, as the latter gains in power to the extent that Jekyll requires drugs only to return to his 'original', socially-sanctioned self.[76] Jekyll's depiction of his abhorrence of Hyde is striking in terms of Kristeva's thesis:

> that insurgent horror was knit to him closer than a wife, closer than an eye; lay caged in his flesh, where he heard it mutter and felt it struggle to be born; and at every hour of weakness, and in the confidences of slumber, prevailed against him, and deposed him out of life.[77]

The image of a muttering Hyde caged in Jekyll's flesh explicitly recalls Kristeva's description of the infant's struggle 'to be born' as a separate, speaking subject, while Jekyll's terror of being annihilated by Hyde reiterates Kristeva's insistence on the ongoing menace to subject-formation that the abject poses.[78] One of the many interesting features of Stevenson's narration is the account of the general 'disgust, loathing and fear' Jekyll in his guise as Hyde provokes.[79] The 'cut-and-dry' apothecary, for example, who tends Hyde's first victim, is portrayed as turning 'sick and white with the desire to kill him', while the women watching are transformed into 'harpies' by the hatred Hyde instils.[80] This description of Hyde's pervasive impact can be linked to Kristeva's argument that the abject threatens collective, social – as well as individual – configurations. In becoming Hyde, Jekyll realises that he has 'voluntarily stripped myself of all those balancing instincts' that normally hold our selfish desires in check.[81] Acknowledging that this lack of constraint brought about Carew's murder, Jekyll reflects in a formulation that recalls Stoker's vampire that Hyde 'that child of Hell had nothing human about him'.[82] Thus Stevenson's tale is ultimately one about the restitution of limits, as the saving grace of our humanity. Paralleling Hélène Cixous's work on the Medusa, what the mythical Jekyll/Hyde displays is the monstrosity that derives from too-rigid a social structure, in which our origins and

nature cannot be owned. Here too it remains a question as to whether
a different topography might render such dangerous duplicities redundant, as Jekyll wonders about a future that would recognise the het-
erogeneity of self.

Emma Tennant has rewritten a number of literary myths, including
Stevenson's *The Strange Case of Dr Jekyll and Mr Hyde*.[83] Her *Two
Women of London: The Strange Case of Ms Jekyll and Mrs Hyde* repeats
many features of the original, such as the names, the adjoining houses,
the use of drugs to effect the metamorphoses, the maid's eyewitness
account, the tell-tale handwriting, the deaths of the doctors who first
learn of Jekyll's 'case', and the description of the hand that reveals to
both Hydes that their transformation has not been accomplished.
There are, however, significant differences between the two fictions.
Whereas in Stevenson's novel the drug that Jekyll discovers enables
him, at least initially, to incarnate the self that society has obliged
him to suppress, in Tennant's reworking the drugs are used by the
depressed and marginalised Mrs Hyde to acquire the youthfulness and
beauty that will win her social approbation. As Steven Connor argues,
the transmutation Tennant's Hyde undergoes is based on an ideal
projection rather than an existing facet of self.[84] This aspect of
Tennants's rewriting links to Fay Weldon's creation of Ruth in *The
Life and Loves of a She Devil*. While in Stevenson Jekyll's use of drugs
to break the 'bounds' that prevent him from indulging his selfish pleasures is demonstrated to be disastrous and the novel consequently
upholds the status quo, the fact that in Tennant Mrs Hyde requires
drugs to obtain work and acceptability is a serious indictment of the
social regime.[85] Thus the restoration that follows Jekyll/Hyde's death
in Stevenson is withheld in Tennant, since the limits society imposes
are not endorsed as vital to our collective well-being but are rather
shown to derive from male definitions which have injurious consequences for women.[86] Tennant's feminist revision can be linked to
Kristeva's work on society's abjection of the feminine in *Powers of
Horror*. In her essay 'From Filth to Defilement', Kristeva explores the
correlations between the emerging infant's struggle against the
omnipotent maternal body and society's endeavour to repress or control the feminine. Her argument that this desire centres on the maternal function illuminates the quasi-phobia that surrounds Tennant's
recasting of Hyde as a divorced mother. The novel opens with
an insistence that Mrs Hyde's 'tatterdemalion house' and children
should not be considered part of the 'desirable' Crescents in which
the action is set, while the most striking features about the slim,

elegant, energetic, successful and cultured Ms Jekyll appear to proclaim her childlessness.[87] The fact that this is a situation which affects
all women and not only the unfortunate Mrs Hyde is indicated in the
narrator's realisation that the solicitor Jean Hastie's obsession with
Mrs Hyde – and it cannot be coincidental that Jean Hastie's initials
repeat those of Jekyll/Hyde – is due to its triggering a 'whole buried
side'.[88] This feminist reinterpretation of Stevenson's fiction replicates
Kristeva's argument that wherever society institutes itself on the basis
of male power, then the oppressed but equally powerful feminine
becomes synonymous with evil.[89]

There are several indications in Tennant's reworking that Mrs Hyde's
predicament is a consequence of the Thatcher regime that governed
the United Kingdom during the 1980s. This administration's valuing
of 'rapaciousness' is expounded by the narrator and is also woven into
the text's imagery, in the prowling figure of the rapist who frequents
the communal gardens, for example, and the opening delineation of the
mown grass which is 'as neat and straight as the lines in a bank book'.[90]
Tennant's decision to link the community that shuns Mrs Hyde to a
specific government suggests Kristeva's hypothesis that the abject
assumes different shapes according to the codings operated by the ruling presidency.[91] In *Two Women of London*, the good/evil binary that
permeates Stevenson's fiction is given a fresh twist through Jean
Hastie's research into the nature of original sin. Her conclusion – that
we are each of us free and responsible for our actions – is only partially
endorsed by the narrative, however, which indicates that while this
may be the case in a collective sense it is not wholly true for individuals, since success, 'goodness', even one's gender, are shown to be
socially determined.[92] The murder Hyde commits in Tennant's rewriting highlights the complexity, since while the man she kills is not the
rapist he is the rapacious Sir James Lister, and it is consequently not
possible to condemn her action as unconditionally 'evil' as it is in
Stevenson's original. Jean Hastie's avowal in an 'afterword' that the
case of Jekyll/Hyde has 'caused a considerable rift in both Christian
and atheist feminist thinking' echoes the pronouncement that
Dr Crane's heart attack occurs as a result of 'the strain of trying to
reconcile opposites', and underscores the difficulties *Two Women of
London* displays of separating personal motivation from social engi-
neering.[93] Perhaps the only response to such an impasse is to remember Kristeva's argument that culture has been and therefore can be
constituted differently, and to broach the 'horror' that any such refiguring of the division between self and other resurrects.[94]

Tennant's *Faustine*, which draws on the Renaissance legend of the mountebank who sold his soul to the devil in exchange for knowledge and power, repeats the central themes of *Two Women of London*.[95] Muriel's metamorphosis into Lisa Crane parallels Mrs Hyde's transformation as Ms Jekyll, except that here the world's idolisation of Lisa is shown to derive as much from the immense wealth she acquires as from her beauty or even her leased youthfulness.[96] In an interesting extension of Byatt and Weldon's 'redundant' middle-aged protagonists, the context in which Muriel's conversion occurs is this time the youth culture of the 1960s. Jasmine Barr, who narrates the story for the benefit of Muriel's granddaughter Ella, argues that this 'was the very worst time in history, probably, to find yourself all of a sudden middle-aged', particularly if you were female.[97] Unlike *Two Women of London*, where the disjointed narration prevents us from empathising with any one character, in *Faustine* the feminist slant operates through the detailed knowledge we are given of – and our consequent sympathy for – Muriel's predicament, as she struggles to care for her daughter and granddaughter and to do a job that makes her 'invisible'.[98] The poignancy of Muriel's situation is also highlighted by her granddaughter, whose quest for Muriel frames the novel, since Ella herself fears what she perceives as the horror of old age.[99] The agency through which Muriel's transformation takes place is not drugs but the media's power to determine what we see. This is portrayed partly by the Devil's conjuring trick in the television showroom that persuades Muriel to sell her soul, and partly through Muriel's own manipulations of the fashion and magazine world that result in her becoming head of the appropriately named 'New Image Corporation, Inc.'. That the media's representations are falsehoods is emphasised in the text, in the description of the lies Muriel must tell as a fashion-writer, for example, and in the posed photographs and videos in Lisa's 'mausoleum' which Ella realises are 'a terrible travesty of life'.[100]

The account of Muriel's Faustian transaction suggests Kristeva's delineation of the circumstances in which what she terms 'an ego wounded to the point of annulment' endeavours to counteract by designing 'a stream of spurious egos' to deal in its place.[101] Kristeva's description recalls Muriel's sense of 'invisibility' as well as the plethora of what Ella perceives to be the 'dead' media images of Lisa Crane.[102] As Kristeva indicates, the problem with this delegation is that the individual cannot engage in a relation with others, a point echoed in Ella's childhood nightmare of Lisa as the Snow Queen with a frozen heart.[103] This implicit critique of Muriel's metamorphosis is made explicit in the depiction of the problems that her alteration of the natural course entails.[104] Since one of the consequences of Muriel's acquisition of youth is her theft of her daughter Anna's lover, Anna experiences her mother's rejuvenation as the negation of her own existence. Muriel's conversion also robs Ella of the beloved grandmother who has been her lifeline – Ella refers to her as her 'constant' star, her 'one sacred thing' – since her new lifestyle cannot accommodate a granddaughter, while simultaneously depriving Muriel who finds it hard to erase her love for Ella.[105] There is also Anna's assertion that Muriel's actions are part of the larger aberrations apparent in contemporary attitudes to the natural world.[106] Perhaps, though, the most interesting comment on Muriel's pact is given by the Devil himself. Arguing that hell is the chaos of 'unendingness', his tale corroborates Kristeva's thesis that boundaries are what make us human.[107] The challenge posed by Tennant's *Faustine* would therefore seem to be to fill the 'blank' the Devil figures with limits that enable rather than destroy.[108]

Vampires, sex-slaves, feminine paragons: the rewritings of Anne Rice and Emma Tennant refuse the restoration of order which their antecedents perform. Rather, their purpose is to reveal the procedures that create society and the self, as well as the horrors that can ensue whenever these processes do not occur, or occur in too repressive a fashion. In this, they fulfill what Kristeva describes as the former function of the sacred, though with an open-endedness that religion has hitherto seldom attained.[109] Despite different mythic models, their strategies and conclusions accord with those of a number of the rewritings discussed so far. In delineating the effect of too much and too little and in refusing to ordinance a solution, Rice and Tennant utilise contemporary understandings to prompt us to think through our parameters for ourselves. By showing us the consequences of this dilemma and by leaving the ultimate responsibility with their reader, their expository fictions present a potent mythopoeia for our time.

6
Bodies of Power
Beauty Myths in Tales by Marina Warner, Emma Donoghue, Sheri Tepper and Alice Thompson

And after the Emperor had appeared naked and no one had dis-
turbed the solemn occasion, one little girl went home in silence and
took off her clothes. Then she said to her mother. 'Look at me,
please, I am an Emperor.' To which her mother replied. 'Don't be
silly, darling. Only little boys grow up to be Emperors.'

Suniti Namjoshi, *Feminist Fables*[1]

There is no power that acts, but only a reiterated acting.

Judith Butler, *Bodies that Matter:*
On the Discursive Limits of 'Sex'[2]

In Marina Warner's rewriting of the story of the Queen of Sheba, the
legend of the Queen's beauty is appropriately intertwined with an
analysis of the power relations that underscored her famous meeting
with King Solomon.[3] This is signalled right at the start of Warner's
retelling, as the modern-day narrator outlines how Solomon's letter to
Sheba warned her of retribution if she failed to yield to his suzerainty.
Warner's narrator is a female academic, attending a conference in
Jerusalem with a group of male colleagues. The tale opens with the
narrator hastily hiding the various beauty items she has brought with
her so that she can take her turn in hosting a drink in her hotel bedroom. Despite her precautions, she quickly finds herself revealing
details of women's beauty procedures in an uncomfortable endeavour
to join in the men's sexist banter. Her desire to be approved of

prompts her to display her legs, an action that explicitly recalls the trick Solomon played on Sheba in order to glimpse what lay beneath her skirts. After her colleagues have left, Warner's narrator upbraids herself for forgetting her feminism in her attempt to curry favour, and ponders the complicated causality that leads women to betray their sex. In her own case, she remembers her mother's ruthless 'assassination' of other women's bodies in her discussions with her friends and the impact their implied ideal had on her own emerging sense of herself as female.[4] This more subtle power nexus, identified by the narrator in the light of her contemporary experience, is then shown to operate in the legend of Sheba alongside the discernible dynamic of the relative inferiority of Sheba's country. In Warner's version, Solomon's freezing of the river into an ice mirror over which Sheba must walk is interpreted in terms of the irregularity of Sheba's position as a beautiful, wise, comparatively wealthy, *single* woman: she must be a sorcerer's illusion, the djinns whisper to Solomon, with diabolic hooves and hairy legs.

In this context, Sheba's seduction of Solomon reads as an astute response to the prevailing power conditions rather than as a straightforward romance. Yet the love story persists, in past tellings of the myth as well as in Warner's reworking. At the end of the conference, the narrator visits the hill near the Old City of Jerusalem where Solomon is reported to have housed his harem. The beauty of the site, with its lemon trees and sweeping views, reawakens the narrator's wish for the romance to be true. Although her tale ends on a feminist note, it is undercut by the sensual pleasures of the location and the poetry of the Solomon–Sheba myth, the latter interwoven into the narrator's strident call to resist temptation and continue the fight through italicised parentheses that repeat Solomon's beguiling entreaties.[5]

The use of the present-day narrator in Marina Warner's retelling of the story of the Queen of Sheba to unpick the complicated patchwork of imperatives that drive women both then and now suggests Naomi Wolf's thesis in her polemical study *The Beauty Myth*.[6] The narrator's memory of the 'scorecards of physical perfections' her mother and her friends devised to judge women by, as well as her own collusion in her male colleagues' patronising repartee, supports Wolf's view that despite the advances made by feminism women are still caught in a debilitating stratagem.[7] For Wolf, a myth of feminine beauty has been resurrected to take the place of those legal and social constraints Western feminism so effectively discredited during the 1970s as detrimental to women's lives. Although Wolf sees the creation of this myth as a response by the magazine and advertising industries to the loss of

revenues that resulted when feminism highlighted the restrictive
nature of the domesticity their products had hitherto enshrined, her
analysis of its wide application by the media, government institutions
and commerce more generally leads her to categorise it as a pervasive
device for ensuring women's continued subordination.[8] In this context, beauty is a currency forged for the benefit of those in power
rather than an intrinsic attribute.[9] Wolf examines women's susceptibility to the operations of the myth, drawing for this purpose on the
work of other feminist commentators, including Marina Warner's history of monuments, with its demonstration of how women rarely figure as named individuals but only as the anonymous, 'beautiful'
accompaniments to great men.[10] Wolf suggests that such traditions
have conspired to teach women to value themselves only in terms of
the way they are perceived. While Wolf does not elaborate on this
point, her argument can be linked to the discussion of other feminist
theoreticians such as Moira Gatens, who draws on the writings of the
cultural historian Michel Foucault to contend that what we think of as
our bodies is less an effect of genetics than the result of historically
and socially specific practices of power.[11] Gatens's notion of the body
as both the target of and the medium for expressing such operations
of power adds a further illuminating dimension to Wolf's thesis.

A number of Emma Donoghue's feminist fairy tales in her collection *Kissing the Witch* illustrate the impact a prescriptive standard of
beauty can have.[12] In her retelling of 'Donkeyskin', for example, the
prince's failure to recognise the princess without her alluring costumes
causes her to rebel. Although the princess's action ultimately makes it
possible for her to see herself, the tale makes it clear that the prince
will continue to suffer.[13] In Donoghue's reworking of 'Cinderella',
the dicta that reduce the protagonist to a domestic drudge are neither
the impositions of a hostile stepmother as in the source tale, nor a
desire to placate a male hegemony as in 'The Legs of the Queen of
Sheba', but, in an interesting elucidation of Gatens's theory, voices
the protagonist has internalised: 'nobody made me do the things I
did, nobody scolded me, nobody punished me but me. The shrill
voices were all inside'.[14] In 'The Tale of the Voice', the protagonist
deliberately assumes a seductive guise in order to procure her man, a
tactic that tellingly includes never speaking. Although, as Naomi Wolf
indicates, the protagonist's conformity initally grants her a degree of
power, this is only within a very limited arena and quickly evaporates
once her man's attentions are caught by a new 'beauty'.[15]

Sheri S. Tepper's novel *Beauty* creates its own beauty myth which
it uses in the service of ecology.[16] Ostensibly a rewrite of the tale

of 'Sleeping Beauty', Tepper's narrative draws on aspects of science fiction in order to show how the world will end unless human beings take a more responsible attitude to the earth's resources. Beauty, the novel's protagonist, is the cursed daughter of the fairy story who nonetheless manages to escape her fate to become the repository of all that is beautiful, as she inadvertently stumbles across a group of documentary-makers from the future and is transported by them into the late twenty-first century. This is a time in which the world has had to reorganise in order to feed its excessive population: the earth is a giant farm for the production of the wafers that give its human inhabitants 'sustenance ... but no pleasure', while living arrangements are confined to cell-like rooms in 'tall, half-buried towers'.[17] The earth's eventual collapse is signalled both in the 'forever pool' which prompts Beauty's fairy aunt to 'curse' Beauty, and in the reports of the refugees from the twenty-second century Beauty meets in the present day. These refugees, who, like Beauty and the documentary-makers who take her into the future, benefit from an anomaly in the time-travel technology to return a hundred years, arrive with stories of exhausted farms and defunct power-generators as people are pushed down the waste-disposal chutes 'a hundred thousand at a time'.[18] Their plight is poignantly illustrated in the story of the mother who kills her six-year-old daughter while singing the future's grim slogans.[19]

The institution of beauty as that which must be preserved in this context of extinction is achieved partly through the insistence on the 'ugliness' of the future when contrasted with the virtues of the fourteenth century and the loveliness of the castle where Beauty is born, and partly through the establishment of a dialectic between beauty and evil. This last antithesis is present in the conflict between the Holy One who made the world in its beauty and the Dark Lord whose 'worship of pain' and death finally threatens the world with total destruction that drives the plot, as well as in the various comparisons between beautiful and evil creation, such as that indicated by Beauty's visit to Baskarone which contains 'everything that men made beautiful' and the 'horro-porn' that is the staple cultural diet of the future.[20] Despite an irritating naivety in its nostalgia for the idealised order and chivalry of the fourteenth century and the occasionally crude distinctions that are drawn between beauty and ugliness/evil, the novel's construction of its myth is more complex than might at first appear, and suggests a number of pertinent parallels with those theories which link the designation of beauty to power.[21] Beauty's mother is a fairy, one of the last of her kind, and Beauty's visit to her realm of Ylles is significant in that it requires Beauty to eat fairy fruit and rub 'elvenroot' into her eyes before she can turn what she first perceives as 'a waste of moorland' into the 'marvels' and perfection of Faery.[22] Later, Beauty is able to achieve such transformations without the aid of magic fruits and herbs. Her discovery that she can create beauty simply by thinking about it causes her to wonder: 'What else could I do, just by thinking?'[23]

This more complex notion of beauty as a deliberate action is qualified by the narrative's depiction of the fairies' visual 'enchantment' of a human couple into deer which they can then hunt, kill and eat without explicitly contravening the pact they have made with the Holy One not to cause humans lasting harm, through their heartless treatment of Thomas the Rhymer, and above all in the account of the fairies' sterility.[24] The solution Beauty's fairy aunt devises to preserve the beauty she incorporates is to hide her away from the machinations of the Dark Lord and his human supporters in the world out-of-time devised by the writer Ambrosius Pomposus. Despite its manifold charms, the narrative shows this world to be untenable, since it is the product of a single mind and consequently limited. The text presents its dissolution as the outcome of its inevitable flaws, detailed in this case as the lack of spontaneity and surprise.[25] The way through the impasse these qualifications to the creation of beauty reveal is paradoxically supplied in the episode during which Beauty is a hostage to the Dark Lord in hell. Here, despite the ugliness and evil graphically portrayed in the descriptions of torture and pain, Beauty uses the power of thought to transform reality not only for her own sake but also for the common good. As in Dante's *Inferno*, the occupants of the Dark Lord's hell experience the consequences of their own injurious inventions, which Beauty endeavours to counter first by inciting individuals to think differently and then by instigating a collective 'magic'.[26] The episode thus underscores both the potency of individual creation and the greater power of collaborative effort, as well as the need for all such action to be ethically responsible.[27]

This view of beauty as an effect of deliberate, accountable designation underscores the novel's ecological project, since the earth is presented as the product of both the Holy One's original and human beings' ongoing acts of creation. The adoption of fairy tale as the main generic model offers an appropriate medium for the moral that the world's future depends on each of us creating caringly rather than greedily, as well as encompassing the frequent time-shifts the narration employs.[28] It also upholds the simplistic characterisation and the grandiose sweeps of the plot.[29] Nevertheless, despite its worthy purpose and the astute use of genre to achieve it, the novel ultimately fails in the manufacture of its myth. The final installation of the protagonist as an icon of the world's beauty, which is to be preserved for a distant future, is at odds with the depictions of beauty as a mode of perception.[30] In a sci-fi variant of the fairy story, Beauty falls asleep at the end of the novel having filled her castle with samples of all that the world contains.[31] Despite her recognition that because the Holy One made the world beautiful in its entirety she must include even those creatures which cause destruction, this does not extend to its human population since she arranges for Sibylla, the woman who might have been her stepmother, who is already asleep in the castle, to be removed. Beauty has overheard Sibylla's scheming to marry into her father's supposed fortune, and interprets this as an indication of her evil rather than as the desperate resort of a woman endeavouring to survive in a society where marriage may have been her only option.[32] Similarly, despite some potentially interesting criticism of human beings' over-reliance on the eye – Beauty, for example, comes to condemn Faery on this count – the concomitant insistence that what actually matters is meaning and not appearance disavows the interrelated nature of the two.[33] These failures to comprehend the complex mechanisms that inform what we do connects to the naive note of cautious optimism with which the novel ends.[34] The narrative emphatically locates the present as the last point at which humankind has the chance to avert the impending ecological disaster, and yet it shows Beauty's attempts to take action to be useless. Its message that the world's salvation ultimately depends not on politics or direct intervention but on men's innate desire 'to make things come out right' undermines its earlier insistence on the need for training and deliberation in all acts of what it has defined as beautiful creation.[35]

Judith Butler's work on the way the body is constructed through performance offers a further illuminating perspective on the designation of beauty.[36] For Butler, individual identity is the product of the way the body repeatedly performs cultural norms. As an example, she examines the shift that is effected when a baby is changed from an 'it' by the pronouncement that it is a 'he' or 'she', a naming which 'boys' the boy and 'girls' the girl by bringing them into the social domain of language and human relationships in particular ways.[37] This process of 'boying' and 'girling' does not, however, end at this point, but is resumed at intervals by different authoritative bodies who continue the process of definition. What is significant in Butler's analysis is that the interpellating agencies in the progress towards self-demarcation are effective only as they are reiterated by the individual. Like the law, power in this context depends on our citation for its impact. This sheds an interesting light on the collusions of Warner's narrator in 'The Legs of the Queen of Sheba', since it suggests that she is right when she reflects that it would have been better if she had articulated an alternative viewpoint, as well as on the difficult options the majority of Emma Donoghue's heroines choose. Although many of Donoghue's tales where the central character disobeys the expected pattern end in uncertainty rather than triumph, Butler's account indicates that their contrary performance may be the starting-point for a new programme.[38]

While Butler is not concerned with the issue of beauty per se, her discussion of the production of the sexed body presents an interesting additional perspective to the theories of beauty I have examined so far. For Butler, one's sex is not simply a function of biological differences, but is rather the result of the way these differences are delineated culturally and then performed by the individual. This analysis offers a further underpinning to the depiction in Tepper's novel of the training the central character must undergo to participate in the culture of Faery.[39] While Beauty's participation is at first engendered by magic, she later learns how to perform the magic on herself. In the episode where the fairies ride out to hunt, for example, Beauty has only to look to see how the others are dressed in order to be able to present herself in the same way.[40] Significantly in terms of Butler's theory, Beauty's action is motivated by her mother's chiding that she is not appropriately attired. It is pertinent to Butler's point that the style Beauty chooses is the 'high boots and flowing skirts on the ladies'.[41]

Another facet of Butler's analysis which chimes with a discussion of Tepper's novel is Butler's account of the way one's sex is constituted in relation to designated and regulating 'ideals'. It is the individual's attempt to reiterate these ideals that cumulatively produce his or her gender, a series of enactments which in turn serves to uphold the ideals. Butler's theory here sheds an instructive light on the performances of Ruth in Fay Weldon's *The Life and Loves of a She Devil*, the protagonist of A. S. Byatt's 'Medusa's Ankles', the young Mary in Christine Crow's *Miss X or the Wolf Woman*, Emma Tennant's *Ms Jekyll/Mrs Hyde* and Muriel/Lisa Crane in *Faustine*, as well as Marina Warner's narrator in her tale of the Queen of Sheba. Butler's insistence on this point is given an interesting twist by James Kirwan in his philosophical investigation into the nature of beauty.[42] Kirwan combines the Augustinian idea of the *musica mundana* (or music of the heavenly spheres) as a model for earthly beauty with the Lacanian notion of the impossibility of satisfying desire, to posit a concept of beauty as that which we yearn for but know we can never attain.[43] His suggestion that it is this simultaneous movement of promise and accepted impossibility which comprises its allure offers a further informative interpretation of Tepper's ending, since it indicates that Beauty's failure to save the world through her actions may be the condition for the preservation of the novel's beauty myth.

Alice Thompson's *Pandora's Box* offers a fascinating illustration of Butler's notion of the delineation of the self in relation to legislating ideals.[44] The novel begins with Dr Noah Close being awoken one night to discover a burning figure on his doorstep. Although the narration stresses that the body Noah rescues is so badly burned that it is impossible to tell whether it is male or female, it is significant that when he arrives at the hospital Noah automatically refers to it as a woman. His apparently thoughtless appellation sets the template for all his subsequent dealings with the body. Noah's medical specialism is 'the reconstruction of human bodies' and it is to him that the seemingly impossible task of repairing the body is allocated.[45] The face in particular is so badly damaged that he must rebuild even the bones. To do this Noah chooses a 'textbook photograph of an idealised woman's face' even though he fully expects that the recovery process will leave the face a mass of scars.[46] Contrary to all his experience, however, both the body and the face heal flawlessly, producing a perfect replica of the textbook's ideal woman which is glossed by the narration as Noah's 'dream come true'.[47]

Noah's marriage to Pandora, her murder and Noah's subsequent search for her also illuminate Kirwan's theory of beauty as an impelling ideal, as Noah's quest leads him to give up first his home, then his job, and finally his most cherished beliefs. Playfully cast in the genre of crime fiction, Noah's determination to discover the truth about Pandora continues to inspire him even after he has been cleared by the police. Significantly in terms of Kirwan's analysis, the truth Noah desires is imaged as completion: 'the oneness he was looking for'.[48] Evoking Lacan's notion of the desire for an impossible plenitude as the mainspring of human motivation, Kirwan suggests that it is this paradox of abundance and lack which is at the heart of beauty's allure, a hypothesis illustrated here in the depiction of Noah's sense that he never fully possessed Pandora despite being married to her.[49] Kirwan's contention that the essence of beauty is that it intimates fulfilment even as it denies its own promise also underscores the reference to the mythical Pandora in the passage from Hesiod that opens the narrative, in which Pandora is given to men so that 'they may all be glad to heart while they embrace their own destruction'.[50]

Lazarus, who may be Pandora's murderer, if only because he is the man she has perhaps become (Pandora risen from the dead), is beautiful in a way that recalls Butler's thesis of the operation of ideals in self-formation. The outside of Lazarus' house is covered in mirrors which reflect the external world while revealing nothing of itself, and Lazarus' beauty is similarly based on his ability to reflect his interlocutors, giving them a heightened portrait of themselves. It is noteworthy that Angela Carter's *The Passion of New Eve*, which will be discussed in the next section, has a comparable character and setting. Yet Thompson's novel goes further than the exposition of the way the individual is drawn to reproduce such a mirroring. Venus, Noah's unwilling aide in his search for Pandora, agrees to lure Lazarus in an attempt to find out what he knows, and in order to do so turns herself into an icon of the women Lazarus desires.[51] When Noah next finds her, the awful mechanisms of this procedure have become apparent since Lazarus has completed the process and turned Venus into a living statue, with Pandora's box nailed to her palms. The cost of such (re)definition is also exposed in the description of the excruciating pain Pandora suffers as Noah surgically transforms her, as well as in the implied distress of her marriage to Noah, experiences which prompt Lazarus to ask Noah if he has ever wondered what it might be like for the person he refashions.[52] These depictions, together with Lazarus' revelation that he wanted to free Pandora from Noah's debilitating idolisation of her, exemplify Butler's account of the distortions we undergo in our endeavours to approximate to a commanding ideal.[53]

Whereas in the texts I have discussed thus far beauty is primarily a visual phenomenon, as the vibrant descriptions of the site of Solomon's harem in Warner's story or the wonders of Faery, Chinanga and Baskarone in Tepper's chronicle exemplify, this insistence on the eye is questioned in Thompson's novel.[54] Noah's search for Pandora takes him to the desert where his experience of a mirage forces him to acknowledge that his eyes can deceive him. This realisation that he can be convinced that he can see something which is not there in reality forces him to question the empiricism that has hereto governed his life.[55] His admission that perception is neither reliable nor neutral is further demonstrated in his suspicion that the world he inhabits after Pandora's departure is an emanation of his own state of mind and above all in his association with Venus, the psychic detective, whose distrust of reality initially places her at the opposite pole to Noah.[56] Although it is Venus' intuitive, imaginative response that eventually leads Noah back to Pandora, her approach is shown to have its problems since it pinions her first inside Noah's hunt and then in the dreams and fantasies of the world he takes her to, captioned in the aptly named hotel 'The Mirage'.[57] Lazarus' blinding of Venus, which Venus explains as an abortive attempt to stop her from seeing the truth, is a further, horrific discrediting of the role of the eye in perception. The ending, which tentatively brings Noah and Venus together, appears to signal that their best chance of accurate vision lies in a careful combination of their respective methods.

Butler's insistence that sex is never a simple fact or condition of the body but a construction achieved through the reiteration of cultural ideals is explicitly demonstrated in Thompson's narrative, in Noah's appellation and surgical creation of the female Pandora and Venus' self-transformation into an icon of seductive femininity. For Butler, though, this process of becoming a man or a woman is always problematic since one's body never quite complies with the given forms. This is demonstrated in the obvious difficulties Pandora has in being Noah's wife, exemplified in her tapestry of the beautiful, naked, full-breasted and wide-hipped woman to which she adds a painstakingly stitched erect penis, and in her own presumed resurr(er)ection as Lazarus.[58] It is also developed through the deliberate gender mixings of the saloon Lazarus frequents, where the statues of the Virgin Mary have black beards painted on them, the figures of Christ wear sequinned dresses, and the staff and customers cross-dress, which precipitate a series of unanswered and perhaps unanswerable questions as to what being a 'real' man/woman means.[59]

For Butler, the process of gender definition is a differential one, involving the creation of an excluded and consequently threatening 'outside' which drives us to persistently rearticulate our position.[60] Her discussion of the equation of this 'outside' with femininity suggests an interesting interpretation of the passage from Hesiod that prefaces Thompson's novel, in which Pandora is given to men so that she may destroy them.[61] It also offers an instructive view of Noah's relation to Pandora, since it indicates why his (re)creation of her becomes his undoing.[62] The fact that Pandora does not speak despite being physically able to do so is similarly illuminated in Butler's delineation of the constructed subject as a body that speaks.[63] In this context, Noah's fantasised devouring of Pandora – an act which releases him from his quest and enables him to live in the 'real' world once more – might be read as his endeavour to incorporate what he has hitherto refused.[64]

Butler's insistence that the maintenance of the legislating forms depends on our continued citation of them suggests that the laws which ordain masculinity and femininity, beautiful or otherwise, are inherently fragile and can be contravened. This possibility is explored in the spoof detective story that is woven into Thompson's narrative, since the police's decision to abandon the case frees Noah to dispense his own law. Yet, as Butler argues, the opportunities for a different performance are limited, and Noah must ultimately rid himself of his creation if he is to avoid psychosis.[65] At the novel's close, neither he nor Venus can dispense with their pasts, despite their mutual recognition of patches of new light.

While Butler and Thompson both signal the difficulties that attach to any reformulation given the prevailing context, neither suggest that the current institution and exercise of power should remain unanalysed or intact. Thompson's novel in particular intimates that an answer may lie in the pooling of procedures, since both Noah's empirical and Venus' imaginative visions are shown on their own to be deficient. Empiricism is discredited because it ignores the presiding power nexus as well as the nature of the act of perception, just as Noah has ignored the abysses that open on either side of the tightrope of facts he has strung across his life.[66] As his initial labelling of Pandora demonstrates, seeing is never neutral but is always directed through the filter of a specific history and culture. Imagination on its own is revealed to be equally inadequate, as Noah's obsession with his invention Pandora impels him to abandon his past self, until all he is left with is a series of gestures that are as meaningless as the mock styles of the bedrooms in the motel he and Venus visit.[67] *Pandora's Box* consequently argues for a recognition of the different facets that collectively comprise vision, including the perspective of the perceiver, the delineating norms which structure vision, and the interplay of experience, understanding and expectation that affects all acts of cognition.[68] Perhaps, in the end, the lesson Noah and Venus learn is that perception is never a reflection but itself a realisation of the truth.[69] Thompson's novel thus offers a more viable conclusion than Tepper's, as its note of wary expectancy is based on comprehension of the dilemma and the attendant dangers of adopting one path at the expense of another. In this, it connects to the presentation of the problems involved in forging an alternative that can be seen in the rewritings discussed so far, particularly since, like them, it refuses to do more than indicate the direction of a solution.

7
New Myths or Old?
Angela Carter's Mirrors and Mothers

Not until all babies are born from glass jars will the combat cease.
Camille Paglia, *Sexual Personae*[1]

Am I fact? Or am I fiction? Am I what I know I am? Or am I what he thinks I am?
Angela Carter, *Nights at the Circus*[2]

In Angela Carter's perplexing tale 'Reflections', the male narrator is forced to kiss himself in a mirror.[3] Since he fully expects the reflected lips to be cold and lifeless, he is astonished when he discovers that they are warm and moist and that the embrace excites his sexual desire. The narrator is drawn through the mirror by the kiss, into the antithetical domain of its other side. Despite the strange, topsy-turviness of this realm, where the reversed laws require the narrator to do the opposite to what he intends, it quickly becomes impossible for the narrator to distinguish between the real world and its reflection. Carter's precise, elaborate descriptions make the hold this mirror world exerts over the narrator entirely convincing.

The mirror is a recurring theme in Carter's fiction. In another short story, 'Flesh and the Mirror', the mirror above the lovers' bed in the 'blue-movie' hotel room they rent for the night has the effect of reducing the lovers to their actions beneath it: 'time, place and person' are annihilated here because in this case there is 'nothing whatsoever beyond the surface of the glass'.[4] The stark reflections of her body engaged in the sexual act force the tale's female narrator to confront her role in fabricating the images of herself she presents to the world. The story is threaded with references to her self-creations, which extend from her deliberately turning up her coat-collar in order to indicate loneliness and manipulate people into talking to her, to her staging of her failed reunion with her lover, to her inability to see her lover as anything other than what she desires him to be.[5] The setting of the tale in the alien city of Tokyo, which the narrator believes to contain 'enormous histrionic resources', underscores the theatrical nature of her constructions, and highlights their Western cultural origin through her frequent appeals to a shared European heritage, ranging from *Madame Bovary* to fugue.[6]

Carter's insistence that our self-images are concocted from a powerful medley of already determined and determining projections and reflections continues the discussion of previous sections and underlies her view of myth. In an essay entitled 'Notes from the Front Line', Carter outlines her intentions as a writer as the 'investigation of the social fictions that regulate our lives', a comment she prefaces by delineating her own slow understanding of the way she herself had been 'created' as a woman 'by means outside my control'.[7] She goes on to describe her interest in myths as influential agents in this process, terming them in a formulation reminiscent of Roland Barthes as 'extraordinary lies designed to make people unfree'.[8] In her controversial reading of the pornographic writings of the eighteenth-century French Marquis de Sade, *The Sadeian Woman: An Exercise in Cultural History*, Carter further develops her analysis of myth.[9] Considering the way that pornographic graffiti reduces men and women to aspects of their biology, Carter suggests how these abstractions are imbued with mythic archetypes of male and female:

> man aspires; woman has no other function but to exist, waiting. The male is positive, an exclamation mark. Woman is negative. Between her legs lies nothing but zero, the sign for nothing, that only becomes something when the male principle fills it with meaning.[10]

She attacks this mythic inscription for dealing in what she calls 'false universals', since it ignores the complexity of individuals as well as the mutability of history.[11] What Carter finds liberating in Sade's work is her perception of his refusal to equate female sexuality with women's reproductive function, which she argues is apparent in the vicious trajectory he devises for the virtuously feminine Justine as well as in the success he awards to the antithetically monstrous Juliette.[12] For Carter, all mythic versions of woman, including and perhaps especially that of the mother, are 'consolatory nonsenses' – a phrase which she suggests is an apt definition of myth.[13] Later in her reading of Sade,

Carter elaborates on her antagonism towards the mythic mother, maintaining that it is 'one of the most damaging of all consolatory fictions' since it exiles those women who subscribe to it from the actuality of the present.[14] Her frustration with 'the timeless, placeless, fantasy land' such archetypes imply underscores her reading of the torture, rape and sterility Sade has Juliette inflict on her mother, since she contends that Sade's account potentially dispels the myth and opens the way for women to return to history.[15]

In *The Sadeian Woman*, Carter completes her critique of the myth of the mother with an examination of the ways in which the womb has come to be figured. Her description of it as the 'potent matrix of all mysteries' and hence the site all men simultaneously long for and fear, presents a further interesting connection with the antithetical world of the mirror in 'Reflections'.[16] This mirror world is explicitly referred to by its guardians as 'the Sea of Fertility': the place of synthesis where division is healed.[17] When the androgynous Anna – so called 'because she can go both ways' – throws the lost object back into the mirror it is reunited with its reflection and order is restored.[18] The narrator terms his own traversal of the mirror a 'giving birth', a delineation which is endorsed by the warm, moist, opening lips that provide his means of passage.[19] Later, when the narrator's struggle to return through the mirror destroys its antithetical world, the guardian accuses him of irrevocably cutting 'the umbilical cord'.[20] Like Anna, the mirror's guardian is androgynous, and it is significant that even after being shown his/her breasts and penis the narrator chooses to refer to her as 'she'. Nevertheless, despite its persuasive portrayal of the force of such 'reflections', the tale is ultimately critical of the premisses on which they depend. This is apparent in the explanations the guardian gives, which range from the vague description of the mirror world as 'the symbolic matrix of *this and that*' to the confusing account of its 'system of equivalences' with its reductive linking of the phallus and the gun.[21] The story's ending, with its insistence on the arrogant victory of the assassinating male, can similarly be interpreted in this light, since the self the narrator envisages himself giving birth to when he passes through the mirror is merely a repetition of the age-old mythic pattern.

This final image of the destroyed matrix by the vanquishing male evokes Camille Paglia's description of what she calls the daemonic struggle between mothers and sons. In her book *Sexual Personae: Art and Decadence from Nefertiti to Emily Dickinson*, Paglia argues that there is truth in the mythic stereotypes of male and female since they are accurately drawn from biology, which she believes plays a vital role in determining our natures as men and women. She consequently views the mother as 'an overwhelming force who condemns men to lifelong sexual anxiety, from which they escape through rationalism and physical achievement'.[22] For Paglia, it is precisely men's need to liberate themselves from the mother's engulfments that leads to their creation of law and art.[23] In Carter's story, however, there is a note of ambiguity in the final lines, since although the male narrator has cut the umbilical cord it is an action that signals 'the world's death'.[24] Exactly what Carter means by this phrase is left unexplained, but it does not suggest the confident and beneficial contribution Paglia outlines.

Despite some similarities between the ending of 'Reflections' and Paglia's thesis, there is an important difference in their respective attitudes to biology. In contrast to Paglia's insistence on a fundamental distinction between the sexes, in Carter's story the matrix is not the province of the female but belongs to an androgyne whom the narrator chooses to regard as a woman.[25] Carter's novel *The Passion of New Eve* explores these issues of reproduction, sexuality and the construction of the individual as masculine or feminine in its extended pursuit of a young male, Evelyn, on his journey across a post-apocalyptic America in which the structures of continuity, commerce and the law have broken down.

The Passion of New Eve opens with Evelyn paying what he imagines to be a final tribute to the screen icon of his youth at a cinema on his last night in London. Billed as 'the most beautiful woman in the world', his goddess is Tristessa de St Ange, a name that effectively heralds her appeal of angelic suffering.[26] Recalling Carter's delineation of mythical woman in *The Sadeian Woman* as the altar of man's desire, Tristessa's allure lies in her passive acceptance of others' projections. Evelyn's journey to America will paradoxically take him to Tristessa, and to the discovery that Tristessa's immaculate femininity depends on his being a man. While the revelation that Tristessa is a transvestite is central to the novel's thesis that gender is not an emanation of one's biological sex, the impact of external mirroring in that formation is figured in Evelyn's relationship with the woman he meets shortly after his arrival in America. Significantly, it remains unclear even at the close of the narrative whether Evelyn is the hunter or hunted in this exchange, and his depiction of Leilah as the 'perfect woman' is imbued with his account of how her elaborate self-compositions in front of her mirror derive from the erotic dreams that the mirror's reflections produce in him.[27] Evelyn's acknowledgement of the role

Tristessa's screen image played in his own burgeoning adolescent sexuality suggests that even these intimate mirrorings are culturally determined.

Strikingly in terms of Paglia's analysis, Evelyn abandons Leilah when he discovers that she is pregnant with his child. In his wanderings through the decaying and violent metropolis, Evelyn has noted the repeated graffiti of a truncated column, and he is captured as he tries to escape from Leilah's maternity by the radical feminist group whose emblem this is. The group's leader is Mother, a self-constituted divinity, who also turns out to be Leilah's mother whom Evelyn has heard about but has pigeon-holed erroneously as 'a poor black scrub-woman'.[28] Mother surgically castrates and transforms Evelyn into a woman, to found a pro-female mythology as the new Eve. Her plan is foiled, however, since the alteration of Evelyn's body does not effect the desired conversion. Significantly in terms of Carter's account of gender, neither a different biological sex nor even exposure to an elaborate programme of new iconography can transform behaviour. It is only once Eve/lyn escapes, and is subjected to the brutal regime of the tyrannical patriarch Zero where s/he must copy the women's demeanour if she is to survive, that s/he finally learns to become a woman. Recalling Judith Butler's thesis, it is Eve/lyn's reiteration of the gestures of femininity that achieves her change of gender.

Appropriately enough, Eve/lyn's meeting with Tristessa takes place in the glass house she has built for herself and filled with the waxwork effigies of Hollywood's stars. The glass tears Tristessa spends her time making image both her name and the nature of the womanhood s/he has constructed: as Eve/lyn eventually realises, Tristessa's impact, like Lazarus' in Alice Thompson's *Pandora's Box*, depends on her mirroring others' desires to an extent no actual woman could accomplish. Zero's brutal exposure of Tristessa ostensibly releases him from the myth he has created, and he and Eve make love as equals. If the glass signifies the medium through which gender images are fabricated and transmitted, then its shattering appears to enable Tristessa and Eve to relate to each other free from the distorting influence of external symbols and impositions.[29]

The novel's opening, which is told in flashback, includes a series of meditations on the nature of symbol and myth. As Eve/lyn watches Tristessa on the screen, he remembers how Hollywood redesigned her image when her incarnation of passive suffering became outmoded, and he reflects how it is we who empower certain narratives and motifs rather than the other way around. Because his thoughts are presented with hindsight, they implicitly draw on Eve/lyn's own story which the text then proceeds to disclose. The climax of this is Eve/lyn's sex-change, performed by Mother in her underground hideaway Beulah. Here, through Mother's endeavours to convince him of her plan to turn him into a new Eve and efforts to brainwash him into realising her scheme through a carefully constructed bombardment of emblems and tales, Eve learns finally that 'myth is a made thing, not a found thing'.[30] This discovery is supported by descriptions of the various theatrical and technological tricks the feminists use to enforce their alternative scheme, which include lighting, sound and even the regulation of temperature. What is striking about Carter's portrayal of this attempt to institute a woman-centred mythology to replace the existing male paradigms is the insistence that it, too, contorts. Recalling Carter's critique of archetypes in *The Sadeian Woman*, Mother's regime is set in a world-out-of-time that is impervious to the motivations and needs of individuals.[31] This is most emphatically revealed in Mother's naive belief that the surgical recasting of Evelyn's body in a female shape will transform him into a woman. It is also signalled in the grotesque caricature of mythical figures of maternity that Mother adopts, which Evelyn's depictions underscore. The double row of breasts that recalls such ancient fertility goddesses as Artemis, for instance, is trivialised in the account of the 'strenuous programme of grafting' Mother performed on herself to obtain them, as well as in their comparison to the dangling bobbles on the fringe of red plush curtains.[32] The general mode of narration, with its knowing wink to the reader as it highlights the 'rolling iambic pentameters' in which Mother holds forth on such grandiose topics as mortality and eternity, for example, completes this process of deflation.[33] The litany Mother's acolytes recite is also a parody in its higgledy-piggledy mix of Ancient Egyptian, Greek, Christian and other sources, a conflation that is continued in the confusion of mythologies the feminists apply to Evelyn, who is to be a new Eve, a new Virgin Mary who will bring forth an antithetical Messiah from the seed raped from him by Mother prior to his castration, and a new Venus. The fact that Mother makes Eve the replica of a *Playboy* centrefold is a further damning indictment of her thinking.[34]

I have already hinted at the part Tristessa plays in Carter's critique of mythology in *The Passion of New Eve*, in Hollywood's deliberate manufacture of his screen image and in the paradox of his perfect womanhood resulting from his ability to fantasise this as a man.[35] Like Mother, Tristessa is surrounded by mythic epithets, that range from the Catholic 'Our Lady of the Sorrows', to Lazarus, the unicorn, the wounded albatross, Ezekiel, Cassandra, and the Uroborus, the sheer plurality of which cancel each other out. Even Eve/lyn realises that Tristessa has 'no ontological status, only an iconographic one'.[36] The critique continues in the figure of Zero, who captures Eve/lyn following her escape from Mother. Zero is the stereotypical male patriach in his obsession with his own virility and brutal treatment of the women he enslaves, and his gospel is appropriately couched with reference to a broad band of Classical, Christian and macho symbolism.[37] What is made clear in the case of Zero is that his monstrous mythology which deprives his women even of their right to speak depends on the women believing it. Though it is possible to interpret his impotency and physical disabilities in a number of ways, one of their effects is to highlight the fact that the women would have little difficulty in overthrowing his rule if only they chose to do so.[38]

The ending to the novel concerns Eve's rediscovery of Leilah, who has changed her name to Lilith and who is now actively involved in the country's civil reorganisation. It is Lilith who tells Eve that Mother has retired, recognising that her campaign to set the old symbols to fresh work has failed. When Eve hears this, she wonders if they, too, should retire all the symbols and wait for the history Lilith is in the process of shaping to generate its own, new iconography. Although Lilith appears to agree with Eve's suggestion, she goes on to give a lengthy explanation of the various mythical resonances behind her changed name. This ambiguity is carried through to the final lines, since despite Eve's acknowledgement that Mother is merely 'a figure of speech' and her mythology bankrupt, her actual last meeting with Mother culminates in Eve's (return?) journey to motherhood and mother-country.[39]

The ambivalent close to *The Passion of New Eve*, with its declaration of Mother's redundancy on the one hand and the highlighting of Eve's maternity on the other, has prompted mixed reactions from critics. If, as some readers have argued, Carter's portrayal of Mother brandishing her castrating scalpel is a depiction of the phallic mother, then, as Mary Jacobus has demonstrated, this obliterates women from the equation.[40] Nicole Ward Jouve, in her study *Female Genesis: Creativity, Self and Gender*, shares this anxiety, and contends that Carter's debunking of Mother derives from a misunderstanding of the nature of the archetype.[41] Although Ward Jouve sees much that is of value in Carter's analysis of the processes involved in the institution of myth, she believes that her relentless attack on the maternal body ignores the fact that both sexes must negotiate a relation to this origin and that this negotiation can be enabling and free from gender-bias. Ward Jouve's discussion of this point parallels Michèle Roberts's insistence on the need to refigure the lost mother outlined above. Drawing on the psychoanalyst D. W. Winnicott's notion of the child's employment of what he terms a 'transitional object' in the trajectory from infancy to individuated selfhood, Ward Jouve maintains that just as the shell or orange the child lights on for this purpose is gender-neutral so our maternal origin is open to the investments and constructive imaginings of men and women.[42] Ward Jouve goes on to show how the accomplishment of subjectivity is a life-long task in which story and symbol play a formative role. The fact that the mother, in Western mythology at least, has been denied or presented negatively does not mean that the origin itself can be simply dispensed with. In contrast to the parody and ultimate failure of Mother's new iconography in *The Passion of New Eve*, Ward Jouve argues that such reinventions are potentially liberating, since they productively transform the archetypes which she suggests are so vital for the configurations of both sexes.

While Ward Jouve's analysis offers an illuminating perspective on the recasting of myth, I think there are two qualifying points to place alongside her critique of Mother in *The Passion of New Eve*. Although Carter's novel reveals the artificiality, emptiness and injurious effects of certain archetypal formulations, I want to suggest that it does not eradicate myth altogether. Merja Makinen, in an essay on Carter, argues that Mother remains a powerful and haunting figure for the reader despite the narrative's denunciation of her cosmogony.[43] Ward Jouve herself wonders if Eve's meeting with the old woman at the close of the novel points to a re-encompassing of the maternal image, and cites the emphasis on return and symbolism of the final passages as evidence for this.[44] My own view is that the concluding pages do indicate a new investment in the myth. Eve comes upon the old woman immediately after her abortive attempt to meet Mother in the sea-caves, and the dove-tailing of Lilith's account with the description of the old woman strongly implies that this is Mother.[45] Unlike the irony and asides that accompany Mother's revamped gospel in Beulah, the mythical allusions here, such as the depiction of the old woman as Medusa or the implication that she will use Eve's gold to pay death's Ferryman, are given uncritically. The portrayal of the ocean as 'mother of mysteries' and the lyricism of the final line which strikingly ends with the word 'birth', also conveys a very different impression to the disparaging and parodic prose used in previous delineations. Starting

from Carter's critique of myth on the grounds that it ignores the par-
ticularity of individual cases, one way of viewing the novel is to suggest that while it exposes the barrenness of Mother as archetype, what
it achieves in Eve's exchange with the old woman is the ground for a
new story based on the actual conditions of existence. In contrast to
the contrived fantasy of Beulah, where even the food is synthetic, the
old woman's life on the beach is governed by her need to eat, drink,
defecate, and, tellingly, sing songs. In *The Sadeian Woman*, Carter
contends that one of the pernicious consequences of the institution of
the Mother Goddess is that it eclipses mortality, and whereas Mother's
discourse in Beulah attempts to surmount time the depiction of the
old woman is emphatically that of someone preparing to die.[46] Unlike
Mother, whose interest in Eve's maternity is an abstract one, based on
the part it will play in her grandiose plan, the old woman's decision to
help the pregnant Eve by allowing her to take her boat is the result
of a transaction between them: Eve's gentle explanations, the old
woman's comprehension, and above all their trade of the boat for the
gold. The implicit transferral from dying Mother to mother-to-be that
occurs here supports the argument that Carter's attack has been
directed against certain manifestations of the archetype rather than the
mother or origin per se. The suggestive final image of Eve setting out
across the ocean in the boat Mother gives up to her indicates a fresh
employment of the age-old symbols and tales that have hypothesised
our origin, which will keep in sight the nature of human transactions.

Although Ward Jouve is right to argue that Carter wants to sever
the link between biology and gender, I do not agree that this is what
she ultimately accomplishes in her work. Unlike Camille Paglia, who
maintains that the only way of resolving the inevitable hatred all offspring (but particularly sons) harbour for their mothers is for science
to develop an alternative means of reproducing, Carter's *The Passion
of New Eve* rejects the technology of Beulah and makes Eve's child the
product of her liaison with Tristessa. While the narration stresses the
absurdity of applying gender labels to the surgically female Eve and
transvestite Tristessa, the details of their love-making bring the physical attributes of male and female explicitly to the fore.[47] Here, then, it
would appear that Carter spurns Paglia's 'glass jars' as a solution to
the problem, positing in their stead the reality of the flesh as it
conducts itself and is experienced in a given situation. The fact that
Eve began the novel as a man becomes increasingly insignificant as
the delineation of her body, coupled with the conventions of naming
and grammar, conspire to persuade us she is unequivocally female.

The self-knowledge s/he acquires through this process, which leads her to recognise herself as a former violator, for instance, aids this progessively unambiguous reading through the increase in our empathy. If there is any common ground with Paglia's glass jar debate it lies not in Carter's renunciation of the female body, but in her implicit echoing of Ward Jouve's contention that unless we rethink our attitude to the origin there is no guarantee that glass jars will be any less free from the destructive effects of gender-bias than wombs.

The insistence on the reality of the body in Carter's depiction of the old woman's material needs and in her making Eve's pregnancy the result of an actual sexual liaison rather than Mother's megalomaniac campaign connects to an additional point that qualifies Ward Jouve's critique of Carter's presentation of mothers. Evoking the mythical hermaphrodite that shadows her novel, it seems to me that what Carter envisions is not the annihilation of the female but the possibility that both sexes might be involved in human reproduction.[48] In *Female Genesis*, Ward Jouve suggests that the obsession with the myth of Oedipus as a means of explaining male and female development has resulted in a fetishising of the father which has screened men's actual historical absence from the act of parenting. Carter's setting of a passage from the early twentieth-century campaigner Emma Goldman's 'The Tragedy of Woman's Emancipation' as a 'reply' to Sade at the end of *The Sadeian Woman* indicates another dimension to this, since Goldman implicitly answers Carter's condemnation of the tyranny of Sadeian sexual relations in her passionate appeal for equality in love.[49] Aidan Day, in his book on Carter, contends that what Carter's fiction demonstrates is that successful human relationships depend on a recognition of the claims of the other, and that this includes comprehension of the complex nature of sexuality rather than mere acceptance of simplistic patriarchal appraisals of it.[50] Central to this recognition of the other is self-understanding of the kind Eve/lyn learns through the course of *The Passion of New Eve*, since its trajectory teaches the cultural production of her former masculinity as well as the origin of the womanly behaviour she copies from Zero's wives.[51] Such understanding enables her to progress beyond the brutalities she imposes as Evelyn on Leilah or endures as Eve under Zero to a relationship with Tristessa in which she is free to love reciprocally. As Carter quotes Emma Goldman arguing in a strikingly Cixousian formulation, this freedom only begins when one 'cut[s] loose from the weight of prejudices, traditions and customs'.[52] In its rejection of reductive patriarchal representations *and* the glass jars of Beulah, what

Carter's novel envisages is the correlation of individuals of both sexes who have worked through the impositions of their culture in the task of furthering humankind.[53] Paralleling Ward Jouve's analysis, the business of procreation becomes the active responsibility of mothers as well as fathers.

One possible point of detraction from this argument in *The Passion of New Eve* concerns Tristessa. From the initial portrayal of Tristessa as a screen goddess at the opening of the novel, to Eve's discovery of her in her desert hideaway simulating her own effigy, the emphasis is on her mythical status. This is underscored in Zero's attribution of his sterility to her, and is not significantly altered in the account of Zero's exposure of him/her or even in the presentation of his part in the liaison with Eve. Here, despite the depiction of Tristessa's male organs and his delight in the experience of making love to a woman as a man, the frequent use of mythical epithets to describe him, his ramblings, the references to his madness, and above all his inability to relinquish his passivity query whether he has learned the lessons of selfhood sufficiently to engage with Eve as an equal. As Sarah Gamble argues in her book on Carter, this question of whether Tristessa remains within his imaginary biography sheds doubt on the depiction of his relationship with Eve as one of comprehending mutuality.[54]

Carter's short-story collections, *The Bloody Chamber* and *Black Venus*, involve the retelling of an eclectic range of myths and common tales.[55] 'The Lady of the House of Love', for instance, is a reworking of the vampire legend, in which the vampires' remaining descendant is a young woman who exploits men's sexual appetites in order to obtain her prey. Despite her 'horrible reluctance' for the task, the narration insists on the inescapability of the past which will repeat itself through her with the same inexorability as the pattern of the Tarot cards she continually turns over.[56] This emphasis on the injurious effects of ongoing historical imperatives – which is conveyed through the young woman's desolation as well as the final image of the soldier's regiment embarking for the trenches of the First World War – has been linked by a number of scholars to Carter's critique of the pernicious timelessness of myth. Mary Kaiser, for example, argues that *The Bloody Chamber* comprises the rewriting of the same source tale in different historical contexts.[57] She contends that this enables Carter to demonstrate how what happens in a tale depends on the particular circumstances that generated it, so that its wider application to a universal truth is proved to be meaningless. Lucy Armitt extends this notion of repetition to the collection as a whole, and traces the re-emergence of

key motifs in successive stories to suggest how their meaning is either
reiterated or altered.[58] Lorna Sage, in her introduction to a volume
of essays on Carter, agrees that the stories in *The Bloody Chamber*
develop Carter's attack on the fraudulent ahistoricity of myth and
symbol, but believes that what Carter does is to 'rewrite them into
mutability, pull them into a world of change'.[59] By inserting what is
apparently incontrovertible into new 'speculative "histories"', Sage
maintains that Carter is able to expose the bankruptcy of past forms
and gainfully reinvest those which still have resonance for us.[60]

Although Sage does not give specific illustrations in her 'Introduction', an example of her point can be found in Carter's use of the
clockword maid in 'The Tiger's Bride'. The tale explores patriarchy's
usurpation and destructive definition of woman through a reworking
of 'Beauty and the Beast'. In Carter's version, a young girl is pledged
to 'The Beast' by her father as a stake in a game of cards.[61] The clock-
work maid 'The Beast' sends to tend her is initially described as her
'twin' since it so exactly mimics the mechanical obedience she has
been required to display, though the figure takes on a different, rebellious connotation when it is sent to the girl's father to act as his
daughter in her place.[62] The title story of *Black Venus* similarly
demonstrates the twists Carter applies to archetypal models. Here, the
notion of woman as a source of artistic inspiration is reconsidered
through the imaginative reconstruction of the life of Jeanne Duval,
the mistress and muse of the nineteenth-century French poet Charles
Baudelaire. While the debilitating impact of such a notion for both
muse and artist is powerfully portrayed in the tale, it is significant that
it ends with Jeanne enacting an appropriate and terrible revenge. Supported by the money Baudelaire has given her and above all by her
own enterprising sale of some of his possessions, Jeanne can now
choose her sexual partners, to whom she transmits the venereal disease
responsible for Baudelaire's death.[63]

The mother is also prominent in these tales. The title story of *The
Bloody Chamber* opens with the mother reluctantly relinquishing her
daughter to her new husband in accordance with patriarchal custom.
One of the interesting features of this tale is that the male-governed
domain of marriage is depicted as a realm apart: the protagonist's
entry to it is described in terms of 'exile', while her husband's castle is
a 'magic place' with walls made of 'foam' that imply its unreality.[64]
Despite the husband's apparent victory over the mother at the start of
the tale, it is the mother who rescues her daughter from his 'Blue-
beard' scenario and returns her to 'normal' life, primarily signalled in

the narrative in the resumption of paid work. Although so
have taken issue with the mother's swashbuckling style of res
seems to me worth emphasising is the manner in which her sudden
appearance is vindicated to the reader.[65] While the daughter glosses
this as 'maternal telepathy', the mother's more prosaic explanation
that she came because her daughter's phonecall had alarmed her
implies a solid connection between mother and daughter that can survive even the most macabre of patriarchy's fairy tales.[66]

'The Cabinet of Edgar Allan Poe' in *Black Venus* gives a different
perspective on the mother, in its fictionalised account of the celebrated
nineteenth-century writer's childhood. Among the many details of the
young Poe's relationship with his mother is his witnessing of his sister's birth, which appears to him as a mysterious act of horror since his
mother's body is screened by a sheet so that all he can see as he hears
her screaming is the midwife's terrible instrument and the stain of her
blood. The tale then explores how this terror translates into Poe's sex-
less marriage, for instance through a dream in which he uses the midwife's tool to extract teeth from the hidden vagina. While this image
recalls Camille Paglia's insistence that the *vagina dentata* is 'a grue-
somely direct transcription' of men's fear of the origin and revulsion
for women's genitalia, what Carter's story shows, on the contrary, is
that such fears are not universal but derive from specific – and usually
tragic – perversions of the mother–child bond.[67] Lest this bond should
itself become gospel as the cause of subsequent adult wrongdoing, the
narrator of 'The Fall River Axe Murders', also in *Black Venus*, rejects
the murderess Lizzie Borden's wishful belief that 'if mother had lived,
everything would have been different'.[68]

Elaine Jordan argues that 'Peter and the Wolf' in *Black Venus* also
concerns the mother's role, and she traces Peter's rejection of what
she terms his grandmother's wisdom in his acquisition of the Latin
language of the male priests.[69] Jordan suggests that the turning-point
in the story comes when Peter catches sight of the cousin who was
taken by wolves suckling her cubs, since she contends that it is this
image that leads him to abandon the seminary and go out into the
world. Jordan's reading raises a further point that links to the exhibi-
tion of the destructive effects mythic paradigms can have on human
interaction that occurs in *The Passion of New Eve*. For Jordan, Peter's
witnessing of his cousin's instinctual act enables him to eradicate the
injunctions that have previously governed his existence, since through
it he acknowledges both his kinship with the female and his own prox-
imity to animal life. This insistence on bestiality as a positive step is a

particularly prominent theme of *The Bloody Chamber*, generating a new ending to the 'Beauty and the Beast' tale in 'The Tiger's Bride', for instance, where the protagonist's spurning of the furs, clothes and jewels her culture values so highly results in a nudity that allows her to relate to 'The Beast' as an equal and without fear. This return to the animal body free from external prescription accords with Aidan Day's view of *The Bloody Chamber*. For Day, the moral of the collection is precisely this stripping away of all existing definitions of sexuality to reach a point of shared humanity, from which men and women can separately and collaboratively build anew.[70] In this endeavour to locate an enabling common denomination, Carter's radical tales suggest a way through the impasse the rejection of consensus has posed in a number of the texts discussed thus far. The ending to the title story of Carter's collection, 'The Bloody Chamber', might similarly be taken as illustrative of such a state, since the blind piano-tuner that the protagonist eventually lives with happily is physically incapable of mirroring any imposing images of the way she should be.[71]

In her essay 'Notes from the Front Line', Carter famously declares herself to be 'in the demythologising business', an assertion that has tended to cloud the new fictionalising that occurs in her work.[72] In her creation of Fevvers, *aerialiste extraordinaire*, in *Nights at the Circus*, Carter invents a figure who simultaneously exposes the fault-lines of existing paradigms and signals vibrant new possibilities. Carter, in an interview, describes Fevvers as 'a metaphor come to life', and the novel abounds in mythical sources for her 'fevvers' that encompass Leda, Cupid and 'The Winged Victory'.[73] One of the difficulties of reading Fevvers in *Nights at the Circus* derives from Fevvers's own emphatic if fluctuating self-proclamations, such as her repetition for Walser's benefit of Lizzie's pronouncement on first seeing her wings that she is the angel of the coming twentieth century 'in which no women will be bound down to the ground'.[74] Fevvers, of course, has commercial reasons for alternately asserting and down-playing her 'difference', an ambiguity she preserves in her choice of publicity slogan: 'Is she fact or is she fiction?'[75] As Walser himself finally comes to realise, her career as a trapeze artist depends on her successfully occupying this border, since any disclosure of herself as fact would relegate her to the category of freak and mean she would not be taken seriously.[76]

The difficulty of deciding whether Fevvers is 'extraordinary woman' or 'marvellous monster' is compounded by the way the narrative itself plays with and exposes as unsatisfactory or fraudulent existing definitions of sex.[77] Fevvers's startling revelation to Walser at the beginning of their interview that she was 'hatched' not born, for instance, is never conclusively resolved, since when Walser finally believes he sees that Fevvers has no navel he is no longer in a position to trust his judgement.[78] If the provenance of Fevvers's natural mother remains obscure, we are given plenty of information about Fevvers's early life in Ma Nelson's brothel, where the question of the mother is further complicated by Fevvers's account of her upbringing as if she were 'the common daughter' to half-a-dozen of the whores.[79] The all-female brothel is portrayed as the antithesis to the tyrannous feminism of Beulah in *The Passion of New Eve*, since it is described by Fevvers as a world 'governed by a sweet and loving reason'.[80] Despite Fevvers's rosy depiction, it is nevertheless a world that services men, a point that is underscored when Ma Nelson dies and her establishment is inherited by her bigoted and heartless brother. It is also telling that when the whores finally open the curtains before they depart, the light of day shows their world to have been an illusion.[81] These perplexing depictions of mothering and women's government connect to an extended questioning of the attributes of male and female that persists through the text. In Ma Nelson's brothel, Fevvers has the task of representing first Cupid and then 'The Winged Victory', and it is the sword from the last of these incarnations that she chooses as her souvenir when the whores are forced to leave the house. The sword protects Fevvers from men, and its role as surrogate phallus transgressively employed in the service of a woman is highlighted in Fevvers's confession of how 'bereft' she feels when it is taken from her.[82] This contravening sport with the phallus is also present in the description of the clowns chopping brilliantly coloured cloth genitalia from the front of each others' trousers, which immediately reappear in even more lurid and fantastical guises. But if *Nights at the Circus* cavorts with the phallus, it also sends up theories of women *à la* Paglia. Rosencreutz's perverse view of the female sex as the 'atrocious hole' which threatens the aspiring penis is exploded when he loses himself in the 'blind alley[s]' of his myth, as well as by Fevvers's deflating and very funny gesture of helping herself to another 'dollop' of his stilton while he pontificates.[83] Even Fevvers's own occasional pronouncements on the nature of her sex are consistently parodied, as when her eloquent portrayal of herself as the winged image of women's freedom is countered by Lizzie's sharp Marxist rejoinder: 'improve your analysis, girl, and *then* we'll discuss it'.[84]

Anne Fernihough, in an interesting commentary on *Nights at the Circus*, suggests that the reason why Fevvers is so hard to decipher is that as readers we tend to locate the problem of her identity in her anatomy rather than in her audience.[85] Fernihough's analysis returns us to the complex correlation between self-projection and the defining reflections of others that permeates Carter's early stories and *The Passion of New Eve*, a correlation that is explored in *Nights at the Circus* through the tricksy world of entertainment as well as Fevvers's tale. When Walser's preoccupation with Fevvers leads him to join the circus in his pursuit of her, the leader of the clowns explains that while it is each clown's unparalleled privilege to choose the face he will present to the world, that face will henceforth subsume his identity to the point that he no longer exists without it. This modelling of the self by one's audience is also apparent in Mignon's story, since her photographic impersonations of dead loved ones are created by the longing and imagination of the bereaved themselves. It is significant that Fevvers shows herself to be aware of such proceedings, for, as she tells Walser, what she learnt nightly in the brothel was the pointlessness of waiting for any metaphorical prince's kiss since this 'would seal me up in my *appearance* for ever!'[86]

The episode of Walser's indoctrination by the Shaman is central to the novel's exploration of the relation between self-determination and the reflecting eyes of others. Walser is trained by the Shaman in his hallucinogenic cosmography, which, as Joseph Bristow and Trev Lynn Broughton point out, is shown to be as dangerous in its distortions of reality as any other whole-scale mythopoeia.[87] The Shaman's theology is one which categorically and terrifyingly cannot distinguish fact from fiction, since, as the third-person narration at this juncture stresses, it depends on a closed system of interpretation that ignores not only history but any other view. Its horrifying effects are starkly depicted in the impact it has on Walser, and by Fevvers's lucid realisation that the Shaman is intent on turning her 'from a woman into an idea'.[88] But if the specific form of the Shaman's magic highlights the pernicious consequences of myth-making, the potency of others' vision is less easily thrown off. When Fevvers tells Walser at the start of their interview that it is 'to the mysteries of the eyes of others that we commit ourselves on our voyage through the world', she touches on a point that resurfaces repeatedly through the novel, despite all the revelations of the partial, often deluded, and always fickle nature of audience response.[89] If it is the Shaman's performance that threatens to annihilate Fevvers when she enters his tent, it is the members of his congregation who paradoxically restore her, since the image of herself she perceives in their eyes is what enables her to reassert herself.

In the final analysis, then, the answer to Fevvers's question appears to be that subjectivity is neither solely 'what I know I am' nor 'what he thinks I am' since both may be misguided or incomplete, but an incessant negotiation between the two. This seems implicit in Anne Fernihough's suggestion that what Fevvers offers is a model of navigation between the impositions of culture in the construction of the self, on the one hand, and the existence of the self-as-body on the other. Fernihough's essay also indicates a way of reading the problematic ending to the novel, in which Carter returns us once again to the particular, this time through the sexual coupling of Fevvers and Walser. While the pleasures of the flesh in the act of making love are foregrounded, the importance of the union for Fevvers appears to reside in the empowering image of herself she sees mirrored in Walser's eyes – as her half-joking, half-serious sense that she is blonder even though she still has no peroxide indicates. The body exists, the novel seems to testify, as Fevvers eats, drinks, belches and farts her way through the narrative, but it is only a part of our self-experience, which also derives, whether we like it or not, from the gaze of others. After all, as Lizzie so pertinently reminds her, Fevvers's livelihood depends primarily on her ability to please the eye. Understanding how our audience's mirrorings operate and endeavouring to intervene when they become restrictive, as Fevvers attempts in her blazonings, may be as much as we can do as we endlessly manoeuvre between the nets and bars of the ring. Perhaps, like the 'O' of the circus ring itself, metaphor for the eye as well as woman's sex, our myth-making will then become a means of enhancing self-understanding rather than 'the wheel of life on which we are all broken'.[90]

Fevvers tells the sceptical Lizzie that her relationship with Walser is not about giving herself but about pleasing herself, and that she fully intends for the enabling effect of seeing herself mirrored by Walser to be reciprocated in the impact she plans to have on him. One striking feature of the closing pages of the novel is the reintroduction of the notion of biological mothering, through the mother and baby Lizzie and Fevvers rescue, and through Fevvers's revelation that her arrival at Ma Nelson's coincided with Lizzie losing a baby so that it was Lizzie's breast she suckled. These depictions of mothering exist alongside Fevvers's account of the New Man she hopes will 'hatch' out of Walser, and her use of the term here indicates a beginning distinct from birth in which others' interventions in the composition of the self are comprehended and, where necessary, improved on or countered.[91] This reading implies a further dimension to Carter's view of mothering, since it suggests that, like the anatomical body itself, being born is only part of the story, and that hatching oneself in relation to the world's mythology is its necessary corollary. In this light, Fevvers's own story of her genesis from broken egg-shells may be no more than a clever deployment of existing iconography, cunningly reconstructed from the available lore so as to make her fabulously rich. Perhaps *this* is the reason for Fevvers's uproarious guffaw at the end, since she will literally have had the last laugh. If this is the case, then its contagion depicted in the final lines can only be a good sign.

Carter's last novel, *Wise Children*, is prefaced with a quote from the legendary Shakespearean actress Ellen Terry, which implies that it will redress Shakespeare's preoccupation with fathers and daughters and focus, instead, on mothers and daughters.[92] There is ample evidence in the text to support such a claim. The novel's narrator, Dora Chance, refers several times to the difficulty of proving paternity compared to the 'biological fact' of maternity, and her anxiety on this point is confirmed in the gloriously farce-like denouement of her natural father's hundredth birthday party, in which a number of assumptions about fathers are revealed to be untrue.[93] Although the woman who brought up Dora and her identical twin sister Nora insists that they are not her real daughters, Dora's narration shows her to have been an excellent mother, implicitly responsible for the 'wise' and happy lives they have been able to lead.

Yet overall the novel does not sustain this thesis. A suspicion is raised in the closing pages as to whether or not Dora and Nora's beloved 'Grandma' was in fact their mother, a doubt which, if it were found to be correct, would raise questions as to why Grandma might choose to deny her maternity. Nora, despite longing for a baby, only becomes a mother at the end by proxy, when Peregrine produces Gareth's twins from the pockets of his jacket. Though this is not quite Paglia's glass jars, the flourish with which Peregrine presents the twins to Dora and Nora as their own birth-day gift contains echoes of a surrogate nativity. In a similar vein, while Dora discredits paternity as a difficult-to-substantiate 'hypothesis', both she and Nora repeatedly acknowledge Peregrine's importance in their lives as stand-in father.[94]

Dora's reason for writing is her desire to tell her own tale. This desire, which coincidentally involves her tracing her entire family's history, is one that is shared by a number of the participants in her account.[95] The generous if unreliable Peregrine, for instance, offers Dora and Nora 'a Chinese banquet' of possible versions of his life, and even Melchior's acting career is presented as emanating from his wish

to replay his father's story.[96] It is a desire that Dora and Nora assume
for Gareth's infant twins, since as Nora astutely realises, 'they'll make
up their own romance out of it' despite what they decide to tell them
about their birth.[97] It is significant that Nora's realisation occurs
immediately after her recognition that she and Dora concocted their
own fantasy of their father Melchior, projecting onto him their hopes,
dreams and wishes. While their fantasy had a basis in fact, Nora perceives how they continually reinvested it in order to keep it alive.

Dora's determination to find an answer to the question 'whence
came we?' and its echo in the parallel stories she tells recalls Nicole
Ward Jouve's intimation that we must each of us find a way of figuring our origin.[98] Michael Hardin, in an essay on *Wise Children*, argues
that because Dora and Nora have no biological mother to mirror
them in the process of individuation they act as mirrors for each other,
and he contends that the fact that they are identical twins enables
them to bypass the hierarchical positions this normally entails and create a basis for identity founded on reciprocity.[99] Though I think
Hardin dismisses the mother too easily from his account, by ignoring
the role Grandma Chance plays in Dora and Nora's upbringing, for
instance, his reading is a suggestive one, and his notion that the twins
equally and constructively mirror each other is supported by Dora's
statement that what they see when they look in the mirror is different
to what other people see, by Dora's insistence that though they are
identical they nevertheless respect each other's 'secrets', and above all
in the pair's outrageous dressing-up for Melchior's birthday.[100] Here
the twins, now well into their seventies, can indulge their whims to
the limit, because although the kids and market-men snigger at their
silver mini-skirts and gold stilettos, they are able to reflect each other's
chosen style in a positive light. It is particularly significant that their
mirroring during this scene is verbal as well as visual, as is illustrated
by Dora's memory of the 'lovely female impersonators' they have
known which attenuates their despondent recognition that their pro-
jected images can no longer be those of attractive young women.[101]
As Hardin also discusses, Dora and Nora's unique relationship permits
them to choose their distinguishing differences, and even to play with
these, as in the episode where with Nora's permission Dora fools her
sister's boyfriend into making love to her by swapping perfumes.

For Hardin, the fact that the twin babies Dora and Nora are left
with at the end are male *and* female indicates a further positive stage
in human development, since he argues that their reciprocal mirrorings
will remove gender as a basis for differentiation from the individuation

process. If Hardin is right, then this implies that the next generation
as Carter imagines it will be able to figure a relation to the origin that
does not derive from the oppositional gender definitions of patriarchy.
But if here Carter appears to support Ward Jouve's analysis, doesn't
the possibility that the new twins will attribute their origin to Peregrine's pockets suggest a denial of woman in the way Ward Jouve
deplores? My own reading is that what Carter presents us with in *Wise
Children* moves us beyond the ending of *The Passion of New Eve*,
which endorsed the role of male and female in the act of procreation,
to the responsible participation of both sexes in the ongoing task of
parenting. As Tiffany tells Tristram when he belatedly considers his
baby: 'there's more to fathering than fucking, you know'.[102] Ward
Jouve's pertinent critique of the problems with Freudian and post-
Freudian accounts is also relevant here, since Carter's depiction allows
for the possibility that a biological mother may not be a child's sole or
primary carer, that a father may be absent, and that identity is in any
case established through relationships with a variety of others. When
Dora and Nora stop on their way home to buy bottles and formula-
milk for the babies, they are assuming an alternative to the maternal
breast, but an alternative that will be founded above all on enduring
commitment. As Dora pointedly reminds Nora, it will be difficult for
them to go out in the evenings for a while. In this light, Carter's attitude to mothering seems not so much a denial as a reappraisal, given
the realities of family life on the one hand, and the needs of the human
infant on the other.[103] Nora's comment at the end of the novel that
she and Dora will have to be mothers *and* fathers to the new twins
corroborates this view, and there is hope in her belief that it is this that
will make them 'wise children'.[104]

In *Female Genesis*, Ward Jouve suggests that literature is itself a
potent transitional object in the ongoing task of individuation, and
the various story-tellings in *Wise Children* appear to support this
thesis. As with the act of parenting, however, the stories are not without consequence, and one of the many pleasures of Carter's text is the
way it gaily exposes or sends up existing irresponsible and damaging
fictions. The gold crown Melchior treasures as the symbol of his
father's greatness is from the first paraded as mere painted cardboard,
and even Shakespeare's exalted status is not exempt from the banal
reductions of musical adaptation or cats shitting on his sacred earth.
Comedy is permissible and even indispensable, but, in contrast to the
enigmatic guffaw that ends *Nights at the Circus*, this is laughter that
must stay in touch with real life. As Dora tells Peregrine, 'wars are

facts we cannot...laugh away'.[105] Although as elected parents Dora and Nora will provide the new twins with a rich repertoire from which to compile their own stories, they do so in the knowledge that one day soon they will 'drop'.[106] This highlighting of mortality returns us to Mother at the end of *The Passion of New Eve*, albeit with a different emphasis. While the issue of origin may be open to our continual reinvention, death is a limit that precedes us and therefore cannot be told away. We may sing while we wait for it, as both Mother in *The Passion of New Eve* and the septuagenarian Chance sisters do, but its inevitability cannot be nullified by myth. It is inexpressibly sad that Carter's own death followed so closely after the completion of this novel.

The question of the mother in Carter's fiction is, then, a complex one, and one which can be fruitfully explored in the light of Ward Jouve's analysis. Carter's inventive story-telling circles in and out of existing paradigms, revealing their dangers and redeploying their power to create new formulations that embrace what it means to be human. In this they amply fulfil Ward Jouve's compelling account of the importance of literature as mirror, in its role of enabling us to know ourselves as many and as one in the encounter with a potentially infinite array of others.[107]

Conclusion

To tell the stories was her work.
... Night in
she'd have us waiting held
breath, for the ending we knew by heart.

Liz Lochhead, The Grimm Sisters[1]

Stories held in common make and remake the world we inhabit.

Marina Warner, Managing Monsters: Six Myths of Our Time[2]

Christine Brooke-Rose's novel *Amalgamemnon* is set in the nightmare
world of the future in which computers controlled by an elite of
'technomaniacs' rule.[3] As the ex-'literature history philosophy' teacher
who narrates the fiction outlines, this is a 'technoidideology' – a pun
that indicates the frightening impersonality of the machine-controlled
ideology which prevents any criticism or counter-thought.[4] Despite the
narrator's initial insistence that the ancient Greek myth of Agamemnon
can have no place in such a scheme, her narrative finally upholds the
necessity of such stories as a crucial means of survival and escape.[5]

Myth, it would appear from the wealth of women's adaptations and
reworkings, is a potent force in contemporary feminist fiction. Yet as
the discussions in this volume show, women's rewritings frequently
alter the form of their source-myths and set them to very different
purposes. The twin themes of beauty and monstrosity in Ovid's tale of
Psyche that opens the first of my readings are pursued in the context
of patriarchy's usurpation and concomitant definition of the feminine
in a number of the texts I consider. Mother's surgically recast New
Eve in Angela Carter's novel, Noah's creation in Alice Thompson's
Pandora's Box, the transposition of Robert Louis Stevenson's Hyde in
Emma Tennant's *Two Women of London*, even Josephine's religious
devotion in Michèle Roberts' *Impossible Saints* – all are illustrations of
the tyranny and appalling consequences the patriarchal imposition of
an ideal has on women. Yet as Marina Warner's retelling of the legend

of the Queen of Sheba or Ruth in Fay Weldon's *The Life and Loves of a She Devil* demonstrate, this prescription is rarely inflicted directly but rather depends on our internalisation of its precepts for its effect. Fictions by Sheri S. Tepper and Carter further reveal how our mirror-images are projections resulting from the complex interplay between the reflections of others and our acceptance or rejection of their perceptions.

This exploration of the dual constructions of female beauty and monstrosity extends to an investigation into the nature of the binaries that more generally structure our thinking. Anne Rice's retelling of the vampire myth, for example, blurs the distinction between good and evil that governs Bram Stoker's *Dracula* in order to display the bias and the contingency of its law. Tennant's *Two Women of London* similarly unmasks the artificiality of social order, which is shown to derive from delineations that are detrimental to women. These expositions point to an important departure from traditional views of myth as a mechanism for explaining the universe, since myth is here used to disclose the motivations and interests that inform all such explanations. An interesting feature of Hélène Cixous's *The Book of Promethea*, A. S. Byatt's 'The Djinn in the Nightingale's Eye' and Roberts's *Impossible Saints* is the highlighting of childhood as a state that precedes the internalisation of external injunctions, the reclaiming of which offers opportunities to refute, redraw and play with the law. Christine Crow's *Miss X or the Wolf Woman* is also concerned with the introduction of adult prescriptions, and, in a comparable manner to Cixous's *The Book of Promethea*, demonstrates how we occupy both positions of any transcendent binary with the result that our identity can never be fixed. Margaret Atwood's novel *The Robber Bride* can be interpreted in this light, since the narration reveals how the supposedly evil Zenia is in fact a projection of each of the characters' repressed selves.[6] This recognition of the complexity of self permeates the preoccupation with religious myth that occurs in Roberts and Rice's work. While both Roberts and Rice's fictions take issue with the way traditional Christian iconography and teaching institute the polarity between good and evil, there is nevertheless a difference in the conclusions they present. Whereas in Rice's 'The Vampire Chronicles' religion is a hindrance that obstructs comprehension of the fundamental meaninglessness of the universe, Roberts's novels argue for a reclamation of its still powerful images and tales.[7] This in turn signals an important distinction in their approach to myth, which I will discuss below in relation to the more general question of whether the existing corpus of myth must be dismantled in order for women's experiences to be made apparent or whether, conversely, the most effective strategy lies in adopting and adding to its store.

While the repudiation of patriarchal paradigms is a persistent theme of the mythic rewritings included here, this is coupled with a corresponding insistence on the need for boundaries as the basis of social interaction. Despite the rejection of imposed definitions in Rice's 'The Vampire Chronicles', her reworking of the myth unveils the horror that ensues when there are no shared parameters from which communication and exchange with others can proceed. Thompson's *Pandora's Box* similarly emphasises the problems refusing the existing structures entails, as well as the psychotic dangers of any unconnected creation. Rice's erotic recasting of 'Sleeping Beauty' and Tennant's protagonists exhibit the stultification of too rigid a code, while the trajectory of Carter's Fevvers in *Nights at the Circus* heralds the success that can occur when practices are understood and agreed to. Dissatisfaction with the existing law is accompanied by an investigation into actual barriers. Carter and Crow's fictions explore the distinction between animal and human, while the texts of Byatt, Roberts, Rice and Tepper probe the relation between the human and supernatural or divine. Death is nonetheless the most consistently examined human limit, and is consequently an important common theme. Gillian Perholt sees the spectre of her death as she lectures in Byatt's 'The Djinn in the Nightingale's Eye', and her subsequent validation of the power of art is in part a response to this vision. Human mortality overshadows Roberts's *Impossible Saints*, through the descriptions of the chapel inlaid with bones that open and close the narrative as well as the repeated intrusions of Josephine's corpse. Rice's 'The Vampire Chronicles' question the desirability of immortality, while death is clearly presaged in the final portrait of Mother in Carter's *The Passion of New Eve* and the Chance sisters' speculations at the end of *Wise Children*. For Cixous, recognition of our mortality is the necessary precondition for all adult interaction and creation. As for Roberts's Josephine, Byatt's Gillian, Rice's Louis and to an extent Tennant's Muriel and Carter's New Eve and Chance sisters, the problem facing the narrator of Cixous's *The Book of Promethea* is that of shaping her existence in a way that will include equal exchange with others in the knowledge of this void.

This exploration of an alternative gauge for social order is coupled with a complementary insistence on the complex nature of identity. Crow and Cixous's writings demonstrate the annihilating impact of labels that do not correspond to the multiple and changing character of the individual, and a number of the fictions discussed here suggest that the process of subject-formation is ongoing. This is an important point, for it radically alters the way the writers view and present mythical figures and, as I shall argue below, contributes to a refusal to posit a solution to any problems raised. Theorist Judith Butler offers a convincing account of the mechanisms whereby we construct our identities through our repeated performance of cultural norms, an operation which I believe is often cast and internalised in the form of a narrative we tell ourselves and to which the widespread currency of myths contributes. Butler's work also crucially indicates that our telling of alternatives is a viable force for change. Gender is an integral part of self-definition and the extent to which many of the texts considered here subvert, transpose or play with traditional gender categories is striking. What emerges in the wake of this undermining of gender certainties is the undeniable presence of the body, whether as a response to the immateriality of God or as a reassertion of the body's experiences and needs. In both cases it provides a fresh critique of detrimental patriarchal paradigms, since it indicates a solution to the mind/body split that has pervaded Western thinking including gender definition – and the terror of the female body in particular which this has produced – as well as a means of testing that regime's cultural prescriptions.

Investigation into the nature of the self is accompanied by a review of relationships with others. Love is consequently a prominent concern, from the angry revelations of the shortcomings of fairy-tale romance in Weldon's *The Life and Loves of a She Devil*, to Fevvers's plans for a fulfilling relationship with her New Man Walser in Carter's *Nights at the Circus*. Yet as both these narratives show, the touchstone for the future is an equality in which individuals can relate to one another freely and in which the needs and complexities of each are fully recognised. This underlies Gillian Perholt's decision to release her djinn in Byatt's tale, is the declared aim of Cixous's narrator in *The Book of Promethea*, and informs Josephine's plans for a new foundation in Roberts's *Impossible Saints*. It extends to homo- as well as heterosexual relationships, as Crow's *Miss X or the Wolf Woman* demonstrates, since in Mary Wolfe's case it is another woman who is responsible for the dictatorial pronouncements that are so damaging to her development. The negative consequences for both sexes of failing to evolve such an equality are portrayed in a number of texts, including Emma Donoghue's rewriting of 'Donkeyskin', in which the Prince's inability to see beyond his Princess's attire prolongs his suffering.

The rejection of the debilitating hierarchy that has governed relationships permeates the refusal to replace the existing male gods with
female equivalents. This can be seen in the savage parody of Mother's
attempts to found a pro-female mythology in Carter's *The Passion of
New Eve*, as well as the extreme presentation of the megalomaniac
Akasha in Rice's *The Queen of the Damned*. Even in texts in which the
notion of a mother-goddess is an enabling concept – such as the insistence on Isis as a potent alternative to the later myth of Oedipus in
Crow's *Miss X or the Wolf Woman*, or Isabel's vision of a female component to the Christian Trinity in Roberts's *Impossible Saints* – this is
embedded within a critique of tyrannous interdicts that negate individual needs. But if the feminist rewriting considered here in the main
declines the return to a former matriarchy, it does exhibit a preoccupation with the maternal: from Mrs Noah's confusion about the
mother's function in Roberts's novel, to the Chance sisters' reinvention of it, aged seventy, in Carter's *Wise Children*. Patriarchy's usurpation of women has meant that the mother's role has been determined
from without, and one of the Gaffer's purposes in *The Book of Mrs
Noah* is to indicate why and how this has occurred. Roberts's insistence that our acts of creation are endeavours to figure our severance
from the maternal body is echoed in a number of other texts, including Carter's tale 'Reflections', Cixous's *The Book of Promethea* and,
perhaps surprisingly, Rice's 'The Vampire Chronicles'. The idea of artistic creation as a mode of navigating our exile into the symbolic arena
is one to which I shall return when I discuss the ongoing relevance of
myth. This review of the mother initiates a fresh look at fatherhood, as
its inflated place as a consequence of Freud's reworking of the Oedipus myth in Roberts and Crow's fictions or the paternal revelations in
Carter's *Wise Children* illustrate.

    In Jeanette Winterson's novel *Sexing the Cherry*, there is a short
episode in which the narrator imagines herself taking a walk through
city streets that have been clouded over by the day's output of
language.[8] The billows of chatter, quarrelling, love-song, cursing and
intellectual debate are cleaned by an army of specially equipped men
and women who patrol the sky in balloons. Some of the words resist
erasure, however, and the incident documents how some continue to
cause damage, some are caught and kept to provide ongoing inspiration, while still others escape and metamorphose into potent new
symbols. This episode in *Sexing the Cherry* presents a striking metaphor
for contemporary feminist rewritings of myth. It suggests, for instance,
the dangers of attempting to institute a wholly new mythology which

fails to take into account the persistent power of the existing repertoire, since it demonstrates that this cannot be dispensed with fully
and will resurface even if it is ignored. Similarly, it indicates that
changes can be made to the inherited corpus through both collective
and individual endeavour. The episode also signals that our speech-
acts have consequences – a point that is echoed in the insistence that
our creations must be undertaken responsibly in a number of the fictions considered here.[9]

In both Byatt's 'The Djinn in the Nightingale's Eye' and Weldon's
The Life and Loves of a She Devil myth provides the starting-point for
laughter. Theories of comedy which outline how we find something
funny when it is different to what we expect confirm that deviations
from the anticipated version can have an impact. It is therefore not
surprising to find comedy present in the majority of the texts
discussed. Winterson's witty interlude implies a further dimension that
is relevant here. Just as the narrator of *Sexing the Cherry* must decide
whether to keep or release her sonnet-memento, so the stalled laugh
at the end of *The Life and Loves of a She Devil* or Fevvers's final, enigmatic guffaw in Carter's *Nights at the Circus* leaves the onus firmly
with the reader. In both cases, the cathartic potential of laughter is
denied. This in turn suggests an important sense in which current
feminist rewriting deviates from extant myth, since it denies the happy
ending traditionally associated with fairy tale, as well as the albeit
frequently tragic resolutions that typically conclude classical myth.
This indicates a point of consensus among the writers included here,
since their fictions tend to deposit a residue of problems or dilemmas
which the narrative refuses to settle. This new task facing the reader of
feminist myth consequently signals a more involved, autonomous and
creative role than was commonly allocated to the receiver of the
conventional repertoire.

It is not only as a template for comedy that feminist writing benefits
from myth's prevalence and power. While in the works discussed here
the narratives are never reproduced unchanged, the citation of a
known pattern provides points of orientation and recognition so that
the resulting fiction contains a greater degree of resonance and applic-
ability than an individual account is generally able to generate.[10] This
shared reference aids the location of a common denominator which
the writings of Cixous and Carter in particular identify as the necessary first step towards establishing a social order that would refuse the
demarcations of the present hegemony. In my view it also creates a
more viable form of postmodern fiction, since it rejects the notion of

an Eternal Truth and avoids its polar nightmare of a chaos of individual viewpoints. While the demolition of the old certainties has resulted in a corresponding refusal in fiction of the conventions of plot, chronology and consistent narration and characterisation, the reference to known models replicates the pleasures and securities these undeniably provided, thereby offering a basis from which the reader may be inspired to a greater degree of transgression and change.

Jane Caputi's otherwise helpful classification of feminist rewriting of myth as either 'patriarchal myth-smashing' or 'woman-identified myth-making' consequently seems inadequate in this light, since it not only fails to encompass the insistence on sexual equality that pervades many of the fictions discussed in this volume, it also renders invisible their reclaiming and re-employment of existing myth.[11] This is not to deny the extent to which the inherited corpus requires alteration. As the ending to Toni Morrison's novel *Beloved* indicates, some stories are best not passed on.[12] As we have seen, the texts considered here engage in 'patriarchal myth-smashing' in a number of ways. Playing out the myth to its bitter end as in Weldon's *The Life and Loves of a She Devil*, exposing its flaws and injustices as Roberts's *Impossible Saints* endeavours to do, or revealing the relative nature of its truth by setting it in different contexts as Carter's tales in *The Bloody Chamber* or Tennant's transpositions to recent cultural imperatives demonstrate, are all illustrations of the techniques adopted. Caputi's notion of 'woman-identified myth-making' is also apparent, as the foregrounding or illumination of women's experience in these texts reveals. I have already mentioned the explorations of motherhood and exposure of the damage the imposition of a feminine ideal has on women, and this is complemented by the presence of female protagonists who are neither sexy nor mothers – indeed, the number of middle-aged or even very old women who would normally be dismissed from patriarchy's limited calculations is striking. This is coupled with a proliferation of the images traditionally associated with women, such as the magic power of Isis' sewing in Crow's *Miss X or the Wolf Woman*, Pandora's weaving in Thompson's novel, the emphasis on food in Roberts and Carter's fictions, make-up and beauty products in Byatt's 'Medusa's Ankles', Weldon's *The Life and Loves of a She Devil*, Cixous's *The Book of Promethea*, Tennant's *Faustine* and Warner's 'The Legs of the Queen of Sheba', and dancing in Roberts's *The Book of Mrs Noah* and Carter's *Wise Children*.

Thus, while Caputi's definition goes a long way towards outlining the practices of feminist rewriting of myth, it fails to cover the degree to which the existing repertoire is redeployed in the fictions discussed here. Straight citation, reversal which would champion women but also replicate the underlying power structure, even wholly new mythopoeia is rejected in favour of innovative combinations of mythic elements as in Carter's Fevvers, the presentation of omitted viewpoints as in the adoption of first-person narration in Rice's *Interview with the Vampire* or the Sibyl's stories filling in the Bible's gaps in Roberts's *The Book of Mrs Noah*, and the reclamation on behalf of women of patriarchally invested images and tales such as Gillian Perholt's endeavour to retrieve a splendid redundancy in Byatt's 'The Djinn in the Nightingale's Eye' or Mrs Noah's reinterpretation of the biblical flood as a metaphor for birth and severance from the mother in Roberts's novel. The technique of interleaving alternative stories alongside the expected or dominant narrative is also prominent in many of the fictions included here, as is illustrated by the lives of the women saints that intersperse Josephine's tale in Roberts's *Impossible Saints* or the interweaving of the narrator's story with the Sheba legend in Warner's reworking. These strategies indicate a general reluctance to relinquish the potency of myth, whether this is couched in the form of Crow's argument that women need to recover myth's power, or the desire of Warner's narrator to preserve and re-experience its poetry.[13] This, then, provides an answer to the dilemma as to whether feminism should destroy or disregard the extant corpus or whether, on the contrary, it should adopt its constructions. The co-option that is shown to be a danger of the latter course in Roberts's *Impossible Saints* must be set alongside the exile and purposelessness that Louis's rejection of the social order produces in Rice's *Interview with the Vampire*. In Byatt's fairy tale, the predicament of 'The Eldest Princess' who is trapped by her story is in the end less acute than that of her story-less sister, since at least the eldest has the possibility of changing her story's course. The insertion of women's experience which has been omitted from patriarchy's account and the fresh deployment of women's images can be seen in this context, supported by Luce Irigaray's argument that the reclamation of those areas which have been marginalised or ignored offers feminism a more viable form of creation than the meaninglessness that would ensue from total rejection. Critic Jean-François Lyotard has argued that the role of the writer today is not to compose new myths but to offer inspiration and models for our own imperative rewritings. My own view is that we can only communicate via the existing cultural currency, that that currency inevitably imposes its structures and prior investments, but that there

or reinterpretation and invention which cumulatively
quo. Feminist mythographers have revealed how early
fs were appropriated by a hierarchical and belligerent
t is tempting to combine their evidence of changes in
mythology with the delineations of the fictions presented here to pre-
dict that equality will be the informing principle of future myth-
making.[14] The collective input that goes into what then becomes
myth accords with such a view, providing it does not constitute a
new despotism in its turn and allows for individual differences. This
chimes, too, with current theories of subjectivity, which indicate that
we must all take up a position within the accepted code of words and
symbols in order to make sense of ourselves and the world. Narrative
is an integral part of this process of definition and understanding, to
which the repertoire of myths we receive contributes. As Warner
argues, myths and fairy tales permit us to dream alternatives which can
then be incorporated into actual practice. It is possible in this light to
see myth as a radical store of alternative patterns the individual can
then reproduce, as well as to see its transformations and magic as a
non-psychotic means of breaking and remaking our relation to the
social contract.

In Maxine Hong Kingston's story of a Chinese immigrant family in
America, 'No Name Woman', the protagonist realises that she has
inadvertently contributed to her aunt's torment by refusing to listen to
and repeat her story.[15] While the non-mimetic conventions of myth
give its narratives elastic possibilities, its operations are more multifarious than Warner's notion of dreaming alternative courses and selves
implies. As Weldon's *The Life and Loves of a She Devil* or Tennant's
Faustine demonstrate, adopting myth's prescriptions directly can have
damaging and material consequences, and Hong Kingston's story
shows the no less harmful effects of failing to heed its telling. The symbolic form of myth inhibits instant and definitive interpretation and
consequently prevents any crude or mechanical acting out of its apparent meaning. Myth's difficult aspects can be important, as the unsatisfactory blandness of Barbara Walker's politically correct sanitising in
her *Feminist Fairy Tales* exhibits.[16] As the texts I discuss here illustrate,
we need to free ourselves from the myths that debilitate women, but
we also need to retain the challenges and revelations myths enfold.
The collective generation of myth is an intrinsic component of this
complexity, since, unlike Ambrosius Pomposus' untenable creation in
Tepper's *Beauty* because it is the product of a single mind, it depends
on the involvement of many. It accordingly has the capacity to expand

our experience, and in this guise as greater-than-ourselves fulfils the former function of the divine. Nevertheless, as Roberts's *The Book of Mrs Noah* highlights, this is emphatically not the punitive dictatorship of patriarchal lore but rather an ongoing 'genesis' to which we all contribute. Creativity – whether this takes the form of story-telling as in Byatt's 'The Djinn in the Nightingale's Eye', or spreads across a range of activities as in the radical foundation Roberts's Josephine plans in *Impossible Saints* – is a crucial element of this alternative configuration. For Cixous and Crow, it is literature and writing in particular that constitute the new divine, since their array of possibilities opens up countless vistas for the reader/writer, with the concomitant impossibility of stasis. Like the text that is finally identified as the missing piece in lieu of Osiris' phallus in Mary Wolfe's detective story of self-discovery in Crow's *Miss X or the Wolf Woman* (and it is apt as well as funny that this text is the doubly erased *The Lesbian Body*), literature is an arena both writers perceive as illuminating the range of human potential. Walker's *Feminist Fairy Tales* consistently reverse the gender binary, bringing women triumphantly out on top, yet what is striking about the fictions I discuss in this volume is their persistent refusal to posit any such resolution. On the contrary, most end in uncertainty with only the sketch of a future direction. In accordance with their rejection of the oppositional hierarchies that have governed patriarchal practice, their intention is not to erect a new tyranny but to indicate the procedures whereby solutions might be achieved. Like the shimmering, evanescent rainbow of stories at the end of Roberts's *The Book of Mrs Noah*, the answer is not the institution of a different power order but the recognition of connection. As the story of the clowns in Carter's *Nights at the Circus* displays, the freedom of initially choosing one's face becomes a subsequent oppression if this freedom is not renewed. Our creation must be continual if the burning bush in Cixous's *The Book of Promethea* is not to solidify into Moses' Law and remain alive to the input of individuals, the changing nature of circumstances and the ongoing process of identity formation.

The myth of her hatching that Fevvers propagates in Carter's *Nights at the Circus* can be interpreted as a second birth, since it signals her ability to apprehend and productively employ the operations of her culture. Nicole Ward Jouve's account of literature as a vital 'transitional object' in the life-long task of individuation underscores this interpretation, highlighting the role narrative in particular has in the organisation, comprehension and communication of our experience. Her view links to Roberts's notion of art as that which enables us to figure the lost maternal body in which we were continuous with the world, imaged in the umbilical rainbow of stories at the end of *The Book of Mrs Noah*. It is also contained in the depiction of the second, adult paradise the narrator must work to achieve in Cixous's *The Book of Promethea*, which incorporates the knowledge of separation and death. Byatt's Gillian Perholt similarly sees art as a means of dealing with human mortality, a point that is echoed in the ending to Carter's *The Passion of New Eve* and *Wise Children* and Rice's *Interview with the Vampire*. Joseph Campbell calls myth a second womb, a phrase which, though richly evocative, nevertheless fails to encompass the metamorphoses of the self or the corresponding mutations in the tales we adopt and tell. Perhaps Virginia Woolf's metaphor of a 'semi-transparent envelope' more accurately conveys the way we navigate the world, in our half-luminous, half-opaque configurations of symbols and stories.[17]

An extraordinary and intriguing message flashed up on my e-mail while I was working on this book, about a woman who believed she had been shot while sitting in her car outside a supermarket. Attendants, worried by the woman's lack of movement, eventually went to ask her if she was all right, only to discover that the 'gun-shot' was an explosion from a cannister of dough left in the sun on the rear-shelf of the car, and that what the woman thought were her brains oozing from the back of her head were dollops of the sticky dough. I was so struck by this story that I immediately sent it to all those on my personal address list. One friend e-mailed me back to tell me she had already received the tale from another source, while another thanked me for my message and said she had forwarded it to everyone on her file. At a conservative estimate the item had already been circulated to tens of thousands of readers world-wide. Brooke-Rose's *Amalgamemnon* presents a grim portrait of a future in which life is controlled by machines programmed by an avaricious and patriarchal elite. Though I am more hopeful than Brooke-Rose that society will not revert to old paradigms, what seems certain is that advances in technology will fundamentally alter our experience. The increasing introduction of mechanical body-parts will have a dramatic impact on the way we perceive gender, and the easy circulation made possible by computers will have equally radical implications for our myth-making. At best, the speed and facilitated interactivity of such communications will promote the collective and continual recreation exhibited as the way forward in the fictions included here. Whether this will prevent the ensuing consensus from forming itself into a new authoritarianism is some only the future will reveal. Perhaps, at least, if – like Itys in Timberlake Wertenbaker's reworking of the Philomela myth – we retain the capacity to question the tales we are told and tell, we can put the lessons of contemporary women's rewriting of myth to good service.

Notes

Note to the Preface

1 Anne Sexton, *Transformations* (Oxford University Press, 1972) see p. 1.

Chapter 1

1 Lewis Spence, *An Introduction to Mythology* (London: Harrap, 1921), pp. 11–12.
2 Michael Bell, *Literature, Modernism and Myth: Belief and Responsibility in the Twentieth Century* (Cambridge University Press, 1997), p. 1.
3 Eric Dardell, 'The Mythic', in *Sacred Narrative: Readings in the Theory of Myth*, ed. Alan Dundes (Berkeley: University of California Press, 1984), p. 232, and Riane Eisler, 'Introduction', *The Woman's Companion to Mythology* (1992), ed. Carolyne Larrington (London: Pandora, 1997), p. viii.
4 R. G. Stone, 'Myth in Modern French Literature', in *Myth and the Modern Imagination*, ed. Margaret Dalziel (Dunedin: University of Otago Press, 1967), p. 177, and John J. White, *Mythology in the Modern Novel: A Study of Prefigurative Techniques* (Princeton University Press, 1971), p. 25. White is drawing here on the work of Howard Nemerov, *The Quester Hero: Myth as Universal Structure in the Works of Thomas Mann* (Cambridge, Mass.: Harvard University Press, 1940), p. 3.
5 Sigmund Freud, *The Psychopathology of Everyday Life* (1901), in *The Standard Edition of the Complete Psychological Works of Sigmund Freud*, 24 vols, trans. James Strachey (London: The Hogarth Press, 1953–66), vol. VI, p. 258; Jean-François Lyotard, *The Lyotard Reader*, ed. Andrew Benjamin (Oxford: Blackwell, 1989), p. 72, and Albert Cook, *Myth and Language* (Bloomington: Indiana University Press, 1980), p. 164.
6 Robert Graves, 'Introduction', *The New Larousse Encyclopedia of Mythology* (1968; London: Hamlyn, 1975), p. v.
7 W. R. Halliday, *Indo-European Folk-Tales and Greek Legend* (Cambridge University Press, 1933), pp. 5–6.
8 F. Max Müller's contentious phrase derives from his etymological tracings, as in Ovid's tale of Daphne's metamorphosis into a laurel. K. K. Ruthven, glossing Müller, shows how behind Daphne is the Sanskrit Dahana or

140

Ahana meaning dawn. Apollo is the sun-god, hence the emblem is that of dawn in the arms of the sun. The word for dawn also means burning, and this is contained in the word for laurel, recalling the fact that laurel is easy to burn (see K. K. Ruthven, *Myth* (London: Methuen, 1976), p. 34). The second reference is Nor Hall, *The Moon and the Virgin* (London: The Women's Press, 1980) p. 28. See below for further explanation of this view of myth as expression of the primal mother.

9 Mircea Eliade, *Myths, Dreams and Mysteries: The Encounter Between Contemporary Faiths and Archaic Reality* (1957), trans. Philip Mairet (London: Fontana, 1970), p. 16 and Dardell, 'The Mythic', p. 231.

10 Lauri Honko, 'The Problem of Defining Myth', in Dundes (ed.), *Sacred Narrative*, pp. 47–8.

11 T. S. Eliot, 'Ulysses, Order, and Myth', in *Selected Prose of T. S. Eliot*, ed. Frank Kermode (New York: Harcourt Brace Johanovich, 1975), p. 177 and Marina Warner, *Managing Monsters: Six Myths of Our Time* (London: Vintage, 1994), p. xiv.

12 J. G. Frazer, *The Golden Bough* (1890–1915, abridged ed. 1922) (Ware: Wordsworth Editions, 1993) see especially pp. 711–13.

13 Raffaele Pettazzoni, 'The Truth of Myth', in *Sacred Narrative*, p. 107.

14 Jessie L. Weston, *From Ritual to Romance* (Cambridge University Press, 1920).

15 Margaret Dalziel, 'Myth in Modern English Literature', and G. R. Manton, 'The Making of Myth', both in *Myth and the Modern Imagination*, p. 27 and pp. 11–17.

16 Manton suggests that this creative art was gradually replaced by rote learning to furnish the origins of a definitive text (see ibid., p. 15).

17 Bronislaw Malinowski, 'The Role of Myth in Life' (ibid., p. 206).

18 Hans Blumenberg, *Work on Myth* (1979), trans. Robert M. Wallace (Cambridge, Mass.: MIT Press, 1985).

19 See Sigmund Freud, 'Creative Writers and Daydreaming', *Complete Psychological Works of Sigmund Freud*, vol. IX, p. 146. For a pertinent discussion of Frazer's influence on Freud see Laurence Coupe, *Myth* (London: Routledge and Kegan Paul, 1997), pp. 126–7.

20 See Freud, *The Interpretation of Dreams*, in *Complete Psychological Works of Sigmund Freud*, vol. IV.

21 Colin Falck, *Myth, Truth and Literature* (1989; Cambridge University Press, 1995) esp. pp. 116–19.

22 Nicole Ward Jouve, *Female Genesis: Creativity, Self and Gender* (Cambridge: Polity Press, 1998) pp. 198–202. Simon A. Grolnick similarly makes this analogy in his work on fairy tale. He argues that fairy tales are told at bedtime which is a potentially difficult moment for a small child and that the tales function as a source of security, which he links to Winnicott's notion of a transitional object. See Simon A. Grolnick, 'Fairy Tales and Psychotherapy', in *Fairy Tales and Society: Illusion, Allusion and Paradigm*, ed. Ruth B. Bottigheimer (Philadelphia: University of Pennsylvania Press, 1986) p. 208.

23 An easy introduction to Joseph Campbell's prolific work on myth is his *The Power of Myth*, with Bill Myers (New York: Doubleday, 1988).

24 See Carl Jung, *The Archetypes and the Collective Unconscious* (1959), trans. R. F. C. Hull, in *The Collected Works of C. G. Jung* (London: Routledge and Kegan Paul, 1969) vol. VIIII, part 1.
25 Carl Jung, 'On the Psychology of the Unconscious', quoted in *Jung: Selected Writings*, ed. Anthony Storr (London: Fontana, 1983) p. 68.
26 Ibid., p. 71.
27 In an essay entitled 'The Undiscovered Self', Jung argues that the technological revolution has altered human experience to the point that we are approaching what he describes as 'a metamorphosis of the gods'. He believes that while art has undertaken an important function in destroying outmoded aesthetic views, it has not been able to furnish a substitute. He suggests that only myth, as the 'primordial manifestation of the human spirit' and process of unconscious symbolisation through the ages, has the capacity to fill this void (ibid., p. 402). It is interesting to restate the premiss of his essay, which was published in 1957, in terms of contemporary feminism.
28 'Psychological Aspects of the Mother Archetype' (ibid. p. 84).
29 Jung, *The Archetypes and the Collective Unconscious*, p. 5.
30 Perhaps the best starting point for Lévi-Strauss's work on myth is his *Myth and Meaning* (London: Routledge and Kegan Paul, 1978).
31 Roland Barthes, *Mythologies* (1957), sel. and trans. Annette Lavers (London: Paladin, 1973), p. 123.
32 Ibid., p. 142.
33 Ibid., p. 134.
34 Ibid., pp. 130 and 143.
35 *Managing Monsters*, p. 13.
36 A recent woman's magazine I leafed through in a doctor's waiting room featured an interview with 'a spirit called Diana' whose responses clearly positioned her as the deceased royal and whose descriptions of her life in heaven and advice to those on earth bizarrely echoed the presentation and role of the gods in classical Greek and Roman myth.
37 Alix Pirani, *The Absent Father: Crisis and Creativity: The Myth of Danae and Perseus in the Twentieth Century* (1988; London: Penguin, 1989) p. 184.
38 Italo Calvino (ed.), *Italian Folktales* (1956), trans. George Martin (London: Penguin, 1980); Marina Warner (ed.), *Wonder Tales: Six Stories of Enchantment* (1994; London: Virago, 1996); and Angela Carter (ed.), *The Virago Book of Fairy Tales* (London: Virago, 1990), p. ix.
39 Jack Zipes, *Breaking the Magic Spell: Radical Theories of Folk and Fairy Tales* (1979; New York: Routledge and Kegan Paul, 1992) p. 23.
40 G. S. Kirk, *Myth: Its Meaning and Function in Ancient and Other Cultures* (Cambridge University Press, 1970) p. 41.
41 Dundes (ed.), *Sacred Narrative*, p. 1, and Mircea Eliade, *Myth and Reality*, trans. Willard R. Task (New York: Harper and Row, 1963); see also Jack Zipes' discussion of Eliade's position in *Fairy Tale as Myth: Myth as Fairy Tale* (The University of Kentucky Press, 1994) pp. 1–3.
42 Marie-Louise Von Franz, *The Feminine in Fairy Tales* (1972; Boston and London: Shambhala, 1993) p. 5 and Zipes, *Fairy Tale as Myth*, esp. pp. 5–6.

Notes 143

43 Dalziel, 'Myth in Modern English Literature', pp. 28–9 and Carter (ed.), *The Virago Book of Fairy Tales*, p. xi.
44 Maria M. Tatar, 'Born Yesterday: Heroes in the Grimms' Fairy Tales', in Bottigheimer (ed.), *Fairy Tales and Society*, p. 100.
45 Ibid., pp. 96 and 101.
46 Kirk, *Myth: Its Meaning and Function in Ancient and Other Cultures*, pp. 37–8.
47 Vladimir Propp, *Morphology of the Folktale* (1928), trans. Laurence Scott (University of Texas Press, 1968), see particularly the section on fairy tale.
48 See Cronan Rose, 'Introduction', *The Voyage In: Fictions of Female Development*, ed. Elizabeth Abel, Marianne Hirsch and Elizabeth Langland (Hanover: University Press of New England, 1983) p. 17 and Bruno Bettelheim, *The Uses of Enchantment: The Meaning and Importance of Fairy Tales* (Harmondsworth: Penguin, 1976) p. 73.
49 Maureen Duffy, *The Erotic World of Faery* (London: Hodder and Stoughton, 1972) p. 20.
50 Calvino, *Italian Folktales*, pp. xviii–xix.
51 Frederic Jameson, *The Political Unconscious: Narrative as a Socially Symbolic Act* (London: Methuen, 1981) p. 105 and Michel Butor, 'On Fairy Tales', quoted in Zipes, *Fairy Tale as Myth*, p. 142.
52 Alison Lurie (ed.), *The Oxford Book of Modern Fairy Tales* (Oxford University Press, 1993), p. xi; see also her *Don't Tell the Grown-Ups: The Subversive Power of Children's Literature* (Boston: Little, Brown, 1990) for some interesting analyses of the genre. See Coupe, *Myth*, pp. 175–7, for a discussion of Ernst Block's contribution to the debate.
53 Rosemary Jackson, *Fantasy: The Literature of Subversion* (London: Methuen, 1981) see especially pp. 33 and 174.
54 The following gloss is taken from Bettelheim, *The Uses of Enchantment*.
55 Ibid., p. 24.
56 See Karen E. Rowe, 'Feminism and Fairy Tales', in Bottigheimer (ed.), *Fairy Tales and Society*, p. 230, Zipes, *Breaking the Magic Spell*, p. 169 and Marina Warner, *From the Beast to the Blonde: On Fairy Tales and their Tellers* (1994; London: Vintage, 1995) pp. 212–13.
57 Zipes' argument here is primarily taken from his *Fairy Tale as Myth*, except where indicated.
58 Jack Zipes, *Fairy Tales and the Art of Subversion* (New York: Routledge, 1991) pp. 7–8.
59 Ibid., p. 56.
60 Alison Lurie's citation of George Cruickshank's 1853 teetotal revision of the Grimms' tales and Kenneth Grahame's pacifist 1898 story 'The Reluctant Dragon' gives two further examples of this trend (see Lurie (ed.), *The Oxford Book of Modern Fairy Tales*, pp. xiii and xv).
61 See *Fairy Tales and the Art of Subversion*, p. 11.
62 Homer's epics are full of instances of women sent to spin while battles and stratagems of crucial importance for their futures are conducted by men. Penelope's famous attempt to delay the suitors by spinning is a prime example (see Homer, *The Iliad*, trans. Robert Fiztgerald (Oxford University Press, 1984), Book XIX, lines 136–61).

144   *Notes*

63 Zipes' argument here is taken from his *Breaking the Magic Spell.*
64 Ibid., p. 17.
65 Warner (ed.), *Wonder Tales*, p. 6. In *From the Beast to the Blonde*, Warner
    suggests that the 'happily ever after' can be viewed as a 'charm'. She
    argues that its critics overlook the knowledge of misery within marriage
    that the story often reveals, p. 217.
66 Warner's argument for the remainder of this section is drawn from *From
    the Beast to the Blonde* unless otherwise indicated.
67 Ibid., p. xvi.
68 Karen E. Rowe similarly offers an interesting etymological account of
    'fairy' and its connections to women, the fates and spinning in her 'To
    Spin a Yarn: The Female Voice in Folklore and Fairy Tale', in
    Bottigheimer (ed.), *Fairy Tales and Society*, p. 63.
69 This is a point made by Angela Carter in her introduction to her
    collection of fairy tales, see Carter (ed.), *The Virago Book of Fairy Tales*,
    p. xi.
70 Warner, *From the Beast to the Blonde*, p. 34.
71 Carter (ed.), *The Virago Book of Fairy Tales*, p. x.
72 Mary Daly, *Gyn/Ecology: The Metaethics of Radical Feminism* (1978;
    London: The Women's Press, 1984) p. 47, Daly's emphasis.
73 The following account is drawn from Monica Sjöö and Barbara Mor, *The
    Great Cosmic Mother: Rediscovering the Religion of the Earth* (San
    Francisco: Harper and Row, 1987).
74 Sjöö and Mor present evidence which suggests that the earliest tools were
    women's digging sticks, that women were the first potters, weavers,
    textile-dyers, hide-tanners and the first to gather and study the medicinal
    properties of plants, as well as the pioneers of language since this is most
    likely to have developed through women's communal work and in the
    interaction with children rather than during the long and often solitary
    periods men spent away from the camp hunting (see ibid., p. 7). They
    also demonstrate how evolution of the female body, involving, for
    example, the change to a menstrual cycle in which sexual activity need not
    lead to reproduction, and the development of the clitoris and breasts as
    organs of sexual pleasure with no reproductive function, transformed the
    development of the human race (see ibid., pp. 10–11).
75 Sjöö and Mor describe how the dead were placed in curled foetal
    positions and painted red during the Neanderthaloid period as a
    preparation for rebirth, and detail a grave found in La Ferrassie in France
    which was covered by a stone slab from which breast-shaped markings
    had been carved to symbolically suckle the reborn occupant. They show
    how in later megalithic times small holes were laboriously chiselled from
    the portal slabs providing a vital birth canal (see ibid., p. 46).
76 Marija Gimbutas, *Goddesses and Gods of Old Europe, 6500–3500 BCE*
    (1974; Berkeley: University of California Press, 1982); see Sjöö and Mor,
    The Great Cosmic Mother, p. 37.
77 Sjöö and Mor trace many fascinating connections between early
    matriarchal religion and its transposition into Judaeo-Christianity, such as
    the inversion of the mother goddess and her son and the survival of the
    horned and hoofed bull-god in iconography of the devil.

78 Margaret Atwood's *The Robber Bride* (1993; London: Virago, 1994) can be read productively in this light, as the central figure Zenia takes on aspects of the novel's very different women characters. The ambiguity that hangs over Zenia's existence also supports this view of her as a pseudo-goddess.

79 As an example, Sjöö and Mor document how in Mesopotamia the transition from matriarchy to patriarchy occurred through the revolt of the queen's consort, on whom she traditionally conferred executive powers by allowing him to adopt her robes, names, sacred instruments and regalia (ibid., p. 217). See also Susannah Rostas' fascinating account of the female goddess in Aztec mythology in 'Mexican Mythology: Divine Androgyny But "His" Story; The Female in Aztec Mythology', in Carolyne Larrington (ed.), *The Woman's Companion to Mythology* (London: Pandora, 1992), pp. 362–87.

80 Adrienne Rich traces the origins of the Hellenic figure of Pandora to the Cretan earth-mother goddess, showing her transformation from a position of 'All-Giver' to a mere girl dowered with gifts by the Olympians and sent to tempt men. Rich argues that Pandora's 'box' was originally a jar in which the goddess stored the bounty of wine, fruit and grain, see Adrienne Rich, *Of Woman Born: Motherhood as Experience and Institution* (1976; London: Virago, 1984), p. 122. Barbara Walker similarly redefines it as a honey-vase from which blessings pour out (see her *The Women's Encyclopedia of Myths and Secrets* (Edison, New Jersey: Castle Books, 1996), p. 12). Rich is drawing on the pioneering work of Jane Harrison for her analysis (see her *Mythology* (New York: Harcourt Brace, 1963), p. 44). Rich believes that the entire Olympian mythology revolves around a fear of the mature, maternal woman, and she cites, as examples, the fact that the most venerated goddess of their pantheon, Athena, is born from the head of her father Zeus and depicted as virginal, childless and obsessed with the outcome of men's wars, while Hera, Zeus' wife, is portrayed as jealous and competitive, and destructive mothers, such as Medea and Clytemnestra, abound (ibid.).

81 The following account is drawn from the later of the two books, *Sacred Pleasure*, see Riane Eisler, *Sacred Pleasure: Sex, Myth and the Politics of the Body* (1995; Shaftesbury: Element Books, 1996).

82 Ibid., p. 15.

83 Eisler studies, for instance, the proliferation of hybrid human and animal figures as well as pointing out the lack of images of men slaying 'monsters' or each other in the art of the Neolithic period, see ibid., p. 76.

84 Eisler links this attitude to the repressive and misogynistic conditions of Greek society, see ibid., pp. 103–12.

85 Robert Graves, *The White Goddess: A Historical Grammar of Poetic Myth* (1948; London: Faber, 1961). Graves suggests that in agricultural communities where there was little warfare goddess worship was the rule, and that it was nomadic herdsmen, whose bulls and rams dominated the herds, who initiated worship of a male sky-god, often imaged as a bull or ram.

86 See Diane Purkiss's essay, 'Women's Rewriting of Myth', in Larrington (ed.), *The Women's Companion to Mythology*, p. 443 for an assessment of the problems Graves's account poses for feminists.

87 See, for example, Joseph Campbell, *Creative Mythology: The Masks of God* (1968; Harmondsworth: Arkana, 1991) p. 626.

88 Campbell traces this episode to Sumerian seals from as early as 35,000 BCE. He argues that the serpent too was originally a positive figure, symbolising death and rebirth in the shedding of its skin, see Campbell, *The Power of Myth*.

89 Eisler, *Sacred Pleasure*, p. 355.

90 See Sjöö and Mor, *The Great Cosmic Mother*, p. 17.

91 Hélène Cixous, 'Sorties', in *The Newly Born Woman* (1975), with Catherine Clément, trans. Betsy Wing (London: I. B. Tauris, 1996) pp. 63–132.

92 See Peggy Kamuf (ed.), *A Derrida Reader: Between the Blinds* (Hemel Hempstead: Harvester Wheatsheaf, 1991), for an excellent introduction to Derrida's work.

93 See also Cixous, 'Sorties', pp. 64–65 on this point.

94 See Hesiod, 'Theogeny', in *Hesiod and Theognis*, trans. Dorothea Wender (London: Penguin, 1973) pp. 26–9, lines 116–210 and pp. 38–48, lines 453–767; I have adopted the more common spellings here.

95 Manton, 'The Making of Myth', in *Myth and the Modern Imagination*, pp. 9–25.

96 See John Creed, 'Uses of Classical Mythology', in *The Theory of Myth*, ed. Adrian Cunningham (London: Sheed and Ward, 1973); Creed cites Euripides as an example of a reader for whom the stories of Homer and Herodotus were true.

97 Cook, *Myth and Language*, p. 164.

98 Quoted in Ruthven, *Myth*, p. 52; Addison exempted authoresses from his ban.

99 See Michel Foucault, *Les Mots et les choses: une archéologie des sciences humaines* (Paris: Gallimard, 1966). It is translated into English as *The Order of Things: An Archaeology of the Human Sciences* (London: Tavistock, 1974).

100 For Edmund Leach, myth's own institution of binary categories is one of its chief characteristics, mirroring our own unchanging process of thought. For Leach, the importance of myth lies in the 'mediation' it offers between such opposing categories as human/superhuman, mortal/immortal, male/female, legitimate/illegitimate, good/bad; he sees this mediation as an anomaly in terms of our normal, 'rational' mode of operating and he links it to the non-natural and 'holy' arena of religion. See Edmund Leach, *Genesis as Myth and Other Essays* (London: Jonathan Cape, 1969), p. 11.

101 See Margaret Whitford (ed.), *The Irigaray Reader* (Oxford: Blackwell, 1991), for an excellent introduction to Irigaray; also my discussion of French feminist work on language in *Language and Sexual Difference: Feminist Writing in France* (Basingstoke: Macmillan – now Palgrave, 1991), for a full account of these ideas.

102 Elisabeth Bronfen, *Over Her Dead Body: Death, Femininity and the Aesthetic* (Manchester University Press, 1992), p. 395.

103 See Toril Moi (ed.), *The Kristeva Reader* (Oxford: Blackwell, 1986).

104 Jenny Diski, *The Vanishing Princess* (London: Weidenfeld and Nicolson, 1995).

105 Derrida here is referring to the notion that meaning in language is a
    result of the differences between signifiers, a notion he elaborates to
    suggest how it is also a product of differentiation with elements that are
    absent or deferred from the linguistic unit under consideration. See, for a
    fuller discussion of these points, Sellers, *Language and Sexual Difference*,
    pp. 2–3 and pp. 20–22.
106 See my *Hélène Cixous: Authorship, Autobiography and Love*
    (Cambridge: Polity Press, 1996), for a detailed examination of Cixous's
    view of writing.
107 I discuss these points at length in my *Language and Sexual Difference*
    (see pp. 48–52 and 98–113).
108 See also Zipes, *Fairy Tales and the Art of Subversion*, for an analogous
    discussion on this point, especially pp. 170–80.
109 See Irigaray's 'The Looking Glass, from the Other Side', in Luce
    Irigaray, *This Sex Which Is Not One* (1977), trans. by Catherine Porter
    (New York: Cornell University Press, 1985), pp. 68–85 for an interesting
    illustration of this tactic; also my discussion in *Language and Sexual
    Difference* of this essay and Irigaray's position generally, pp. 7–13, 22–4,
    52–6, 75–80, 113–18 and 135–8.
110 Judith Butler, *Bodies That Matter: On the Discursive Limits of 'Sex'*
    (New York: Routledge and Kegan Paul, 1993), pp. 36–55.
111 Purkiss, 'Women's Rewriting of Myth', pp. 441–57.
112 Barbara G. Walker, *Feminist Fairy Tales* (New York: HarperCollins,
    1996), pp. 27–34 and 63–70; Angela Carter, 'The Company of Wolves',
    The Bloody Chamber (1979; Harmondsworth: Penguin, 1981), pp.
    110–18; and Alison Fell, *The Mistress of Lilliput* (London: Doubleday,
    1999).
113 See 'Spivak and the Subaltern', in Peter Childs and Patrick Williams,
    Post-Colonial Theory (Hemel Hempstead: Prentice Hall Europe, 1997),
    pp. 157–84; the more general problem of co-option is explored by Mark
    Currie in the introduction to his edited volume *Metafiction* (London:
    Longman, 1995), see pp. 8–9.
114 Camille Paglia, *Sexual Personae: Art and Decadence from Nefertiti to
    Emily Dickinson* (New Haven, Conn.: Yale University Press, 1990); for
    Paglia, mythology's identification of woman with nature is correct so
    that rewriting is both unnecessary and pointless since this truth will
    always re-emerge.
115 Bronfen, *Over Her Dead Body*, p. xii.
116 See Daly, *Gyn/Ecology, Pure Lust: Elemental Feminist Philosophy* (Boston:
    Beacon Press, 1984); and *Websters' First New Intergalactic Wickedary of
    the English Language* (1987; London: The Women's Press, 1988).
117 Daly, *Pure Lust*, p. 408.
118 These are all taken from Daly's *Wickedary*.
119 Kamuf (ed.), *A Derrida Reader*, p. 168.
120 Maria J. Valdés (ed.), *A Ricoeur Reader: Reflection and Imagination*
    (University of Toronto Press, 1991), p. 9.
121 Marina Warner, 'Now You See Me', *The Mermaids in the Basement*
    (1993; London: Vintage, 1994), pp. 121–36.
122 Jackson, *Fantasy: The Literature of Subversion*.

123 Ibid., p. 41; Jackson does, however, maintain that the happy endings of fairy tale have a counter-effect since they work to re-cover desire (p. 4). It is significant in this context that Ovid chose the title *Metamorphoses* for his collection of mythic tales.

124 Carol Shields, *Larry's Party* (London: Fourth Estate, 1997).

125 See, for example, Cixous's *Neutre* (Paris: Grasset, 1972), an extract of which is translated into English in Susan Sellers (ed.), *The Hélène Cixous Reader* (London: Routledge, 1994), pp. 3–16.

126 The causes are roughly these: the Phoenicians steal Io, princess of Argos, the Greeks retaliate by invading Tyre and claiming Europa with a second attack on Colchis and the kidnapping of Medea; in reponse Paris, son of Priam of Troy, captures Helen of Sparta.

127 Odysseus' serving-women are snared like birds 'to make them die the most piteous death', *The Odyssey*, Book XXII, line 472, p. 276.

128 Paglia, *Sexual Personae*, p. 29.

129 Though this died away in the second half of the twentieth century under the influence of more progressive educational practice, its effect is not to be underestimated, permeating subsequent literature and thought. Latin was still routinely taught in my own school-time and it remains an option, together with Classical Civilization, on the curricula of many independent schools. It is also interesting that a number of primary schools are reintroducing the language through the new *Minimus* Latin course initiative.

130 George Eliot, *The Mill on the Floss* (1860; Ware: Wordsworth Editions, 1993), pp. 123–41, quotation on p. 126.

131 Virginia Woolf, *A Room of One's Own* (1928; Harmondsworth: Penguin, 1975) pp. 48–50. Alicia Ostriker argues that one of the reasons why women writers return to myth is that by choosing a story which exists in the public domain they confer authority on their writing, see 'The Thieves of Language: Women Poets and Revisionist Mythmaking', in Elaine Showalter (ed.), *The New Feminist Criticism: Essays on Women, Literature and Theory* (1985; London: Virago, 1996), p. 317.

132 Ward Jouve, *Female Genesis*, pp. 187–8.

133 Don Cupitt, *What is a Story?* (1991; London: SCM Press, 1995).

134 This is also a point made by Nicole Ward Jouve, who follows Ricoeur to argue that our exposure to the text can equip us with expanded models for living, see *Female Genesis*, p. 187.

135 Nicole Ward Jouve, 'The Red Road' in Sue Roe, Susan Sellers and Nicole Ward Jouve, *The Semi-Transparent Envelope: Women Writing – Feminism and Fiction* (London: Marion Boyars, 1994), pp. 158–62.

136 Mary Shelley, *Frankenstein or the Modern Prometheus* (1818; Oxford University Press, 1969). It is interesting to note that the relationship to Prometheus may have been detected initially by a male friend, the poet Lord Byron, who was classically educated, see M. K. Joseph's 'Introduction' to the Oxford edition, p. vi.

137 Barthes' evocative phrase is 'myth is speech *stolen and restored*' (his italics, *Mythologies*, p. 125).

138 Cupitt also argues that oral myth is more potent in this respect than
    written myth since writing is 'visible all-at-once', a capacity which
    generates an impression of simultaneity and timelessness. He argues that
    oral myth more exactly mirrors the way we speak and act in time, see
    What is a Story?, p. 2.
139 Cixous, 'Sorties', pp. 72–8.
140 This is the purpose of Ellen Cronan Rose's attack, which takes issue with
    fairy tale on the grounds that it gives boys the active, adventurous role
    and girls the passive one, see 'Through the Looking Glass: When
    Women Tell Fairy Tales', in Abel, Hirsch and Langland (eds), *The Voyage
    In: Fictions of Female Development*, pp. 209–27.
141 Kay F. Stone, 'Feminist Approaches to the Interpretation of Fairy Tales',
    in Bottigheimer (ed.), *Fairy Tales and Society*, pp. 229–36.
142 Stone is quoting Leah Kavablum's Freudian reading in *Cinderella:
    Radical Feminist, Alchemist* (New Jersey: Guttenberg, 1973), p. 231.
    This position can be allied to Bruno Bettelheim's argument that
    tampering with the tales is unnecessary since we automatically rework
    them. We are not passive recipients of the text, Bettelheim maintains,
    and the tales should be left as they are for the individual child to adopt,
    reject or alter (see *The Uses of Enchantment*, p. 151).
143 Lurie (ed.), 'Introduction', *The Oxford Book of Modern Fairy Tales*, p. xi.
144 Hélène Cixous outlines her practice of feminine reading in
    'Conversations', in my edited *Writing Differences: Readings from the
    Seminar of Hélène Cixous* (Milton Keynes: The Open University Press,
    1988), pp. 141–54.
145 See Julia Kristeva, *Revolution in Poetic Language* (1974), trans. Margaret
    Waller (New York: Columbia University Press, 1984) and *Desire in
    Language: A Semiotic Approach to Literature and Art* (1980), trans.
    Thomas Gora, Alice Jardine and Leon S. Roudiez (Oxford: Blackwell,
    1981), for a full account of her views.
146 Jacques Derrida gives an example of this type of reading in his essay
    'Plato's Pharmacy'. He shows how Plato's intention to rid a word of its
    ambiguities 'violently destroys' it. He suggests that we must endeavour
    to read in 'stereograph', listening with both ears (see 'Plato's Pharmacy'
    and 'Tympan' in Kamuf (ed.), *A Derrida Reader*, pp. 112–39 and
    146–68).
147 Nina Auerbach and U. C. Knoepflmacher (eds), *Forbidden Journeys:
    Fairy Tales and Fantasies by Victorian Women Writers* (The University of
    Chicago Press, 1992).
148 Ibid., p. 3.
149 See Edward Said, *The World, the Text and the Critic* (London: Faber and
    Faber, 1984).
150 Lévi-Strauss, *Myth and Meaning*.
151 Ibid., p. 44.
152 Carter, 'Introduction', *The Virago Book of Fairy Tales*, pp. xvi–xvii.
153 Zipes, *Fairy Tale as Myth*, p. 9.
154 Quoted in Olson (ed.), 'Introduction', *Myth, Symbol and Reality*,
    p. 3.

Chapter 2

1 Hélène Cixous, 'The Laugh of the Medusa', in *New French Feminisms* (1980), ed. Elaine Marks and Isabelle de Courtivron (Brighton: Harvester, 1981), p. 255.

2 Sigmund Freud, *Jokes and their Relation to the Unconscious* (1905), trans. James Strachey (Harmondsworth: Penguin, 1976), p. 149.

3 Apuleius, *The Golden Ass or Metamorphoses* (*circa* 170 CE), trans. E. J. Kenney (Harmondsworth: Penguin, 1998), pp. 50–1.

4 There are obvious echoes of 'The Story of Cupid and Psyche' in the tales of 'Beauty and the Beast', 'Snow White' and 'Cinderella'. Marina Warner discusses the links between Apuleius and 'Beauty and the Beast' variants in *From the Beast to the Blonde: On Fairy Tales and their Tellers* (1994; London: Vintage, 1995), see pp. 273–97.

5 *The Golden Ass*, p. 73.

6 Ibid., p. 79.

7 A. S. Byatt, *The Djinn in the Nightingale's Eye: Five Fairy Stories* (1994; London: Vintage, 1995), pp. 93–277.

8 Ibid., p. 121. In Shakespeare's *A Winter's Tale* Leontes falsely accuses Hermione of treason and adultery and imprisons her. Sixteen years pass before she is reunited with a repentant Leontes and her daughter Perdita.

9 Byatt, *The Djinn in the Nightingale's Eye*, pp. 41–72.

10 Ibid., p. 100. The reference is to John Milton's *Paradise Lost* (1667; Harmondsworth: Penguin, 1968), Book IX, p. 207, lines 499–505.

11 Byatt, *The Djinn in the Nightingale's Eye*, p. 118.

12 Ibid., p. 114.

13 Gillian reflects that the majority of her ancestresses would not have reached the age she has (ibid. p. 104); 'Medusa's Ankles' is in *The Matisse Stories* (1993; London: Vintage, 1994), pp. 3–28.

14 Ibid., p. 3.

15 Ibid., p. 28 and p. 25

16 Fay Weldon, *The Life and Loves of a She Devil* (London: Hodder and Stoughton, 1983).

17 Ibid., pp. 29–30.

18 The narrative opens with a description of the 'lies' Mary Fisher writes (ibid., p. 7, see also p. 192).

19 See ibid., pp. 10 and 29.

20 See ibid., p. 71.

21 Ibid., p. 62.

22 See ibid., p. 254.

23 Finuala Dowling, *Fay Weldon's Fiction* (Cranbury, NJ: Associated University Presses, 1998), p. 14.

24 Weldon, *The Life and Loves of a She Devil*, p. 186. It is noteworthy that the doctor reiterates the question of women's desire here: 'tell me ... what it is you *really* want'.

25 Ruth's tactics are parodied in a letter she receives from her mother informing her that her mother can no longer write to Ruth because her new husband does not wish it, and that the religion she now subscribes to

in which she has found peace preaches women's obedience to their marital Master as God's representative on earth (ibid., p. 34).

26 Cixous, 'The Laugh of the Medusa', pp. 245–64. Cixous's work on the Medusa myth is echoed in Sandra M. Gilbert and Susan Gubar's insistence that the female monster 'is simply a woman who seeks the power of self-articulation', *The Madwoman in the Attic: The Woman Writer and the Nineteenth Century Literary Imagination* (New Haven, Conn.: Yale University Press, 1979) p. 79.

27 Michiko Kakutani's review in the *New York Times*, 21 August 1984, col. 17, for instance, sees Ruth as 'a bitter harridan bent on using her sexual wiles and a 1970s license for self-indulgence to inflict hurt on others'. Finuala Dowling discusses such reactions in *Fay Weldon's Fiction*, pp. 108, 111–12.

28 In Eileen Gillooly, 'Women and Humor', *Feminist Studies*, 17: 3 (1991) pp. 473–92.

29 Fay Weldon, *Down Among the Women* (1971; Harmondsworth: Penguin, 1973), p. 171.

30 Weldon, *The Life and Loves of a She Devil*, p. 213.

31 This lack of sisterhood is shown to be all-pervasive, present in Mary Fisher's novels as well as her disregard for Ruth, and in Ruth's vendetta against Mary. Even Ruth's relationship with Nurse Hopkins is sacrificed in the pursuit of her goal.

32 Ann Marie Hebert, 'Rewriting the Feminine Script: Fay Weldon's Wicked Laughter', in *Journal of Women and Gender*, 7: 1 (1993), pp. 21–40.

33 Ibid., p. 25. The reference is to John Austen, *How to Do Things with Words* (Cambridge, Mass.: Harvard University Press, 1975).

34 Weldon, *The Life and Loves of a She Devil*, p. 239.

35 According to Ovid, Pygmalion is so horrified by women's 'wickedness' that he opts to remain celibate and carves an ivory statue of a woman 'more beautiful/Than ever woman born'. His desire to find a wife in the image of his statue is granted by Venus who brings the statue to life (see Ovid, *Metamorphoses*, trans. A. D. Melville (Oxford University Press, 1986) Book x, lines 240–50). The reference to Pygmalion in *The Life and Loves of a She Devil* is p. 238. Dr Black describes the metamorphosed Ruth as 'Venus ... risen freshly from her conch-shell' (ibid.). Lilith, according to Maria Leach (ed.), *Standard Dictionary of Folklore, Mythology and Legend* (London: New English Library, 1972) p. 622, is the spurned first wife of Adam, queen of the demons and occasionally wife of the devil, who becomes locked in a cycle of revenge and punishment. L. S. Schwartz argues that Weldon's characters more generally are the stock of fairy tale and cites the 'scorned Queen turned Witch; selfish, vain younger Queen; Ugly Ducking Princess denied her rightful place ... and confused King ruled by Female Powers' – all of which have resonance in *The Life and Loves of a She Devil* – as examples ('Quartet Plus Ghost', *Village Voice*, 3 January 1977, p. 58). The Frankenstein references are on pp. 238, 240, 248 and 250 of *The Life and Loves of a She Devil*.

36 Henri Bergson, *Laughter: An Essay on the Meaning of the Comic*, trans. by Cloudesley Brereton and Fred Rothwell (London: Macmillan, 1911),

see for example p. 8. See also Freud, *Jokes and their Relation to the Unconscious*, pp. 256, 262.

37 Fay Weldon, *The Cloning of Joanna May* (1989; London: Flamingo, 1993).

38 Ibid., p. 107.

39 The abandoned and redundant first wife is a recurrent theme in Weldon's fiction.

40 These include the discrepancies between what the eye desires to see and actually sees and the 'plucking' of Joanna's 'I' through Carl's cloning of her.

41 It is also significant that Gillian's second wish is prompted by her jealousy of the djinn's former owner whom he loved.

42 Ibid., p. 104.

43 My sources here are the essays by Bakhtin translated in Pam Morris (ed.), *The Bakhtin Reader* (London: Edward Arnold, 1994).

44 These are on pp. 100, 178 and 256 of 'The Djinn in the Nightingale's Eye'.

45 *The Life and Loves of a She Devil*, p. 256.

46 See, for example, Ruth's 'acknowledgement' of Mary Fisher (ibid., p. 245).

47 Hebert's discussion focuses on the more recent Weldon novel *The Heart of the Country* (London: Hutchinson, 1987), in which an actual carnival takes place, though her point is relevant here (see Hebert, 'Rewriting the Feminine Script', p. 27). Finuala Dowling also examines the carnival in *The Heart of the Country* in her *Fay Weldon's Fiction*, pp. 130–3.

48 See Freud, *Jokes and their Relation to the Unconscious*.

49 In fact, Freud suggests that unless a joke is 'innocent', in other words 'an aim in itself', jokes are either '*hostile* ... (serving the purpose of aggressiveness, satire, or defence)' or '*obscene* ... (serving the purpose of exposure)' (ibid., p. 140).

50 Freud discusses the 'Janus-like, two-way-facing' nature of a joke which he describes as 'a double-dealing rascal who serves two masters' (ibid., p. 208).

51 It is also significant that for Freud one of the areas that must be repressed for socialisation to occur is what he terms our 'hostile impulses' towards others (see ibid., p. 147). Ruth's exaggerated campaign against Mary Fisher can be fruitfully viewed in the light of this suggestion.

52 I discuss Kristeva's position in *Language and Sexual Difference: Feminist Writing in France* (Basingstoke: Macmillan – now Palgrave, 1991), pp. 98–113.

53 In this sense, it can be argued that Weldon's joke 'fails' in Freud's terms since it does not produce pleasure in the recipient but rather frustration which it is left to us to negotiate (see *Jokes and their Relation to the Unconscious*, p. 144).

54 See, for example, *The Life and Loves of a She Devil*, p. 29: 'And I tell you this ...'.

55 Ibid., p. 10.

56 Susan Sontag (ed.), *A Barthes Reader* (London: Cape, 1982), p. 409.

57 See, for example, *The Life and Loves of a She Devil*, p. 174.

58 Ruth's success at the Blacks' party, coupled with her knowledge of Mary's terminal cancer and Bobbo's complete submission in prison, might have persuaded her not to complete her merciless programme.

59 There are thirty-four chapters in the novel and a significant number of the paragraphs consist of a single sentence. An example of the easy, slogan-like prose is Ruth's comparison of herself with Jesus: 'he offered the stony path to heaven: I offer the motorway to hell' (ibid., p. 174).

60 'It takes a little time to become wholly she devil. One feels positively exhausted at first, I can tell you' (ibid., p. 54).

61 These are, of course, all abundantly present in Weldon's novel.

62 Stella Duffy, *Singling the Couples* (London: Sceptre, 1998). In Duffy's novel, a she-devil princess embarks on a campaign to destroy couples in love. The parallels with Weldon's novel include the princess's ability to remake herself in the image of another's desire as well as her ruthlessness. The jilted fiancée's programme of revenge involves such clichéd tactics as destroying her former lover's clothes and keeping the car he has registered in her name as a tax dodge (ibid., p. 45).

63 The comparison is between Ruth's 'peel away the wife, the mother, find the woman, and there the she devil is' (*The Life and Loves of a She Devil*, p. 50) and her tribute to Mary: 'she is a woman: she made the landscape better. She devils can make nothing better, except themselves. In the end, she wins' (ibid., p. 245). Ruth's defiant 'I will be what I want, not what He ordained ... I will defy my maker, and remake myself' (ibid., p. 170) is also highly ironic in the context of the appearance she chooses which is, as one of her surgeons puts it, 'one of His feebler and more absurd images' (ibid., p. 249).

64 Berman, quoting Patricia Meyer Spacks, argues that a female character's laughter is not always an indication of her recognition of the injustices of patriarchal society and her means of affirming herself over these, but may be – as in Wendy Wasserstein's view – a way of exorcising the pain of disappointment and rejection (see Jaye Berman, 'Women's Humor', in *Contemporary Literature*, 31: 12 (1990), pp. 251–60).

65 Freud, *Jokes and Their Relation to the Unconscious*, p. 219.

66 Ibid., p. 227.

67 Apuleius, *The Golden Ass*, p. 197. It is interesting that through a loop-hole in the narration we never discover whether Pamphile's own successful metamorphosis resulted in her obtaining her man.

68 Though there is a final ironic touch in Ruth's decision not to publish the romance (see *The Life and Loves of a She Devil*, p. 256).

69 Gillian's sense of her impending death is reiterated by the goddess figures she sees during a visit to a Turkish museum. It is noteworthy that Gillian's guide to the museum explains the primacy of the ancient goddesses and their subsequent demise in terms that repeat the feminist accounts summarised in the preceding section (see pp. 17–22 above).

70 In fact, the djinn explicitly tells Gillian that he cannot grant her wishes in perpetuity since it is not in her nature to be immortal (see *The Djinn in the Nightingale's Eye*, pp. 195–6). It is interesting that Gillian's more moderate requests are followed by the story in which she confesses to the djinn that the power of her young adult body to attract men terrified her (see ibid., pp. 241–2).

71 In the myth as retold to Gillian, Gilgamesh successfully discovers the flower he has been informed holds the secret to eternal youth, but the

flower is eaten by a serpent while he is bathing (see ibid., pp. 143–51). Gillian's critique of the ending to *A Winter's Tale* similarly hinges on this point, as she argues that the daughter's reappearance in the guise of Persephone restored from the Underworld to return the world to Spring is a falsification of the nature of human mortality (see ibid., pp. 113–14 and 120). Her suggestion that tales function as a corrective to such vain attempts to deny fate is on ibid., p. 120.

72 In fact, the working through of this image is extremely complex, involving the snake in the Gilgamesh myth already cited, the explicit comparisons between Gillian's first, petrifying apparition and Milton's poem (see above, also ibid., pp. 158 and 170), and the narrator's own relation to Gillian's story (see ibid., p. 100; it is significant, for instance, that Gillian's tale is itself presented as a myth – see the opening paragraph, p. 95). In an interview with Juliet Dusinberre, Byatt links the manifold image of the snake that informs her early novel *The Game* (1967; London: Vintage, 1992), to the myth of the Medusa and suggests that 'the serpent is both sex and destruction, and imagination and preservation, and that these two are curiously and intimately connected' (*Women Writers Talking*, ed. Janet Todd (New York: Holmes and Meier, 1983), p. 193, quoted in Richard Todd, *A. S. Byatt* (Plymouth: Northcote House, 1997), p. 12).

73 Gillian emphatically links the glass paperweights to art more generally in an impromptu lecture she gives to the men who own the shop (see *The Djinn in the Nightingale's Eye*, p. 275). The connection Gillian makes between Hermione's appearance as a statue and her 'miraculous' restoration to life and happiness in *A Winter's Tale* is also relevant here (*The Djinn in the Nightingale's Eye*, p. 113).

74 Ibid., p. 272, the earlier figure is described as being of 'many colours, and all of them grey, grey' (ibid., p. 118), while the vibrant colours of the paperweight float 'like uncurling serpents' (ibid., p. 272). The brilliant colours reinforce Gillian's own release from the 'grey void of forced inactivity' that is typically women's script (see above).

75 Just as the 'grey men' that petrified her as a child vanished when she started to describe them, Gillian realises that if only she can relate her first apparition it will disappear (ibid., p. 122). She later tells the djinn of her childhood creation of the 'golden boy' who told her stories and appeared in her dreams (see ibid., p. 234), as well as the fiction she wrote to fill the loneliness of her boarding-school years in which the protagonist was a boy and her endeavour to imagine 'the Other' (ibid., p. 232).

76 The allusion is to Charles Perrault, author of the famous 1697 fairy-tale collection *Histoires ou contes du temps passé*.

77 See *The Djinn in the Nightingale's Eye*, p. 119: 'all her stoppered and stunted energy'.

78 As has been suggested, these are the classical myth of Pygmalion (in which happiness is restored only through Aphrodite's divine intervention) and the débâcle of Frankenstein.

79 Ibid., p. 103. In a formulation that sheds an interesting light on Weldon's text, Orhan argues that the way women are presented as wielding power in these stories, given their underlying powerlessness, is as 'deceitful,

unreliable, greedy, inordinate in their desires, unprincipled and simply dangerous' (ibid., p. 124).

80 It is significant that Gillian includes pythonesses in her description of this venerated tradition of women story-tellers (see ibid., p. 103), and that in her retelling of Chaucer she argues that the unleashing of Griselda's pent-up energies when her children are restored to her is petrifying to the male narrator because it threatens his script (see ibid., p. 119). It is also noteworthy that Gillian sees Paulina in *A Winter's Tale* taking on the role of story-teller as she restores Hermione to life through the fabrication of art (see *The Djinn in the Nightingale's Eye*, p. 113).

Chapter 3

1 'The Love of the Nightingale', in *Timberlake Wertenbaker: Plays* (London: Faber, 1996), p. 316.

2 Christine Crow, *Miss X or the Wolf Woman* (London: The Women's Press, 1990), p. 133.

3 Hélène Cixous, 'Sorties' in *The Newly Born Woman* (1975) with Catherine Clément, trans. Betsy Wing (London: I. B. Tauris, 1996) p. 99.

4 Philomela's story is told in Book VI of Ovid's *Metamorphoses* (Oxford University Press, 1986), pp. 134–42, lines 412–683. It is interesting in the light of what follows that as the text's translator, A. D. Melville, points out, the word Ovid uses to denote the weaving of the tale is *carmen*, which he translates literally as 'spell' and indicates the magical nature of writing (ibid., p. 412). In Wertenbaker's play, the cloth becomes two dolls sewn by Philomela/Philomel which re-enact the rape.

5 *Timberlake Wertenbaker: Plays*, p. 351.

6 It is noteworthy that the word for 'bird' also means 'omen' in both Greek and Latin.

7 A prime instance of this occurs when the novel's protagonist Mary Wolfe accuses Miss X's mother of causing her daughter's unhappiness. Mary later reflects that '**language itself, Annabel's "Law of the Father", had spoken with its foul, poisoned tongue through my mouth**' (*Miss X or the Wolf Woman*, p. 174, bold in original).

8 Ibid., p. 31; see also p. 8.

9 This is the version cited in *New Larousse Encyclopedia of Mythology* (London: Hamlyn, 1975), pp. 17–19.

10 Mary Orr, in her extremely insightful essay on *Miss X*, notes other key appearances of the number fourteen as well as the repetition of the goddess's name in the River Isis (see Mary Orr, 'Crossing Divides: *Miss X or the Wolf Woman*', in Caroline Gonda (ed.), *Tea and Leg-Irons: New Feminist Readings from Scotland* (London: Open Letters, 1992), p. 162).

11 Nicki Hastie, in her essay 'Lesbian Bibliomythography', points out that Monique Wittig's initials duplicate Mary Wolfe's, in Gabriele Griffin (ed.), *Outwrite: Lesbianism and Popular Culture* (London: Pluto Press, 1993), p. 82.

12 Although it is interesting that Mary's retrospectively imagined love-scene with Miss X borrows an explicitly male discourse, as Terry Castle, in *The Apparitional Lesbian: Female Homosexuality and Modern Culture* (New York: Columbia University Press, 1993), pp. 57–9, notes. The exposure of psychoanalytic theory occurs on a number of levels in *Miss X*, ranging from an investigation into Freud's hypotheses in *Totem and Taboo* to the comedy of discovering from an autopsy that the dachsund Sigmund's agoraphobia was genetic rather than the result of trauma.

13 See *Miss X*, p. 153.

14 In an interview with Caroline Gonda, Christine Crow discusses the double-edged nature of labelling, suggesting that in writing *Miss X* her plan was 'to try to give the reader a feeling of entering into that space where the label or the name was perceived as both necessary to give a shape to an identity, but also very harming the other way round, because it objectifies subjective consciousness' (see Caroline Gonda, 'An Other Country? Mapping Scottish/Lesbian/ Writing', in Christopher Whyte (ed.), *Gendering the Nation: Studies in Modern Scottish Literature* (Edinburgh University Press, 1995), p. 12). While Crow recognises the reality of homophobia and the importance of naming oneself as a lesbian, she feels that when the term crosses the 'boundary from political to subjective, private experience' then the women who use it are 'oppressing their own open-endedness, their own growth' (ibid.).

15 Miss X's exhortations include the retrospectively remembered 'if in doubt, *don't*, Mary' and 'take what you want and pay for it, said God!', maxims which Mary comes to understand in the context of Miss X's 'sense of community … a sense which, for the infinite goodness of God (sic) the Father (sic), to be fully exercised on this Earth … required the constant sacrifice of one's immediate lusts and shameful (sic) personal desires, flaws in an otherwise perfect design' (*Miss X*, p. 109).

16 This involves not only the transfer of Mary's feelings to Miss X but also her joining Miss X in ridiculing Miss P. The fact that Miss P is subsequently revealed to be Miss X's lover is yet a further indication of Miss X's torturous double-dealings.

17 Ibid., p. 18.

18 Miss X's extended appellation 'Mary my lamb' reoccurs frequently. There is a further instance of Miss X's annihilating impact on Mary in her forcing Mary to pursue her own subject French rather than Mary's preferences for Classics or English.

19 The allusion to Philomela's weaving is explicit in the text (see ibid., pp. 96, 97 and 131).

20 'But the goat, on which the lot fell to be the scapegoat, shall be presented alive before the Lord, to make an atonement with him, and to let him go for a scapegoat into the wilderness' (Leviticus 16:10).

21 Before she writes her novel, Mary embarks on a study of the origins of Tragedy in which she endeavours to sort out 'all that compleX business about the *Scapegoat*' by exploring the correlations between the Greek sacrifice to Dionysus and 'all that sado-masochistic fiXation in our culture on the death of Xt' (*Miss X*, p. 132). Her conclusion is that both derive from the same 'self-generated Cooking-Pot fuelled by the false

oppositions of language itself' (ibid., p. 133). This assessment reflects
Julia Kristeva's analysis of the role of 'a scapegoat victim' in the
foundation of Western culture and her suggestion that this should be
replaced 'by the analysis of the potentialities of *victim/executioner* which
characterize each identity, each subject, each sex' (see Julia Kristeva,
'Women's Time', in Toril Moi (ed.), *The Kristeva Reader* (Oxford:
Blackwell, 1986), p. 210).

22 See, for example, the list of possible meanings of P.B. in *Miss X*, p. 190.
The repetition of P.B. in the conundrum of Pandora's Box is a good
illustration of this process of disclosure, since the mythical image is taken
to figure the 'secret' of woman's sex (see ibid., p. 83). In a recent private
letter, dated Tuesday, 29 June 1999, Christine Crow suggests that the
importance of myth lies precisely in its potential revelation of 'the
already-there-but-not-yet-fully-known'.

23 Crow describes the X as 'both a censoring device and a mark of the
unknown' in the interview with Gonda (see *Gendering the Nation*, p. 11).

24 Annabel's argument that feminists must hijack the plane of patriarchy
(see *Miss X*, p. 151) is answered in the plane crash that metaphorically
signals Mary's realisation that in these terms '**total identity is death**'
(see ibid., p. 223, bold in original).

25 Ibid., p. 205, bold as in original.

26 Hastie, 'Lesbian Bibliomythography', p. 80. The metaphor of blind
monovision appears in the myth of the Cyclops which recurs through
Mary's narrative as well as in the visor-like dark glasses 'bunched like a
single, blind eye' on the forehead of the analyst whose abortive interview
opens and closes the novel (*Miss X*, pp. 1 and 233).

27 Ibid., p. 60.

28 This is carefully distinguished from Annabel's feminist critique of Mary's
use of myth as politically suspect because of its universalising and exclusive
tendencies which can prevent change (see ibid., p. 149).

29 'The great Mother Isis, solar disk and horns of a cow … travels the world
to find the fourteen scattered pieces … in order to stitch them together
again and turn Osiris back into a god' (ibid., p. 66). The link with
Philomela's weaving is clearly emphasised here. In her letter cited in note
22, Crow argues that writing itself offers an opportunity to pursue what
may not yet be fully known, and suggests that it 're-enacts and undoes or
revivifies' these 'mysteries' that myths enshrine.

30 Mary Orr explores Virginia Woolf's role in the novel as a gradually
emerging role-model of a woman writer for Crow's protagonist (see
'Crossing Divides', pp. 171–2). As Orr points out, Woolf's name figures
in Mary's 'crying wolf' that marks her assumption of her identit/ies
(see ibid. and *Miss X*, p. 229).

31 See Mary's rejection of all labels (ibid., pp. 188–9) and her realisation
that there is 'no such thing as a human identity fiXed to the flagpole prior
to its own rebirth' (ibid., p. 189).

32 Ibid., pp. 232 and 204. In an interview, Christine Crow describes the
creative capacity of imagination in the following terms: 'imagination can
take us to a different place, a different self – and where imagination leads,
reality can follow. Daring to imagine is the first step' (see Alison Hennegan,

'The Extraordinary Miss X: Christine Crow Talks About Her New Novel', *The Women's Press Bookclub Catalogue*, October–December 1990).

33 Hélène Cixous, 'Sorties', pp. 63–132, see especially pp. 63–4.
34 Hélène Cixous, *The Book of Promethea* (1983), trans. by Betsy Wing (Lincoln: University of Nebraska Press, 1991).
35 Hesiod, 'Theogony', in *Hesiod and Theognis*, trans. Dorothea Wender (Harmondsworth: Penguin, 1973), p. 41, lines 563–69.
36 *The Book of Promethea*, p. 154. Cixous outlines this notion of the feminine gift-that-gives in contradistinction to the gift that requires some form of return in 'Sorties', pp. 86–87.
37 *The Book of Promethea*, p. 7, see also p. 56 and the account of how her former life relied on electricity – in other words, artificial means – for its warmth, p. 24. The long list of personal items contrasts with the depiction of Promethea's nudity (see, for example, p. 10).
38 Ibid., p. 7.
39 Ibid., p. 81. The pun develops into an account of all the changes the narrator has had to undergo in order to love and to be loved by Promethea.
40 This impossibility of final translation is expressed in *The Book of Promethea* in the narrator's recognition of her absurd attempts to 'write out' Promethea's fire, ibid., p. 24. For a good example of the way fire is woven into the text, see ibid., p. 171.
41 This failure to attend usually results from the narrator relapsing into her former intellectualising (see ibid., p. 40). The fire as inspiration is illustrated in the narrator's account of the 'morning … without fire' when she cannot write (ibid., p. 93).
42 Emma Wilson, 'Hélène Cixous: An Erotics of the Feminine', in Alex Hughes and Kate Ince (eds), *French Erotic Fiction: Women's Desiring Writing, 1880–1990* (Oxford: Berg, 1996), pp. 121–45.
43 *The Book of Promethea*, p. 9.
44 See ibid., p. 33.
45 Ibid., p. 6. See, for an example of the affirmation of the maternal, p. 34, and, as an example of the impetus given to her writing by Promethea's female body, the narrator's description of herself writing with her left hand between Promethea's breasts, p. 53.
46 Ibid., p. 101; see also p. 21.
47 Ibid., p. 15.
48 There is an explanation of this decision on ibid., p. 11.
49 This signals an important difference from the rewriting of *Miss X or the Wolf Woman*, where the albeit playful orderings of the treasure-hunt, for instance, are an integral component.
50 *The Book of Promethea*, p. 210. This 'it's all up to *you* now' (ibid.) is a direct echo of the address to the reader at the conclusion to *Miss X*.
51 *The Book of Promethea*, p. 63; 'The Notebook of Metamorphoses' begins on p. 138.
52 Ibid., pp. 6, 11 and 12. Some of these operations are inevitably lost in translation.
53 Ibid., p. 112.
54 Hesiod, 'Theogony', p. 40, lines 524–30.

55 See *The Book of Promethea*, p. 79.
56 Ibid., p. 43. See the narrator's realisation that 'I suddenly understood that I had to change every part of my being, not merely turn my gaze in the direction of a new world and discover it, but one by one I had to replace each of my old organs' (p. 42). See also her exhortation to Promethea to rip out her heart because it is 'too small to hold so much love' (p. 77).
57 This metaphor reoccurs through the text. An example is: 'I want this: slowly to sink into her body, slow and breathless to go down inside her heaving breast, to let my soul sink down far from duties, from conversations, far from myself, toward her' (ibid., p. 101).
58 See ibid., p. 179.
59 This aspect of the lovers' story parallels Cixous's discussion of the love affair between Antony and Cleopatra in Shakespeare's play, see 'Sorties' pp. 122–30.
60 There is also an echo of this aspect of the myth in the 'torture' the narrator undergoes in order to avoid damaging Promethea in her writing of her (see ibid., p. 5).
61 For a lucid account of Cixous's idea of other-love see her contribution to 'Conversations', in Susan Sellers (ed.), *Writing Differences: Readings from the Seminar of Hélène Cixous* (Milton Keynes: The Open University Press, 1988), pp. 146–8.
62 See, for example, the narrator's confession of her difficulty in keeping 'myself ever so slightly together around a minuscule point of myself' when confronted with Promethea's blaze (see *The Book of Promethea*, p. 150).
63 Ibid., p. 59.
64 See, for example, the narrator's insistence that what she must do is 'record Promethea's right-now', 'before memory … had begun its embalming and forgetting and story-telling' (ibid., p. 91).
65 Ibid., p. 93.
66 *Miss X*, p. 229; see, for an example of Mary's denouncement of others' tyranny, her rejection here of the '**You** who alone stigmatise, eXtirpate, erase, omit … the Other, the different' (p. 228, bold as in original).
67 Ibid., p. 230. Given the strong French leanings of the text, indicated, for instance, in Mary's reading and the large number of untranslated French passages, it is perhaps not insignificant in terms of Mary's surname that in French the letter 'e' is the mark of the feminine. It is also striking that Mary's account of herself as the she-wolf emphasises the transmission of her knowledge to her young (ibid., p. 229).
68 The wolf, as Mary stresses, is neither sheep nor goat. Mary's proclamation of herself as 'wolf(e)' is also a response to the presentation of the predatory lesbian in the male literature she has read.
69 Hélène Cixous, 'Love of the Wolf', in *Stigmata: Escaping Texts* (London and New York: Routledge, 1998), pp. 84–99. The essay is originally titled 'L'amour du loup' and is translated here by Keith Cohen.
70 See ibid., p. 90.
71 Ibid., p. 85.
72 Ibid., p. 93.

160 Notes

73 Ibid.

74 In 'The Love of the Nightingale', the chorus exposes the way 'the child's instinct' to question is 'suppressed in the adult' (see *Timberlake Wertenbaker: Plays*, p. 318). Cixous's insistence that for the adult recipient of 'Little Red Riding Hood', 'the split between grandmother and wolf has taken place in advance of the story's narrative' suggests why Red Riding Hood's famous observations appear so weakly comic (see *Stigmata*, p. 93).

75 *Miss X*, p. 189. There are numerous references to Promethea's positive savagery, such as that in *The Book of Promethea*, p. 123, as well as descriptions of Promethea's childlike nature (for instance p. 162), and her equation with prehistory (for example pp. 16–17).

76 *Stigmata*, p. 91. It is interesting in this context that the X in *Miss X* can also be equated with the image of the lighthouse beam. See, for example, Mary's disquisition on imagination – already coupled with the X – as 'my first and only truly sighted, truly reciprocal Lighthouse Lamp' (*Miss X*, p. 213). Mary Orr's essay has an interesting section unravelling the metaphor of the lighthouse beam in the novel (see 'Crossing Divides' p. 171).

77 There is a fascinating account of Cixous's own endeavours to pass to this 'other' world in writing in her essay 'Writing Blind' (see *Stigmata*, pp. 139–52).

78 In 'Writing Blind', Cixous warns against seeing this 'other' world writing gives access to as 'an ideal kingdom': 'on the other side there is good *with* evil. Good in evil, evil in good and above all: difficulty' (ibid., p. 143). See also her account of words as our fairy-tale 'workers in the mines of language' (ibid., p. 147).

79 See, for example, *The Book of Promethea*, p. 55, for an account of the positive effects of their 'cannibalistic tendencies' on the narrator.

80 Ibid., p. 13 and p. 103.

81 See p. 70 for an account of the 'descent' 'to where bodies communicate'. It is striking that this account is followed by a passage from which the 'I' disappears.

82 Ibid., p. 154.

83 See ibid., pp. 44–5.

84 Ibid., p. 45.

85 This desire to write affirmatively despite death is comically depicted in the account of the tussle between the 'demons' who 'want there not to be, not to be' and Promethea who 'wants there to be, to be' (ibid., p. 164).

86 There are clearly echoes here of the role of loss in our construction as independent subjects, since it is our perception of ourselves as distinct from the subsequently 'lost' maternal body that propels us towards language. I discuss the role of loss in the formation of autonomy in relation to Cixous's work in detail in *Language and Sexual Difference: Feminist Writing in France* (Basingstoke: Macmillan – now Palgrave, 1991), pp. 39–60.

87 See, for example, 'writing is walking on a dizzying silence setting one word after the other on emptiness' (*The Book of Promethea*, p. 27). Cixous gives a moving account of loss in her own trajectory as a writer in 'Writing Blind' (*Stigmata*, pp. 148–9).

88 See the reference to the 'Present Absolute' in *The Book of Promethea*, p. 33, also the narrator's description of how the present moment contains 'its radiant procession of reminiscences, forebodings, impending transmutations', etc. (p. 111). It is Promethea's paradoxical capacity to live as if she is mortal that constitutes what the narrator perceives as her 'divinity' (ibid., p. 157).

89 'I want no other god than the idea I have of not-lying. Only to this god am I responsible' (ibid., p. 28, see also p. 59).

90 Ibid., pp. 185 and 190.

91 Ibid., p. 190.

92 These ideas are reiterated in the text, for instance in the passage on ibid., p. 87 in which the narrator reflects on how love transports us beyond the self and how in order to live the 'ordeal' of paradise we must continually recreate.

93 Ibid., p. 103.

94 Ibid., p. 99.

95 It is significant, in this context, that one of Mary Wolfe's desires is to 'encounter that rare being capable of containing our metamorphoses' (*Miss X*, p. 31), a desire she later equates, through the medium of the 'X', with the imaginative criss-X of writing (see ibid., p. 213). In 'Writing Blind', Cixous offers the following account of this view of god (the French word for god – '*dieu*' – is retained in the translation to reiterate its echo with the French word for eyes – '*yeux*'):

> I have never written without *Dieu*. Once I was reproached for it. *Dieu* they said is not a feminist. Because they believed in a pre-existing God. But God is of my making. But god, I say, is the phantom of writing, it is her pretext and her promise. God is the name of all that has not yet been said. Without the word *Dieu* to shelter the infinite multiplicity of all that could be said the world would be reduced to its shell and I to my skin. *Dieu* stands for the names that have not yet been invented. *Dieu* is the synonym. (*Stigmata*, p. 150)

Chapter 4

1 Luce Irigaray, 'Divine Women', in *Sexes and Genealogies* (1987), trans. by Gillian C. Gill (New York: Columbia University Press, 1993), p. 71.

2 E. Allison Peers (ed.), *The Complete Works of Saint Teresa of Jesus*, vol. II (London: Sheed and Ward, 1946), pp. 88–9.

3 Michèle Roberts, *Impossible Saints* (1997; London: Virago, 1998). The incident concerning the fat lady is on pp. 127–9.

4 The model for the 'lives' that interleave Josephine's story is, as Roberts makes clear in her 'Author's Note', *The Golden Legend*, a thirteenth-century text giving an abbreviated life-history of key figures in the Catholic pantheon. See Jacobus de Voragine: *The Golden Legend: Readings on the Saints*, 2 vols, trans. William Granger Ryan (Princeton University Press, 1993). The mythical status of this text, particularly for women from the thirteenth century onwards, is signalled in *Impossible*

Saints by Josephine's continual reading of it as a girl and by Sister Maria's reliance on its optimism after Josephine's death. Although the father plays a primary role in almost all the alternative 'lives' Roberts includes, the stories of St Thais and St Dympna are especially striking: Thais' father acts as her mirror so that 'without him looking at her she did not exist' (p. 169), while Dympna reveres her father 'as though he were a god' (p. 201).

5 Ibid., p. 63.

6 Irigaray's essay is partly a response to Ludwig Feuerbach's *The Essence of Christianity* (1881), trans. George Eliot (New York: Harper, 1957). Except where otherwise indicated all references here are to 'Divine Women', though see also Irigaray's 'The Existence of a Female Divine', in *An Ethics of Sexual Difference* (1984), trans. Carolyn Burke and Gillian C. Gill (London: Athlone Press, 1993), pp. 68–71.

7 *Impossible Saints*, p. 190.

8 Maureen Duffy offers a fascinating account of the reasons for sexual repression in the early Christian Church in her *The Erotic World of Faery* (London: Hodder and Stoughton, 1972), pp. 14–25. See also Riane Eisler, *Sacred Pleasure: Sex, Myth and the Politics of the Body* (1995; Shaftesbury: Element Books, 1996), pp. 152–5 and Monica Sjöö and Barbara Mor, *The Great Cosmic Mother: Rediscovering the Religion of the Earth* (San Francisco: Harper and Row, 1987), p. 288.

9 In an interesting demonstration of Irigaray's notion of becoming, Josephine is partly influenced by Magdalena's radiant beauty which, she realises, derives from her having fulfilled herself (see *Impossible Saints*, p. 153).

10 Ibid., p. 29.

11 Although I am following the argument of 'Divine Women' here, this idea is more fully elaborated in Irigaray's essay 'Sexual Difference' (see *An Ethics of Sexual Difference*, pp. 5–19).

12 Julia Kristeva endorses Irigaray's views on this point, arguing that monotheistic unity can only be sustained by a radical separation of the sexes. She contends that the localisation of the desiring body in the other sex makes it possible to postulate a principle of One Law as transcendent guarantor (see 'About Chinese Women', in Toril Moi (ed.), *The Kristeva Reader* (Oxford: Blackwell, 1986), p. 141).

13 Michèle Roberts, *Food, Sex and God: On Inspiration and Writing* (London: Virago, 1998) see especially the essays 'Mary Magdalene', 'The Place of Women in the Catholic Church: On the New Roman Catholic Catechism' and 'The Flesh Made Word' (pp. 27–44).

14 Although I do not have space to discuss this here, Roberts's novel *The Wild Girl* is a fascinating attempt to reconstruct the story of Mary Magdalene (see *The Wild Girl* (London: Minerva, 1984)). The close link between the names of Mary Magdalene and Magdalena in *Impossible Saints* emphasises their similarity.

15 It is noteworthy that Josephine's dream of a new establishment for women mirrors the one created on board the ark in Roberts's *The Book of Mrs Noah* (London: Methuen, 1987), see below.

16 Kristeva's essay 'About Chinese Women', which suggests how the social-symbolic order cannot accommodate woman, sheds an interesting light on this point.

17 *Impossible Saints*, p. 182.
18 Ibid., p. 308.
19 Luce Irigaray, 'Love of Self', in *An Ethics of Sexual Difference*, pp. 59–71.
20 *Impossible Saints*, p. 289.
21 Ibid.
22 Ibid., pp. 288–9.
23 For a full account of Irigaray's work here, see 'Plato's *Hystera*',
    pp. 243–364, and 'The Blind Spot of an Old Dream of Symmetry',
    pp. 13–129, in *Speculum of the Other Woman* (1974), trans. Gillian C.
    Gill (New York: Cornell University Press, 1985).
24 *Impossible Saints*, p. 307.
25 It is also the starting-point of *The Wild Girl* which presents the lost gospel
    of Mary Magdalene and, developing hints in the Bible, turns her into
    Jesus' lover and the mother of his daughter, thereby positing her as
    Christ's feminine equal.
26 *The Book of Mrs Noah*, p. 51.
27 It is also significant in terms of Irigaray's insistence that in order to
    establish a vision women need to seek within and beyond themselves,
    that the protagonist of Roberts's novel imagines the journey to the ark as
    an internal descent into her bowels (figured as a 'Ladies' room occupied
    by grandmothers sitting on commodes) and as an ascent towards the
    heavens (imaged by the grandmother gazing through her telescope),
    see ibid., pp. 14–15. Like Josephine's convent, which offers a refuge for
    women who are not married, one of the rationales for the ark is as a
    '*Salon des Refusées*' and '*Refusantes*', a 'cruise ship for the females who are
    only fitted in as monsters: the gorgons, the basilisks, the harpies, the
    furies, the viragos, the medusas, the sphinxes' (ibid., pp. 19–20).
28 The final story in the novel offers a graphic illustration of a terrifying
    female regime in which no new values have been established. The word
    'cunt' may have been rescued as indicating 'real woman' but it is a term
    reserved only for the 'Prime Ministress': other women as well as men are
    subject to repressive controls (ibid., pp. 250–66). The problems of
    reversal also preoccupy the 'Correct Sibyl'. She argues that the goddess
    worshippers who merely substitute 'she' for 'he' are not offering an
    alternative and that 'the myth starts when *he* meets *she*' (ibid., p. 191).
29 It is noteworthy in the light of the above that the new story of Daphne
    and Apollo Mrs Noah tells is presented as an ancient, obliterated version
    which can nevertheless still be heard 'yelping' in the 'elegant pauses'
    between the lines of the male poets (see ibid., p. 52).
30 Ovid, *Metamorphoses*, trans. A. D. Melville (Oxford University Press,
    1986), Book 1, pp. 14–18, lines 450–568.
31 In the 'official' version given in *The Book of Mrs Noah*, it is Mother Earth
    who transforms Daphne into a tree rather than Ovid's river-god.
32 *Food, Sex and God*, p. 12.
33 Ibid.
34 Ibid., p. 20.
35 The fact that Angelina is discovered to be a man adds a further twist to
    this complex story, figuring, perhaps, men's appropriation of the maternal
    role and the need to repress the mother in order to become a man.

Angelina's maleness links the story to the widespread myth of the gods of
the waxing and waning years competing for love of the goddess, see
Chapter 1 above. The ritual murder can also be linked to the mother via
Julia Kristeva's insistence that the acquisition of language, which derives
from the break in the mother–child continuum, is often figured as an act
of murder and represented by a killing, of which the Christian crucifixion
is only one example (see Moi (ed.), *The Kristeva Reader*, p. 119).

36 *Food, Sex and God*, p. 21.
37 *The Book of Mrs Noah*, p. 242.
38 Ibid., p. 209. The story is paralleled in Mrs Noah's own. The final phrase
of her narrative is a reiteration of the first with the addition of the words
'I write'.
39 Ibid., pp. 270–1.
40 Ibid., p. 273.
41 Ibid., p. 274.
42 Ibid. The colours and dancing associated with the rainbow also link the
image to Irigaray's suggestion that it is in these repressed elements that
women may find alternative values.
43 Discussing what she describes as 'the psychic dismemberment of the
female in this culture', Roberts suggests that this effort to 'reassemble' is
at the origin of her own myth-making (see 'Questions and Answers', in
Michelene Wandor (ed.), *On Gender and Writing* (London: Pandora
Press, 1983), pp. 66–7). Her description here presents fascinating
parallels with the deployment of the myth of Isis in Christine Crow's
Miss X or the Wolf Woman.
44 *The Book of Mrs Noah*, p. 288.
45 See *Food, Sex and God*, pp. 43–4.
46 The story of the Beguines, which in many ways parallels Josephine's
narrative in *Impossible Saints*, offers a powerful and moving incarnation of
woman as equal participant in the act of creation (see *The Book of
Mrs Noah*, pp. 121–5). There are also potent symbols in the celebratory
prayers to the Mother on board the ark (ibid., pp. 42–4), as well as in
Mrs Noah's alternative vision of the Annunciation where the Word is the
Virgin's recreation which in turn evokes the mythical figure of Daphne as
goddess-author (ibid., pp. 214–15).

Chapter 5

1 Bram Stoker, *Dracula* (1897; Ware: Wordsworth Editions, 1993), p. 55.
The editor of this edition, David Rogers, glosses the second sentence as
follows: 'these curses and ghosts and apparitions and harbingers of death
and hobgoblins and all concerning them is only fit to set children and
half-witted women a-crying' (see ibid., p. 317). He offers 'learned
people' for 'beuk-bodies' and 'scare half-wits' for 'skeer an' scunner
hafflin's' (ibid.).
2 Robert Louis Stevenson, *The Strange Case of Dr Jekyll and Mr Hyde*
(1886; London: Penguin, 1994), p. 70.

3 Julia Kristeva, *Powers of Horror: An Essay on Abjection* (1980), trans. Leon
   S. Roudiez (New York: Columbia University Press, 1982), p. 4.
4 See the opening citation and note 1.
5 See *Dracula*, pp. iv–v. Catherine Belsey suggests fascinating links between
   Dracula and Zeus in her *Desire: Love Stories in Western Culture* (Oxford:
   Blackwell, 1994), p. 173. In her *No Go the Bogeyman: Scaring, Lulling
   and Making Mock* (London: Chatto and Windus, 1998), Marina Warner
   argues that one of the principle functions of scary stories is to assuage fear
   (see p. 6).
6 In Stoker's novel, Dracula can assume a variety of guises, including that of
   a bat, a wolf and a grey mist. His transgressive function in gender terms is
   signalled by the androgynous nature of his mouth, the full red lips of
   which contrast with the 'peculiarly sharp' teeth (see *Dracula*, p. 17).
7 Ibid., p. 267. An example of the hellish imagery used to describe Dracula
   is Harker's account of his wrathful eyes 'as if the flames of hell-fire blazed
   behind them', ibid., p. 34. Dracula is powerless against such symbols of
   Christianity as the crucifix.
8 Ibid., pp. 175 and 180.
9 Ibid., p. 201.
10 To date, Anne Rice has written four vampire novels: *Interview with
   the Vampire* (1976; London: Warner Books, 1998); *The Vampire Lestat*
   (New York: Alfred A. Knopf, 1985); *Queen of the Damned* (1988;
   London: Warner Books, 1995); and *The Tale of the Body Thief* (New York:
   Alfred A. Knopf, 1992). Together these comprise 'The Vampire
   Chronicles'. My discussion here will centre on *Interview with the Vampire*,
   though reference will also be made to *Queen of the Damned* and *The
   Vampire Lestat*.
11 Dracula is given no direct voice among the various testimonies and
   records that comprise Stoker's novel. The use of a tape-recorder in Anne
   Rice's rewrite brings Dr Seward's phonograph diary appropriately up to
   date.
12 *Interview with the Vampire*, p. 358.
13 The interviewer, Daniel, finally achieves his aim in *Queen of the
   Damned*.
14 *Interview with the Vampire*, p. 19.
15 Ibid., p. 158.
16 See *The Vampire Lestat*, p. 404.
17 See, for example, *Queen of the Damned*, pp. 346 and 268.
18 See ibid., p. 427.
19 *Dracula*, p. 34 and see p. 176.
20 *Interview with the Vampire*, p. 226 and see p. 18.
21 This is most true of the first of the 'Chronicles', *Interview with the
   Vampire*. It is appropriate as well as ironic that the most detailed account
   of blood-exchanges in *Dracula* are those that take place between Lucy
   and the group of men who love her, under Van Helsing's medical
   direction.
22 See *Interview with the Vampire*, p. 47. It is, however, noteworthy that
   while there are descriptions of vampiric activity among females in the
   'Chronicles' – an example is the passionate encounter between Maharet

and Jesse in *Queen of the Damned*, see pp. 281–2 – this is significantly less than that between men. See, for further analysis of this point, the discussion of Rice's erotic fiction below.

23 'I *am* the Queen of Heaven. And Heaven shall reign on earth finally', Akasha tells the doubting Lestat (see *The Queen of the Damned*, p. 349, original emphasis).

24 Lestat, in his version of vampire history, points out that Isis' failure to restore Osiris' phallus has a pertinent equivalent in the vampires' inability to procreate (see *The Vampire Lestat*, p. 289).

25 Akasha's figuration of the evil mother is underscored in her destruction of her own vampire offspring as well as in her plans for mankind.

26 *Interview with the Vampire*, pp. 212 and 259.

27 Ibid., p. 76. The reiteration of 'mindless', which had been used to describe the Transylvanian vampires, is noteworthy here, particularly in the light of the Chronicles' apparent insistence that thinking beings require limits, see below.

28 Claudia explicitly underscores Louis's realisation when she reminds him: 'your quest is for darkness only ... The myths of men are not your myths' (ibid., p. 181).

29 Lestat, for example, remembers Marius' prophesy as Akasha outlines her new religion: 'that the old religion, Christianity, was dying, and maybe no new religion would rise: "Maybe something more wonderful will take place," Marius had said, "the world will truly move forward, past all gods and goddesses, past all devil and angels ... " ' (*The Queen of the Damned*, p. 427). Bette B. Roberts, in her book *Anne Rice* (New York: Twayne, 1994), suggests how vampire history as told in *The Vampire Lestat* and *The Queen of the Damned* draws on ancient fertility rites as well as ancient Egyptian, Greek and Christian mythology (see pp. 64–6, also p. 51 for an interesting discussion of the links between Lestat's rock performances and the cult of Dionysus).

30 Despite Rice's skilful handling of the grandiose scale of 'The Vampire Chronicles' and her undeniable powers as a storyteller, their mythic potential is also diminished through the frequently weak writing.

31 *Interview with the Vampire*, p. 266. An example is the dress code to which the vampires adhere.

32 See ibid., p. 267. In *The Queen of the Damned*, this law is further generalised in a direct evocation of societal taboos against parental murder, since Akasha's death entails the destruction of the entire vampire race. In Rice as in Stoker, vampires can die if their bodies are exposed to fire or sunlight or if they are dismembered; see also note 39 below.

33 'It struck me suddenly what consolation it would be to know Satan, to look upon his face, no matter how terrible that countenance was, to know that I belonged to him totally ... To know, to believe, in one or the other ... that was perhaps the only salvation for which I could dream' (*Interview with the Vampire*, p. 177).

34 Claudia's message to Louis is 'let the flesh instruct the mind', ibid., p. 134. In fact, the child Claudia, who never learned human morality, is the only vampire who appears able to endure immortality in *Interview with the Vampire*. There are indications that both Armand and Lestat will

die because of their inability to cope with the limitlessness of their
situation (see ibid., pp. 361 and 358).
35 See ibid., p. 345.
36 Although the implication that Louis has told his story as a warning to
some extent undercuts his resolution not to intervene. The vampires'
successful campaign against Akasha in *The Queen of the Damned* reiterates
Louis's resolution, since it leaves humanity free to pursue its course.
37 Kristeva, *Powers of Horror*. The gloss that follows derives mainly from the
ideas presented in the first essay in the collection, 'Approaching
Abjection' (pp. 1–31).
38 See 'Semiotics of Biblical Abomination' (ibid., pp. 90–112, p. 94).
39 It is significant in this respect that vampires are unable to eat or drink in
the ordinary way in both Stoker's and Rice's accounts.
40 There is a fundamental difference between Stoker's and Rice's narratives here, since in Stoker all Dracula's victims will potentially become
vampires whereas in Rice it is only those victims who receive vampire
blood who will be transformed.
41 Kristeva's analysis of the taboos erected around menstrual blood in 'From
Filth to Defilement' (ibid., pp. 56–89) as that which threatens
constructed identity is also pertinent here. Significantly, in 'Semiotics of
Biblical Abomination', Kristeva suggests that the Christian ban on certain
types of food is an endeavour to counteract Eve's transgressive eating of
the apple 'in order to forestall the chaos that would result from the
identification of man with the immortality of God' (ibid., p. 95).
42 See *Interview with the Vampire*, p. 23.
43 *The Vampire Lestat*, p. 430.
44 Louis's insistence that the vampiric act cannot be described in words is
highly significant in this context, see note 20 above.
45 *Interview with the Vampire*, p. 34.
46 It is interesting that at the end of his interview Louis describes his
reunion with Lestat as triggering the painful emotions of loss he
experienced after his brother's death, feelings his mind continually veers
away from, ibid., p. 356; the child's role in this encounter is also striking.
Lestat's charisma is explicitly linked to the myth of Faust, as Louis realises
that he has sold his soul for the shifing lights in Lestat's eyes (see ibid.,
p. 299 and below).
47 It is significant that there is no mention of Louis's own father at this point
in the narrative.
48 It is also the case that in rejecting first Lestat and then Armand, Louis
cuts himself off from contact and exchange with his own kind.
49 See Elisabeth Bronfen, *Over Her Dead Body: Death, Femininity and the
Aesthetic* (Manchester University Press, 1992) p. x. Bronfen's analysis
presents pertinent links with Kristeva's summary, particularly in the
delineation of the feminine as the site of cultural alterity. It is interesting
in this light to speculate on the impact of the *male* corpse in 'The
Vampire Chronicles', perhaps functioning as stand-in for the limiting
Father whose 'death' the nascent subject desires?
50 See Kristeva's discussion of this point in 'From Filth to Defilement',
Powers of Horror, p. 72.

51 I am referring here to the three novels that comprise 'The Beauty Trilogy'; *The Claiming of Sleeping Beauty* (1983; London: Warner Books, 1997); *Beauty's Punishment* (New York: Plume Books, 1984); and *Beauty's Release* (New York: E. P Dutton, 1985). Rice has written two other erotic novels to date, under the pseudonym of Anne Rampling: *Exit to Eden* (1985; New York: Dell Publishing, 1989) and *Belinda* (1986; New York: Jove, 1988).

52 See Amalia Ziv, 'The Pervert's Progress: An Analysis of *Story of O* and the Beauty Trilogy', in *Feminist Review*, no. 46 (Spring 1994), pp. 61–75, p. 63.

53 It is noteworthy that the depiction of Beauty's awakening through the Prince's rape recalls the vampire act: 'he sucked on her lips, he drew the life out of her into himself' (see *The Claiming of Sleeping Beauty*, p. 3).

54 Though there is an indication of a master/slave dynamic between vampires in Stoker's *Dracula* and 'The Vampire Chronicles', in Renfield's reaction to Dracula, for instance, and in Claudia's perception of Armand's mastery in *Interview with the Vampire*, (see p. 270, also p. 93).

55 See Marina Warner's *No Go the Bogeyman* for a pertinent discussion of this debate in relation to mythology, p. 17.

56 Ziv sketches some of this terrain in relation to the construction of a female self, see 'The Pervert's Progress', p. 66. As Ziv herself points out, while these analyses have relevance to texts like *Story of O*, their application to the different gender perceptions that appear to underpin the Beauty trilogy is more limited.

57 Rice, *The Claiming of Sleeping Beauty*, p. 176.

58 Ibid., p. 142.

59 See ibid., p. 166 for a good illustration of how, rejected by her masters, Beauty feels as if she is no more than an object. It is also relevant that at the end of the first novel Beauty deliberately chooses what is considered by both masters and slaves as the ultimate ordeal. Although I do not have space to explore this here, there are pertinent parallels between Kristeva's account of the pleasures of humiliation, the mappings of the body into zones of permission and taboo and the jouissance that fear produces, and Rice's depiction of the slaves' experience.

60 The text's revelation that the Prince 'liked to think of himself as a sword' shortly after he has cut down the 'awesome vines' that surround the sleeping castle and raped Beauty awake is one instance of the trilogy's naïve reliance on cliché (ibid., pp. 2 and 5).

61 See ibid., p. 57.

62 'The Pervert's Progess', p. 68.

63 Prince Alexi's account of his torment by the slave Princess Lynette is an example of this role reversal (see *The Claiming of Sleeping Beauty*, pp. 223–30). Ziv points out that there is little sexual contact between women in the trilogy (see 'The Pervert's Progress', p. 68).

64 It is significant that Kristeva sees both 'too much strictness on the part of the Other' and 'the lapse of the Other' as causes of abjection, see *Powers of Horror*, p. 15 (both phrases are italicised in the original).

65 Pat Califia, *Macho Sluts: Erotic Fiction* (Boston: Alyson Publications, 1988), pp. 243–62. I am grateful to Gill Plain for pointing this story out to me.

66 It is also interesting that Iduna explains her name in terms of ancient Norse mythology as the guardian of the golden apples of immortality, ibid., p. 254.
67 Ibid., p. 258.
68 Ibid., p. 259.
69 Ibid. The text continues with: 'adults are usually not lucky enough to re-experience this infantile pleasure'.
70 The final line is literally a question, see ibid., p. 262.
71 See Kristeva's 'Powers of Horror', in *Powers of Horror*, pp. 207–10.
72 Stevenson, *The Strange Case of Dr Jekyll and Mr Hyde*, p. 69.
73 Ibid., p. 73.
74 See, for example, Jekyll's account of the strange novelty and disorder of his sensations, and how he feels 'younger, lighter, happier in body' as Hyde, ibid., p. 72; see also his portrayal of how as Hyde he is able to 'strip off' the trappings of 'respectability' and 'like a schoolboy... spring headlong into the sea of liberty', p. 75. It is also significant that he describes his murder of Carew as the act of a 'sick child', p. 80.
75 'Haunt' is Kristeva's word to describe the harried subject, see *Powers of Horror*, p. 1, though it is interesting that in Stevenson's fiction both Jekyll and the lawyer Utterson use this analogy to recount the effect Hyde has on them, see *The Strange Case of Dr Jekyll and Mr Hyde*, pp. 20 and 86. The fact that in both cases the analogy is used in terms of sleep reinforces the connection with a pre-conscious/unconscious self. It is also interesting that Jekyll describes the effect of the drug as altering the 'fortress of identity', p. 71, see also p. 74.
76 Ibid., p. 79.
77 Ibid., p. 86. Jekyll's analogy with the feminine is also noteworthy, particularly in terms of Kristeva's work on the feminine as that which society abjects.
78 Kristeva's account of being on 'the edge of non-existence and hallucination, of a reality that, if I acknowledge it, annihilates me', *Powers of Horror*, p. 2, similarly strikes a chord with Jekyll's refusal to refer to Hyde as 'I'. See *The Strange Case of Dr Jekyll and Mr Hyde*, p. 84.
79 Ibid., p. 23.
80 Ibid., p. 12.
81 Ibid., p. 80.
82 Ibid., p. 84.
83 Three of these – *The Bad Sister* (1978), which is a rewriting of James Hogg's *Memoirs and Confessions of a Justified Sinner*, *Two Women of London: The Strange Case of Ms Jekyll and Mrs Hyde* (1989) and *Faustine* (1992) – are collected in *Travesties* (London: Faber and Faber, 1995). Tennant's *Queen of Stones* (London: Cape, 1982) is a reworking of William Golding's *Lord of the Flies*, while *Alice Fell* (London: Cape, 1980) draws on the myth of Persephone and the biblical notion of a 'fall'.
84 Steven Connor, 'Rewriting Wrong: On the Ethics of Literary Reversion', in Theo D'haen and Hans Bertens (eds), *Liminal Postmodernisms: The Postmodern, the (Post-)Colonial, and the (Post-)Feminist* (Amsterdam: University of Rodopi Press, 1994), pp. 79–97, 83.
85 *The Strange Case of Dr Jekyll and Mr Hyde*, p. 30.

86 Annegret Maack makes the point that in Tennant the narrative deliberately disrupts any movement towards finality, since the video footage that is presented as evidence is frequently affected by technical malfunctions and Mrs Hyde simply disappears at the end (see 'Translating Nineteenth Century Classics: Emma Tennant's Intertextual Novels', in Irmgard Maassen and Anna Maria Stuby (eds), *(Sub)Versions of Realism – Recent Women's Fiction in Britain* (Heidelberg: Universitätsverlag C. Winter, 1997) pp. 71–82, 74–5). Though Maack does not make this point, it is also the case that the rapist who stalks the part of London in which the novel is set remains uncaught.

87 *Travesties*, p. 181, see also the description of how the gardener must protect the saplings he is planting in the communal gardens from Mrs Hyde's children (ibid.). Although I do not have space to pursue this here, the obsession with boundaries that is displayed in Tennant's account of the Crescents offers an interesting illustration of Kristeva's study of the abject as that which threatens designated borders. The repellent filthiness of Mrs Hyde's flat can also be productively interpreted in the light of Kristeva's analysis.

88 Ibid., p. 250.

89 'It is always to be noticed that the attempt to establish a male, phallic power is vigorously threatened by the no less virulent power of the other sex, which is oppressed ... That other sex, the feminine, becomes synonymous with a radical evil that is to be suppressed', *Powers of Horror*, p. 70. It should, however, be pointed out that there are indications of Hyde's femininity in Stevenson, for example in his butler Poole's description of his terrible weeping 'like a woman' (*The Strange Case of Dr Jekyll and Mr Hyde*, p. 55).

90 *Travesties*, p. 182. A good example of the narrator's pronouncements is his interjection that 'the media leaves us in no doubt that rapaciousness and a "loadsamoney" economy have come to represent the highest values in the land' (ibid., p. 184).

91 It is, of course, ironic – as well as illustrative of Kristeva's thesis that the feminine will be signalled as evil wherever the controlling power is a phallic one – that this administration, which is exhibited as detrimental to women, is headed by a woman.

92 Margaret Elphinstone points out that the successful femininity which Ms Jekyll incarnates is a highly fragile construction, signalled by the face of Mara's composite woman (see 'Contemporary Feminist Fantasy in the Scottish Literary Tradition', in Caroline Gonda (ed.), *Tea and Leg-Irons: New Feminist Readings from Scotland* (London: Open Letters, 1992), pp. 45–59).

93 *Travesties*, pp. 279 and 184.

94 There is an interesting parallel to the depiction of Jean Hastie's research in *Two Women of London* in Kristeva's essay ' ... Qui Tollis Peccata Mundi', in which she explores the changes wrought to the social fabric by Christianity (see *Powers of Horror*, pp. 113–32).

95 There are various literary versions of the legend, of which the most famous are Christopher Marlowe's *Faustus* (probably written in 1592), Johann Wolfgang von Goethe's two-volume *Faust* (1808 and 1832) and

Thomas Mann's *Doctor Faustus* (1947). In contrast to *Two Women of London*, where the links with Stevenson's *The Strange Case of Dr Jekyll and Mr Hyde* are obvious, it is less clear which of these antecedents Tennant is using in *Faustine*, though its derivation from the myth is explicit in such details as the quasi-comic account of Harry's goat-like legs, Greg's explanation of Muriel's metamorphosis as a 'magic pact with the Devil', and the Devil's own tale of his transaction with Muriel where, in an ironic feminist twist, he asks why a woman shouldn't be offered what was given to Dr Faustus (*Travesties*, pp. 350, 376 and 407).

96 See, for example, ibid., pp. 353 and 378, also the Devil's account of his part in keeping 'the cauldron of greed simmering' (p. 406).
97 Ibid., p. 345, and see her declaration that 'growing old ... was probably the worst thing that could happen to a woman in a free, consumerist society' (p. 325).
98 Ibid., p. 328, see also pp. 405–6.
99 It is interesting in terms of Kristeva's work on abjection that Ella terms this 'the abyss' (ibid., p. 321, see also pp. 341 and 385).
100 Ibid., pp. 306 and 374. It is significant that Muriel sees the lies she had to concoct as a seller of clothes and jewellery as contributing to her desire for metamorphosis (see ibid., p. 322). 'The Devil's Tale' that closes the narrative also presents the media as false (see ibid., p. 407).
101 'Something to be Scared Of', in *Powers of Horror*, pp. 32–55, p. 47.
102 See note 98 above and *Travesties*, p. 304.
103 See ibid., p. 380.
104 It is significant in this respect that Lisa is repeatedly referred to as a 'monster' (see ibid., pp. 307, 352 and 380).
105 Ibid., pp. 330 and 342. Although it is the case that Jasmine's story of Muriel/Lisa needs to be read suspiciously given the Devil's revelation that she is his 'handmaiden' (ibid., p. 408).
106 It is noteworthy that Anna links this specifically to ancient myth – notably the myth of Demeter and Persephone – which is seen to contain truths mankind has forgotten or ignored (see ibid., p. 387).
107 Ibid., p. 407.
108 Ibid., p. 405.
109 See *Powers of Horror*, p. 26, also p. 72.

Chapter 6

1 Suniti Namjoshi, *Feminist Fables* (1981; London: Sheba, 1990) p. 8.
2 Judith Butler, *Bodies that Matter: On the Discursive Limits of 'Sex'* (New York: Routledge, 1993), p. 9.
3 Marina Warner, 'The Legs of the Queen of Sheba', in *The Mermaids in the Basement* (1993; London: Vintage, 1994), pp. 137–60.
4 Ibid., p. 138.
5 '*Make haste, my beloved, and be thou like to a roe or to a young hart upon the mountains of spices*' (ibid., p. 160).
6 Naomi Wolf, *The Beauty Myth: How Images of Beauty are Used against Women* (1990; London: Vintage, 1991).

7 'The Legs of the Queen of Sheba', p. 140.
8 Although I do not have space here to elaborate on Wolf's thesis, her arguments as to the way women's appearance is used to support a '$33-million-a-year diet industry', for example, make compelling reading (see *The Beauty Myth*, p. 17).
9 Wolf presents as an instance of this a fascinating analysis of the institution of the abnormally 'thin' female fashion model as a response to women's liberation, (see ibid., p. 11).
10 Ibid., p. 58. The reference is to Marina Warner's *Monuments and Maidens: The Allegory of the Female Form* (London: Weidenfield and Nicolson, 1985).
11 Moira Gatens, 'Power, Bodies and Difference', in M. Barrett and A. Phillips (eds), *Destabilizing Theory* (Cambridge: Polity Press, 1992).
12 Emma Donoghue, *Kissing the Witch* (1997; Harmondsworth: Penguin, 1998).
13 'These were my feet ... This was my hand ... I looked down and recognized myself' (ibid., p. 153).
14 Ibid., p. 3. Interestingly in this context, Marina Warner presents a historical analysis of the power relations that would have caused stepmothers to guard against the progeny of an earlier marriage in her study of fairy tale *From the Beast to the Blonde: On Fairy Tales and their Tellers* (1994; London: Vintage, 1995), see pp. 201–40. Riane Eisler suggests that the 'Cinderella' story contains the message that for a girl to escape from a life of servitude her body must conform to certain specifications (see *Sacred Pleasures: Sex, Myth and the Politics of the Body* (1995; Shaftesbury: Element Books, 1996), p. 268).
15 This tale recalls Luce Irigaray's contention that to succeed a woman must constitute herself as 'an instrument of seduction' (see 'Divine Women', in *Sexes and Genealogies* trans. Gillian C. Gill (New York: Columbia University Press, 1993) p. 65). Her argument that female beauty has always been thought of as a 'garment' rather than as an aspect of interiority similarly casts an interesting light on Donoghue's reworking of 'Donkeyskin' (ibid.).
16 Sheri S. Tepper, *Beauty* (1991; London: HarperCollins, 1995).
17 Ibid., pp. 85 and 105.
18 Ibid., p. 105.
19 See ibid., p. 100.
20 Ibid., pp. 435 and 436.
21 Beauty declares herself and her daughter to be beautiful and the unfortunate Gloriana to be 'an ugly girl' (ibid., p. 264, p. 12). Nina Lykke succinctly delineates the nostalgic longing to return to a 'good', originary, organic world that marks certain strands of ecofeminist debate. See her essay in *Between Monsters, Goddesses and Cyborgs: Feminist Confrontations with Science, Medicine and Cyberspace*, ed. Nina Lykke and Rosi Braidotti (London and New Jersey: Zed Books 1996), p. 23 (Lykke's essay takes the title of the collection). This is underscored in Tepper's novel by the central character's surprisingly persistent and incongruous longing for her 'Mama'.

22 *Beauty*, pp. 213–14. Beauty describes her new vision of Faery thus: 'every aspect thrilled. Every structure was perfect from every angle' (ibid., p. 215). Although I do not have space to explore this point here, Tepper's novel accounts for the demise of the fairies in terms of the encroachments of organised religion with its own dogmatic rules of vision. Her outline parallels Maureen Duffy's thesis in this respect, in her detailed history of fairies in Britain, *The Erotic World of Faery* (London: Hodder and Stoughton, 1972).

23 *Beauty*, p. 228.

24 Ibid., p. 229. The starvation and ageing Beauty's body shows each time she returns from Faery further highlights the hollowness of its illusions of beauty (see, for example, ibid., pp. 251–2).

25 Robert A. Collins, in an interesting article on the realm in question, argues that the problem of Chinanga is not only that it is the invention of a single mind but that this creation is '"present" through the limiting agency of a single text'. He consequently wittily reads the episode as 'a sly dig at deconstruction' (see Robert A. Collins, 'Tepper's "Chinanga": A Parable of Deconstruction', in *Journal of the Fantastic in the Arts*, 8/4 32 (1997), pp. 464–71, quotes on pp. 468 and 469).

26 That this is an ethical version of the ability to perceive differently which Beauty has learned in Faery is made clear in the account of how she 'enchants' an alternative into existence as well as in the explicit equating of the collective chanting she instigates with magic (see *Beauty*, pp. 408 and 218, also p. 323).

27 In this respect, Tepper's novel strikes chords with Camille Paglia's insistence on the need for society to police individual action, as is demonstrated in Tepper's preference for the controls of the fourteenth century to the permissiveness of the present, see Camille Paglia, *Sexual Personae: Art and Decadence from Nefertiti to Emily Dickinson* (London and New Haven: Yale University Press, 1990) and *Beauty*, p. 410. It should, however, be pointed out that the ethics of Tepper's vision are debatable, as her inclusion of anti-abortionists in the Dark Lord's hell demonstrates, (see ibid. p. 408).

28 Although the main source tale is 'Sleeping Beauty', numerous other fairy tales such as 'Cinderella', 'Snow White', 'The Frog Prince' and 'Rapunzel' are explicitly woven into the narrative.

29 An example of the former is the crude opposition between the good Giles and the evil Jaybee.

30 A further instance of this last point is contained in Beauty's reflection after her visit to Baskarone that if the eye 'has never seen beauty, how can it know' it (ibid., p. 439). I am referring here both to the fairies' creation of Beauty as their emblem in their war against the Dark Lord and to the role Beauty is given by her fairy aunt and her supporters in the hoped-for future. The end of the novel confirms that the reason why Beauty is so important is that she contains the beauty of the world in miniature within her (see ibid., p. 473).

31 The biblical stories of Adam and Eve and Noah are also drawn on here.

32 Marina Warner offers a pertinent analysis of this point in relation to fairy tale in *From the Beast to the Blonde* (see Chapter 1).

33 See *Beauty*, pp. 310 and 388.
34 There are other inconsistencies and problems which the narrative fails to deal with, such as the unexplained contradiction in the presentation of the central character as both the repository of what has already been made beautiful and its source (p. 178).
35 Ibid., p. 419.
36 My reading of Butler here is taken from *Bodies that Matter*.
37 See ibid., p. 7.
38 The ending of 'The Tale of the Hair', for instance, with its 'we lay there, waiting to see what we would see' rather than the traditional 'happy-ever-after' of the genre, is typical of the ambivalent close to these stories (see *Kissing the Witch*, p. 93).
39 Butler's analysis also suggests a critique of Tepper's presentation of the beauty of the natural world as something that is created independently of our reproductions of it (see *Bodies that Matter*, p. 4).
40 'I looked up to see everyone clad in riding clothes. ... As soon as I saw it, I was dressed the same as they, but it had taken my perceiving them to do it. I had done it myself' (see *Beauty*, p. 228).
41 Ibid.
42 James Kirwan, *Beauty* (Manchester University Press, 1999).
43 Kirwan draws on a number of other philosophies in order to reach his conclusion, including the Kantian notion of 'vain wishing'.
44 Alice Thompson *Pandora's Box* (London: Little, Brown and Company, 1998).
45 Ibid., p. 5.
46 Ibid., p. 14. It is significant in the context of Butler's theory that the hospital and by extension medical practice in general is likened by Noah to 'an idealised body' (see ibid., p. 5).
47 Ibid., p. 7.
48 Ibid., p. 133.
49 This is underscored in the trope of glass imagery the narration uses. Pandora's box, for instance, is made of glass, and Noah imagines while he is married to Pandora that she too is made of glass. Yet the glass retains its mystery. Even though Noah believes he can see straight through Pandora – as on the operating table he could see straight through her body – he realises that there is a part of her she retains for herself. It is Noah's determination finally to open Pandora's glass box that drives his quest. Naomi Wolf to some extent parallels Kirwan's view here when she argues that beauty only exists in 'the gap between desire and gratification' (see *The Beauty Myth*, p. 176).
50 *Pandora's Box*, p. i.
51 See ibid., p. 103.
52 See ibid., p. 123.
53 Specifically, Lazarus accuses Noah of wanting Pandora to be a goddess (see ibid., p. 140).
54 Camille Paglia's argument that the power given to the eye in Western culture is linked to the illusion that we have intellectual control over nature is also relevant to the discussion that follows (see *Sexual Personae*, pp. 32–4).

55 See *Pandora's Box*, p. 103.
56 See ibid., p. 42.
57 These are described as 'the dreams of the western world' (ibid., p. 93).
58 Sewing is one of the gifts the gods bestow on Pandora (see ibid., p. i). Her addition of an erect penis to her tapestry of a woman can also be productively read in the light of Butler's insistence that the phallus is itself an 'idealization, one which no body can adequately approximate' and may consequently be viewed as 'a transferable phantasm' (see *Bodies that Matter*, p. 86).
59 Delilah, one of the bar-tenders, tells Noah that Lazarus does not like 'real' men, a pronouncement that leads to a discussion with Venus as to what a 'real' woman might be (see *Pandora's Box*, pp. 101–2).
60 *Bodies that Matter*, p. 8.
61 Butler's discussion of construction theories which see gender as the marking of passive (feminine) bodies is also illustrated in the various references to the physical imprints on Pandora's skin in Thompson's novel (see *Pandora's Box*, p. 4).
62 The novel's opening plays on the idea that Noah invents Pandora in a dream, and the narration is full of references to Noah's enjoyment of his creation of her (see, for example, *Pandora's Box*, p. 21).
63 Though Pandora's tapestries can of course be read as an ironically 'feminine' discourse.
64 It is interesting in this respect that Noah's quest involves him in a homosexual liason, although the narrative omits any account of this (see ibid., p. 118).
65 Butler makes this point with reference to Lacan's notion that the symbolic cannot be contravened without psychosis (see *Bodies that Matter*, p. 14). The penultimate pages of Thompson's novel illustrate this as Noah becomes increasingly prey to what he interprets as Lazarus' devilish fantasies (see *Pandora's Box*, p. 142).
66 See ibid., p. 13.
67 See ibid., pp. 49 and 63, also p. 139.
68 Kirsten Gram-Hanssen offers some pertinent observations on the nature of perception in relation to the philosophies of Husserl and Merleau-Ponty in this vein in her essay 'Objectivity in the Description of Nature: Between Social Construction and Essentialism', in Lykke and Braidotti (eds), *Between Monsters, Goddesses and Cyborgs*, pp. 88–102. In particular, her discussion of Husserl's notion that perception involves different acts of consciousness such as memory and imagination presents interesting parallels with Thompson's depiction.
69 See *Pandora's Box*, p. 100.

Chapter 7

1 Camille Paglia, *Sexual Personae: Art and Decadence from Nefertiti to Emily Dickinson* (London and New Haven: Yale University Press, 1990), p. 19.

2 Angela Carter, *Nights at the Circus* (1984; London: Picador, 1985), p. 290.
3 Angela Carter, 'Reflections', in *Fireworks* (1974; London: Virago, 1987), pp. 81–101.
4 Angela Carter, 'Flesh and the Mirror', in ibid., pp. 61–70. The quotations are from pp. 68, 64 and 65, respectively.
5 The narrator recognises that her turned coat-collar is 'predatory' (ibid., p. 61) and that her lover is an 'object' she has created 'solely in relation to myself': 'his self … was quite unknown to me' (ibid., p. 67).
6 Ibid., p. 63. There are numerous other fascinating parallels between this tale and 'Reflections' which I do not have space to explore here, such as the description of Tokyo in terms which recall the reverse side of the mirror in 'Reflections' (see ibid., p. 62), and the narrator's realisation that her projections cause her to fall through one of the 'holes' that are 'the entrances to the counters at which you pay the price of the way you live' (ibid., p. 67).
7 Angela Carter, 'Notes from the Front Line', in *Shaking a Leg: Collected Journalism and Writings* (1997; London: Vintage, 1998), pp. 36–43, quotations on p. 38. Carter's 'Notes for a Theory of Sixties Style', in its astute analysis of the way the clothes we choose to express ourselves are already encoded within our wider cultural setting, offers an interesting further discussion of these issues (see ibid., pp. 105–9).
8 Ibid., p. 38.
9 Angela Carter, *The Sadeian Woman: An Exercise in Cultural History* (London: Virago, 1979).
10 Ibid., p. 4. It is appropriate as well as ironic in the light of this comment that Eve's teacher in femininity in Carter's *The Passion of New Eve* (1977; London: Virago, 1993) is a tyrannical patriach named 'Zero' (see below).
11 Ibid., p. 5. It is at this point that Carter's analysis becomes polemical, as she suggests that pornographers are women's enemies only because pornography refuses to change in this regard (see ibid., p. 3).
12 The references are to Sade's *The Misfortunes of Virtue* and *The Prosperities of Vice*.
13 *The Sadeian Woman*, p. 5.
14 Ibid., p. 106.
15 It is to be emphasised in the light of the discussion that follows that Carter does not think that Sade fully achieves the dispelling of the myth, since she argues that he draws back from the ultimate transgression of the mother's orgasm (see ibid., pp. 131–3).
16 Ibid., p. 108. Carter's account of the womb's symbolism here offers interesting parallels with Eve's journey to Mother through the sea-caves towards the end of *The Passion of New Eve*.
17 'Reflections', p. 89.
18 Ibid.
19 'I gave birth to my mirror self' (ibid., p. 93).
20 Ibid., p. 101.
21 Ibid., p. 92, my emphasis, and p. 91.
22 Paglia, *Sexual Personae*, p. xiii. It is noteworthy in the context of *The Sadeian Woman* that Paglia explicitly aligns herself with Sade in this, though her reading of him is different to Carter's (see ibid., p. 2).

23 It should be pointed out that Paglia does not believe that women are as capable of this production as men because of their different biological relation to the maternal source, thus offering a further point of divergence from Carter's position.

24 'Reflections', p. 101.

25 It is significant that what finally prompts the narrator to call the guardian 'she' are the 'female garments' s/he is wearing (see ibid., p. 87).

26 Carter, *The Passion of New Eve*, p. 5. It is significant, too, that Madame de Saint-Ange is the instructress in Eugénie's sexual education in Sade's *Philosophy in the Boudoir*, since, as Carter argues, she is responsible for Eugénie's 'final ambivalent triumph over the female principle as typified in the reproductive function' (see *The Sadeian Woman*, p. 117).

27 Leilah's renaming as Lilith and her revelation that it is her mother Evelyn was captured by indicate a more dominant role than Evelyn's final realisation that Leilah only existed as 'the projection' of his own 'lusts and greed and self-loathing' (see *The Passion of New Eve*, p. 175). Evoking Carter's analysis of femininity in *The Sadeian Woman*, Evelyn's initial account of Leilah includes a description of 'the exquisite negative of her sex' and suggests how she is a 'perfect woman' because 'like the moon, she only gave reflected light' (see *The Passion of New Eve*, pp. 27 and 34).

28 Ibid., p. 36.

29 This is perhaps most apparent in Eve's realisation that the pleasure they derive from their love-making cannot be conveyed in speech as it exists (see ibid., p. 149).

30 Ibid., p. 56.

31 Merja Makinen, in her essay on Carter, 'Sexual and Textual Aggression in *The Sadeian Woman* and *The Passion of New Eve*', points out that because of the long gestation period of *The Sadeian Woman* the two texts overlapped in their writing (see Joseph Bristow and Trev Lynn Broughton (eds), *The Infernal Desires of Angela Carter: Fiction, Femininity, Feminism* (London: Longman, 1997), p. 156 (essay on pp. 149–165).

32 *The Passion of New Eve*, p. 59 and see p. 64.

33 Ibid., p. 77.

34 It is significant in this light that in 'Notes from the Front Line', Carter refers to *The Passion of New Eve* as her 'anti-mythic novel' (see *Shaking a Leg*, p. 38).

35 In an interview, Carter explicitly describes Tristessa as 'a male projection of femininity' (see Sarah Gamble, *Angela Carter: Writing from the Front Line* (Edinburgh University Press, 1997), p. 127).

36 *The Passion of New Eve*, p. 129.

37 See, for instance, ibid., p. 100, where Zero's rhetoric terms the deserted town in which he takes refuge the New Jerusalem and his sex 'a bow of burning gold'.

38 There are other characters who continue this exposure of myth in the novel, such as the child crusader whose campaign is based entirely on his random memory of his nurse's bible-reading and intermittent radio broadcasts.

39 Ibid., p. 184.

40 'If the mother is phallic, then there is nothing but masculinity after all; women are really men' (see Mary Jacobus, *First Things: The Maternal Imaginary in Literature, Art and Psychoanalysis* (London: Routledge, 1995), p. 17). The implications of Carter's depiction of Mother as possessing the phallus are discussed by Maria Aline Seabra Ferreira, in her article 'The Uncanny (M)other: Angela Carter's *The Passion of New Eve*', in *Paradoxa*, vol. 3, nos 3–4 (1997), pp. 471–88, see pp. 481–6.
41 Nicole Ward Jouve, *Female Genesis: Creativity, Self and Gender* (Cambridge: Polity Press, 1998), see especially her essay on Carter ' "Mother is a Figure of Speech ...": Angela Carter', pp. 141–62.
42 See especially ibid., pp. 196–204 for Ward Jouve's discussion of Winnicott.
43 See Makinen 'Sexual and Textual Aggression in *The Sadeian Woman* and *The Passion of New Eve*', pp. 162–3.
44 See *Female Genesis*, pp. 155 and 216.
45 There are other indications, too, such as the description of the old woman's hands resembling those of a surgeon, Mother's former profession (see *The Passion of New Eve*, p. 189).
46 See *The Sadeian Woman*, p. 110. The old woman's impending death is acknowledged by herself as well as by Eve (see *The Passion of New Eve*, pp. 189 and 190).
47 Indeed, some critics have taken issue with Carter precisely on this account (see, for instance, Patricia Duncker's essay 'Queer Gothic: Angela Carter and the Lost Narratives of Sexual Subversion', *Critical Survey*, vol. 8, no. 1 (1996), pp. 58–68).
48 It is possible to read the figure of Eve/lyn him/herself in this light.
49 See *The Sadeian Woman*, p. 151. The essay Carter refers to is printed in Emma Goldman, *Anarchism and Other Essays* (New York: Dover Publications, 1969).
50 Aidan Day, *Angela Carter: The Rational Glass* (Manchester University Press, 1998) see p. 151.
51 The text is explicit on this last point and suggests that all womanly behaviour is such an 'imitation' (see *The Passion of New Eve*, p. 101).
52 *The Sadeian Woman*, p. 151.
53 I see Eve's realisation that the sea-caves are empty in this light, as instances of the bankruptcy of the imagery rather than the redundancy of the state: Eve is after all pregnant when she journeys through them. It is noteworthy in this context that Carter suggests that the sea and cave are the common images for the womb (see *The Sadeian Woman*, p. 108).
54 Gamble argues that 'Tristessa remains a static, introverted figure, incapable of any real development, or of love for anything beyond her own idealised self-image. ... While Eve falls in love with Tristessa ... Tristessa will not, or cannot, disentangle herself from her "fictive autobiography" which renders all her experience into the stuff of tragic theatre' (see her *Angela Carter: Writing from the Front Line*, p. 127).
55 Angela Carter, *The Bloody Chamber* (1979; Harmondsworth: Penguin, 1982) and *Black Venus* (1985; London: Picador, 1986).
56 *The Bloody Chamber*, p. 95.

57 Mary Kaiser, 'Fairy Tale as Sexual Allegory: Intertextuality in Angela Carter's *The Bloody Chamber*, in *The Review of Contemporary Fiction*, vol. 14, no. 3 (Fall, 1994), pp. 30–6.

58 Lucie Armitt, 'The Fragile Frames of *The Bloody Chamber*', in Bristow and Broughton (eds), *The Infernal Desires of Angela Carter*, pp. 88–99.

59 Lorna Sage, 'Introduction', in Lorna Sage (ed.), *Flesh and the Mirror: Essays on the Art of Angela Carter* (London: Virago, 1994), pp. 1–23, quote on p. 16.

60 Ibid.

61 *The Bloody Chamber*, p. 51.

62 Ibid., p. 60.

63 It is interesting that Carter's depiction of the poet's relation to Jeanne parallels Evelyn's relation to Leilah at the beginning of *The Passion of New Eve*, a connection that is strengthened by the descriptions of the naked dances each performs and by their erotic blackness. There is work to be done on Carter's presentation of black women as sexually enticing in these two texts: Evelyn's delineation of Leilah's blackness in relation to her 'dissolution', in particular, raises a number of problematic questions (see *The Passion of New Eve*, p. 14).

64 *The Bloody Chamber*, pp. 12 and 8.

65 Nicole Ward Jouve, for instance, argues that the mother's appearance at the end of this tale 'contradict[s] all motherly representations' (see *Female Genesis*, p. 153).

66 *The Bloody Chamber*, p. 40.

67 Paglia, *Sexual Personae*, p. 13.

68 *Black Venus*, p. 114.

69 Elaine Jordan, 'Enthralment: Angela Carter's Speculative Fictions', in Linda Anderson (ed.), *Plotting Change: Contemporary Women's Fiction* (London: Edward Arnold, 1990), pp. 19–40.

70 I am paraphrasing from Day, *Angela Carter: The Rational Glass*, p. 147, here.

71 In the first part of the story, it is emphatically the Marquis's eyes that impose on the protagonist (see *The Bloody Chamber*, p. 20).

72 Carter, *Shaking a Leg*, p. 38. This point is also made by Elaine Jordan, who contends that in Carter 'the demythologising business is not only a rational process but a making of new fictions' ('Enthralment: Angela Carter's Speculative Fictions', p. 35).

73 John Haffenden, 'Interview with Angela Carter', *Novelists in Interview* (London: Methuen, 1985), pp. 76–96, quote on p. 93. In the interview, Carter makes it clear that one of the models for Fevvers is the Classical Greek statue known as 'The Winged Victory'. In fact, Fevvers's association with mythical imagery extends beyond explicitly winged symbols, and includes Helen of Troy, Venus, an unspecified Hindu Goddess and Lady Godiva.

74 *Nights at the Circus*, p. 25. Harriet Blodgett sees this as a reference to Virginia Woolf's reworking of the spectre of the nineteenth-century poet Coventry Patmore's angel of good womanhood, which Woolf identified as inhibiting women's free expression (see 'Fresh Iconography: Subversive Fantasy by Angela Carter', in *The Review of Contemporary Fiction*,

vol. 14, no. 3 (Fall, 1994), pp. 49–55). Blodgett's depiction of Fevvers's wings as a symbol of women's freedom is particularly pertinent (see ibid., p. 52).
75 *Nights at the Circus*, pp. 34 and 7.
76 See ibid., p. 161.
77 Ibid.
78 Ibid., p. 7.
79 Ibid., p. 21.
80 Ibid., p. 39.
81 Similar doubts are also raised about the other woman's utopia in the novel, when Lizzie wonders what the women will do with any male children their frozen sperm-pool inadvertently produces (see ibid., p. 240).
82 Ibid., p. 247.
83 Ibid., p. 77.
84 Ibid., p. 286, Carter's emphasis.
85 Anne Fernihough, ' "Is She Fact or is She Fiction?" Angela Carter and the Enigma of Woman', in *Textual Practice*, vol. 11, no. 1 (1997), pp. 89–107.
86 *Nights at the Circus*, p. 39, Carter's emphasis.
87 See Bristow and Broughton, 'Introduction', *The Infernal Desires of Angela Carter*, pp. 1–23.
88 *Nights at the Circus*, p. 289.
89 Ibid., p. 39.
90 Ibid., p. 107.
91 Ibid., p. 281. This reading is also indicated in Fevvers's use of the expression to describe the negative education of the Shaman (see ibid., p. 290), and in Walser's own account of how he must begin again, newly hatched (p. 293).
92 'How many times Shakespeare draws fathers and daughters, never mothers and daughters' (Angela Carter, *Wise Children* (1991; London: Vintage, 1992), Preface).
93 Ibid., p. 216, see also pp. 21, 174 and 223. The birthday party not only reveals that Melchior's daughters are his brother Peregrine's, but also produces Father Gareth's illicit offspring.
94 Ibid., p. 223.
95 Dora makes the point early on that she has become the 'chronicler' of the family 'in the course of assembling notes towards my own autobiography' (ibid., p. 11).
96 Ibid., p. 31. Melchior's re-enactment of his father's story is highlighted in Dora's narration (see ibid., pp. 20–25), in Lady A's confession (see ibid., p. 215), and above all in his dressing up as his father complete with his father's cardboard crown for his hundredth birthday (see ibid., p. 224).
97 Ibid., p. 230.
98 Ibid., p. 11.
99 Michael Hardin, 'The Other Other: Self-Definition Outside Patriarchal Institutions in Angela Carter's *Wise Children*', *The Review of Contemporary Fiction*, vol. 14, no. 3 (Fall, 1994), pp. 77–83.

100 *Wise Children*, p. 231, see also pp. 95 and 191.
101 Ibid., p. 192. There is also, of course, a linguistic marker of their difference in the distinguishing first letter of their names.
102 Ibid., p. 211.
103 The account of Grandma Chance's 'invented' family is noteworthy in this context (see ibid., p. 35).
104 Ibid., p. 230.
105 Ibid., p. 221.
106 Ibid., p. 11, see also p. 230.
107 See *Female Genesis*, p. 188.

Notes to the Conclusion

1 Liz Lochhead, *The Grimm Sisters* (London: Next Editions, 1981), p. 11.
2 Marina Warner, *Managing Monsters: Six Myths of Our Time* (London: Vintage, 1994), p. 93.
3 Christine Brooke-Rose, *Amalgamemnon* (1984; Illinois: Dalkey Archive Press, 1994), see, for example, p. 77. It is particularly interesting in the light of my discussion that the novel envisages the new regime as a return to patriarchal order that will deny women equal status (see, for example, ibid., pp. 60, 135).
4 Ibid., pp. 5 and 22, see also p. 54. It is noteworthy that the narrator opens with the words 'I shall soon be quite redundant', a phrase that echoes Gillian Perholt's self-assessment in Byatt's 'The Djinn in the Nightingale's Eye' (see Chapter 2 above).
5 This is apparent both in the way the narrator herself uses the Agamemnon and other myths, and in a number of incidents such as the account of 'the miracle in the prison camp', in which the unexpected discovery of a paperback copy of Herodotus provides 'an hour or so of utterly other discourses', carving a way through 'the dungeon walls' (see ibid., p. 20).
6 Margaret Atwood, *The Robber Bride* (1993; London: Virago, 1994).
7 Rice's view of religion accords with Carter's notion of myth as 'consolatory nonsense' (see Chapter 7 above).
8 Jeanette Winterson, *Sexing the Cherry* (1989; London: Vintage, 1990), see pp. 17–19.
9 Examples are the demonstration that pronouncements generate their own reality in Crow's *Miss X or the Wolf Woman*; the insistence on responsible creation in Tepper's *Beauty*; and the notion that our story-telling must be continually recommenced afresh in both Cixous's *The Book of Promethea* and Roberts's *The Book of Mrs Noah*.
10 Indeed, the portrait of Mother in Carter's *The Passion of New Eve* suggests that mere repetition of myth is a highly dubious and possibly pernicious activity.
11 Jane Caputi, 'On Psychic Activism: Feminist Mythmaking', in *The Woman's Companion to Mythology, 1992*, ed. Carolyne Larrington (London: Pandora, 1997), pp. 425–40, quote on p. 427.

12 Toni Morrison, *Beloved* (1987; London: Picador, 1988), see pp. 274–5.
    As the indented, single-line repetitions of the insistence that this was not a
    story to pass on demonstrate, it is clearly not, however, Morrison's point
    that the story should be forgotten.
13 In the private letter dated Tuesday, 29 June 1999 quoted in Chapter 3,
    Crow argues that women writers must be careful not to reverse or undo
    myth to the point where we lose its power. As Mary Wolfe's gradual
    understanding of the relevance of Petrus Borel to her situation in Crow's
    novel *Miss X or the Wolf Woman* demonstrates, one of the strengths of
    myth is its resistance to instant and final interpretation.
14 Margaret Atwood's novel *The Handmaid's Tale* (1985; London: Vintage,
    1996) provides a chilling demonstration of the way the manipulation of
    myth can construct new truths.
15 Maxine Hong Kingston, 'No Name Woman', in *The Woman Warrior*
    (1975; London: Picador, 1981), pp. 11–22.
16 Barbara Walker, *Feminist Fairy Tales* (New York: HarperCollins, 1996).
17 Virginia Woolf, 'Modern Fiction', in *The Crowded Dance of Life: Selected
    Essays*, vol. 2, ed. Rachel Bowlby (London: Penguin, 1993), pp. 5–12,
    quote on p. 8.

Bibliography

Abel, Elizabeth, Marianne Hirsch and Elizabeth Langland (eds), *The Voyage In: Fictions of Female Development* (Hanover: University Press of New England, 1983).

Anderson, Linda (ed.), *Plotting Change: Contemporary Women's Fiction* (London: Edward Arnold, 1990).

Apuleius, *The Golden Ass or Metamorphoses*, trans. E. J. Kenney (Harmondsworth: Penguin, 1998).

Armitt Lucie, 'The Fragile Frames of *The Bloody Chamber'*, *The Infernal Desires of Angela Carter: Fiction, Femininity, Feminism*, ed. Joseph Bristow and Trev Lynn Broughton (London: Longman, 1997).

Atwood, Margaret, *The Handmaid's Tale* (1985; London: Vintage, 1996).

——, *The Robber Bride* (1993; London: Virago, 1994).

Auerbach, Nina and U. C. Knoepflmacher (eds), *Forbidden Journeys: Fairy Tales and Fantasies by Victorian Women Writers* (University of Chicago Press, 1992).

Austen, John, *How to Do Things with Words* (Cambridge, Mass.: Harvard University Press, 1975).

Barrett, M. and A. Phillips (eds), *Destabilizing Theory* (Cambridge: Polity Press, 1992).

Barthes, Roland, *Mythologies* (1957), trans. Annette Lavers (London: Paladin, 1973).

——, *A Barthes Reader*, ed. Susan Sontag (London: Jonathan Cape, 1982).

Bell, Michael, *Literature, Modernism and Myth: Belief and Responsibility in the Twentieth Century* (Cambridge University Press, 1997).

Belsey, Catherine, *Desire: Love Stories in Western Culture* (Oxford: Blackwell, 1994).

Bergson, Henri, *Laughter: An Essay on the Meaning of the Comic*, trans. Cloudesley Brereton and Fred Rothwell (London: Macmillan, 1911).

Berman, Jaye, 'Women's Humor', *Contemporary Literature*, 31:12 (1990), pp. 251–260.

Bettelheim, Bruno, *The Uses of Enchantment: The Meaning and Importance of Fairy Tales* (Harmondsworth: Penguin, 1976).

Blodgett, Harriet, 'Fresh Iconography: Subversive Fantasy by Angela Carter', in *The Review of Contemporary Fiction*, vol. 14, no. 3 (Fall 1994), pp. 49–55.

Blumenberg, Hans, *Work on Myth* (1979), trans. Robert M. Wallace (Cambridge, Mass.: MIT Press, 1985).

Bottigheimer, Ruth B. (ed.), *Fairy Tales and Society: Illusion, Allusion and Paradigm* (Philadelphia: University of Pennsylvania Press, 1986).

Bristow, Joseph and Trev Lynn Broughton (eds), *The Infernal Desires of Angela Carter: Fiction, Femininity, Feminism* (London: Longman, 1997).

Bronfen, Elisabeth, *Over Her Dead Body: Death, Femininity and the Aesthetic* (Manchester University Press, 1992).

Brooke-Rose, Christine, *Amalgamemnon* (1984; Illinois: Dalkey Archive Press, 1994).

Butler, Judith, *Bodies that Matter: On the Discursive Limits of 'Sex'* (New York: Routledge and Kegan Paul, 1993).

Byatt, A. S., *The Game* (1967; London: Vintage, 1992).

——, *The Matisse Stories* (1993; London: Vintage, 1994).

——, *The Djinn in the Nightingale's Eye: Five Fairy Stories* (1994; London: Vintage, 1995).

Califia, Pat, *Macho Sluts: Erotic Fiction* (Boston: Alyson Publications, 1988).

Calvino, Italo (ed.), *Italian Folktales* (1956), trans. George Martin (Harmondsworth: Penguin, 1980).

Campbell, Joseph, *Creative Mythology: The Masks of God* (1968; Harmondsworth: Arkana, 1991).

——, *The Power of Myth*, with Bill Myers (New York: High Bridge/Parabola, 1988).

Caputi, Jane, 'On Psychic Activism: Feminist Mythmaking', in *The Woman's Companion to Mythology 1992*, ed. Carolyne Larrington (London: Pandora, 1997), pp. 425–7.

Carter, Angela, *The Sadeian Woman: An Exercise in Cultural History* (London: Virago, 1979).

——, *The Bloody Chamber* (1979; Harmondsworth: Penguin, 1981).

——, *Nights at the Circus* (1984; London: Picador, 1985).

——, *Black Venus* (1985; London: Picador, 1986).

——, *Fireworks* (1974; London: Virago, 1987).

—— (ed.), *The Virago Book of Fairy Tales* (London: Virago, 1990).

——, *Wise Children* (1991; London: Vintage, 1992).

——, *The Passion of New Eve* (1977; London: Virago, 1993).

——, *Shaking a Leg: Collected Journalism and Writings* (1997; London: Vintage, 1998).

Castle, Terry, *The Apparitional Lesbian: Female Homosexuality and Modern Culture* (New York: Columbia University Press, 1993).

Childs, Peter and Patrick Williams, *Post-Colonial Theory* (Hemel Hempstead: Prentice Hall Europe, 1997).

Cixous, Hélène, *Neutre* (Paris: Grasset, 1972).

——, 'The Laugh of the Medusa', *New French Feminisms* (1980), ed. Elaine Marks and Isabelle de Courtivron (Brighton: Harvester, 1981).

——, *The Book of Promethea* (1983), trans. Betsy Wing (Lincoln: University of Nebraska Press, 1991).

——, *The Newly Born Woman* (1975), with Catherine Clément, trans. Betsy Wing (London: I. B. Tauris, 1996).

——, 'Love of the Wolf', *Stigmata: Escaping Texts*, trans. Catherine A. F. MacGillivroy, Keith Cohen and Eric Pranowitz (London and New York: Routledge, 1998).

——, *Stigmata: Escaping Texts* (London and New York: Routledge, 1998).

Collins, Robert A., 'Tepper's "Chinanga": A Parable of Deconstruction', in *Journal of the Fantastic in the Arts*, 8/4, 32 (1997), pp. 464–71.

Connor, Steven, 'Rewriting Wrong: On the Ethics of Literary Reversion', *Liminal Postmodernisms: The Postmodern, the (Post-)Colonial, and the (Post-)Feminist*, ed. Theo D'haen and Hans Bertens (Amsterdam: University of Rodopi Press, 1994).

Cook, Albert, *Myth and Language* (Bloomington: Indiana University Press, 1980).

Coupe, Laurence, *Myth* (London: Routledge and Kegan Paul, 1997).

Creed, John, 'Uses of Classical Mythology', in *The Theory of Myth*, ed. Adrian Cunningham (London: Sheed and Ward, 1973).

Crow, Christine, *Miss X or the Wolf Woman* (London: The Women's Press, 1990).

Cunningham, Adrian (ed.), *The Theory of Myth* (London: Sheed and Ward, 1973).

Cupitt, Don, *What is a Story?* (1991; London: SCM Press, 1995).

Currie, Mark, *Metafiction* (London: Longman, 1995).

Daly, Mary, *Gyn/Ecology: The Metaethics of Radical Feminism* (1978; London: The Women's Press, 1984).

——, *Pure Lust: Elemental Feminist Philosophy* (Boston: Beacon Press, 1984).

——, *Websters' First New Intergalactic Wickedary of the English Language* (1987; London: The Women's Press, 1988).

Dalziel, Margaret (ed.), *Myth and the Modern Imagination* (Dunedin: University of Otago Press, 1967).

Dardell, Eric, 'The Mythic', in *Sacred Narrative: Readings in the Theory of Myth*, ed. Alan Dundes (Berkeley: University of California Press, 1984).

Day, Aidan, *Angela Carter: The Rational Glass* (Manchester University Press, 1998).

D'haen, Theo and Hans Bertens (eds), *Liminal Postmodernisms: The Postmodern, the (Post-)Colonial, and the (Post-)Feminist* (Amsterdam: University of Rodopi Press, 1994).

Diski, Jenny, *The Vanishing Princess* (London: Weidenfeld and Nicolson, 1995).

Donoghue, Emma, *Kissing the Witch* (1997; Harmondsworth: Penguin, 1998).

Dowling, Finuala, *Fay Weldon's Fiction* (Cranbury, NJ: Associated University Presses, 1998).

Duffy, Maureen, *The Erotic World of Faery* (London: Hodder and Stoughton, 1972).

Duffy, Stella, *Singling the Couples* (London: Sceptre, 1998).

Duncker, Patricia, 'Queer Gothic: Angela Carter and the Lost Narratives of Sexual Subversion', *Critical Survey*, vol. 8, no. 1 (1996), pp. 58–68.

Dundes, Alan (ed.), *Sacred Narrative: Readings in the Theory of Myth* (Berkeley: University of California Press, 1984).

Dusinberre, Juliet, 'Interview with A. S. Byatt', *Women Writers Talking*, ed. Janet Todd (New York: Holmes and Meier, 1983).

Eisler, Riane, *Sacred Pleasure: Sex, Myth and the Politics of the Body* (1995; Shaftesbury: Element Books, 1996).

——, 'Introduction', *The Woman's Companion to Mythology 1992*, ed. Carolyne Larrington (London: Pandora, 1997).

Eliade, Mircea, *Myth and Reality*, trans. Willard R. Task (New York: Harper and Row, 1963).
——, *Myths, Dreams and Mysteries: The Encounter Between Contemporary Faiths and Archaic Reality* (1957), trans. Philip Mairet (London: Fontana, 1970).
Eliot, George, *The Mill on the Floss* (1860; Ware: Wordsworth Editions, 1993).
Eliot, T. S., 'Ulysses, Order, and Myth', in *Selected Prose of T. S. Eliot*, ed. Frank Kermode (New York: Harcourt Brace Jovanovich, 1975).
Elphinstone, Margaret, 'Contemporary Feminist Fantasy in the Scottish Literary Tradition', *Tea and Leg-Irons: New Feminist Readings from Scotland*, ed. Caroline Gonda (London: Open Letters, 1992).
Falck, Colin, *Myth, Truth and Literature* (1989; Cambridge University Press, 1995).
Fell, Alison, *The Mistress of Lilliput* (London: Doubleday, 1999).
Fernihough, Anne, ' "Is She Fact or is She Fiction?" Angela Carter and the Enigma of Woman', in *Textual Practice*, vol. 11, no. 1 (1997), pp. 89–107.
Ferreira, Maria Aline Seabra, 'The Uncanny (M)other: Angela Carter's *The Passion of New Eve*', in *Paradoxa*, vol. 3, nos 3–4 (1997), pp. 471–88.
Feuerbach, Ludwig, *The Essence of Christianity* (1881), trans. George Eliot (New York: Harper, 1957).
Foucault, Michel, *Les Mots et les choses: une archéologie des sciences humaines* (Paris: Gallimard, 1966); trans. *The Order of Things: An Archaeology of the Human Sciences* (London: Tavistock, 1974).
Frazer, J. G., *The Golden Bough* (1890–1915, abr. edn 1922; Ware: Wordsworth Editions, 1993).
Freud, Sigmund, *The Standard Edition of the Complete Psychological Works*, 24 vols, trans. James Strachey (London: Hogarth Press, 1953–66).
Gamble, Sarah, *Angela Carter: Writing from the Front Line* (Edinburgh University Press, 1997).
Gatens, Moria, 'Power, Bodies and Difference', *Destabilizing Theory*, ed. M. Barrett and A. Phillips (Cambridge: Polity Press, 1992).
Gilbert, Sandra M. and Susan Gubar, *The Madwoman in the Attic: The Woman Writer and the Nineteenth-Century Literary Imagination* (New Haven, Conn.: Yale University Press, 1979).
Gillooly, Eileen, 'Women and Humor', *Feminist Studies*, 17: 3 (1991), pp. 473–92.
Gimbutas, Marija, *Goddesses and Gods of Old Europe, 6500–3500 BCE* (1974; Berkeley: University of California Press, 1982).
Goldman, Emma, *Anarchism and Other Essays* (New York: Dover Publications, 1969).
Gonda, Caroline (ed.), *Tea and Leg-Irons: New Feminist Readings from Scotland* (London: Open Letters, 1992).
——, 'An Other Country? Mapping Scottish/Lesbian/Writing', *Gendering the Nation: Studies in Modern Scottish Literature*, ed. Christopher Whyte (Edinburgh University Press, 1995).
Graves, Robert, 'Introduction', *New Larousse Encyclopedia of Mythology* (1968; London: Hamlyn, 1975).

——, *The White Goddess: A Historical Grammar of Poetic Myth* (1948; London: Faber, 1961).

Griffin, Gabrielle (ed.), *Outwrite: Lesbianism and Popular Culture* (London: Pluto Press, 1993).

Grolnick, Simon A., 'Fairy Tales and Psychotherapy', *Fairy Tales and Society: Illusion, Allusion and Paradigm*, ed. Ruth B. Bottigheimer (Philadelphia: University of Pennsylvania Press, 1986).

Haffenden, John, 'Interview with Angela Carter', *Novelists in Interview*, ed. John Haffenden (London: Methuen, 1985).

Hall, Nor, *The Moon and the Virgin: Reflections on the Archetypal Feminine* (London: Women's Press, 1980).

Halliday, W. R., *Indo-European Folk-Tales and Greek Legend* (Cambridge University Press, 1933).

Hardin, Michael, 'The Other Other: Self-Definition Outside Patriarchal Institutions in Angela Carter's *Wise Children*', *The Review of Contemporary Fiction*, vol. 14, no. 3 (Fall 1994), pp. 77–83.

Harrison, Jane, *Mythology* (New York: Harcourt Brace, 1963).

Hastie, Nicki, 'Lesbian Bibliomythography', *Outwrite: Lesbianism and Popular Culture*, ed. Gabrielle Griffin (London: Pluto Press, 1993).

Hebert, Ann Marie, 'Rewriting the Feminine Script: Fay Weldon's Wicked Laughter', in *Journal of Women and Gender*, 7: 1 (1993).

Hennegan, Alison, 'The Extraordinary Miss X: Christine Crow Talks about Her New Novel', *The Women's Press Bookclub Catalogue*, October–December 1990.

Hesiod, 'Theogeny' and 'Works and Days', in *Hesiod and Theognis*, trans. Dorothea Wender (Harmondsworth: Penguin, 1973).

Homer, *The Iliad*, trans. Robert Fitzgerald (Oxford University Press, 1984).

Honko, Lauri, 'The Problem of Defining Myth', *Sacred Narrative: Readings in the Theory of Myth*, ed. Alan Dundes (Berkeley: University of California Press, 1984).

Irigaray, Luce, *An Ethics of Sexual Difference* (1984), trans. Carolyn Burke and Gillian C. Gill (London: Athlone Press, 1993).

——, *This Sex Which Is Not One* (1977), trans. Catherine Porter (New York: Cornell University Press, 1985).

——, *Speculum of the Other Woman* (1974), trans. Gillian C. Gill (New York: Cornell University Press, 1985).

——, *Sexes and Genealogies* (1987), trans. Gillian C. Gill (New York: Columbia University Press, 1993).

Jackson, Rosemary, *Fantasy: The Literature of Subversion* (London: Methuen, 1981).

Jacobus, Mary, *First Things: The Maternal Imaginary in Literature, Art and Psychoanalysis* (London: Routledge, 1995).

Jameson, Frederic, *The Political Unconscious: Narrative as a Socially Symbolic Act* (London: Methuen, 1981).

Jordan, Elaine, 'Enthralment: Angela Carter's Speculative Fictions', *Plotting Change: Contemporary Women's Fiction*, ed. Linda Anderson (London: Edward Arnold, 1990).

Jung, Carl, *The Archetypes and the Collective Unconscious* (1959), trans. R. F. C. Hull, in *The Collected Works of C. G. Jung* (London: Routledge and Kegan Paul, 1969).

Jung, Carl, 'On the Psychology of the Unconscious', quoted in *Jung: Selected Writings*, ed. Anthony Storr (London: Fontana, 1983).

Kaiser, Mary, 'Fairy Tale as Sexual Allegory: Intertextuality in Angela Carter's *The Bloody Chamber*', in *The Review of Contemporary Fiction*, vol. 14, no. 3 (Fall 1994), pp. 30–6.

Kamuf, Peggy (ed.), *A Derrida Reader: Between the Blinds* (Hemel Hempstead: Harvester Wheatsheaf, 1991).

Kavablum, Leah, *Cinderella: Radical Feminist, Alchemist* (New Jersey: Guttenberg, 1973).

Kermode, Frank (ed.), *Selected Prose of T. S. Eliot* (New York: Harcourt Brace Johanovich, 1975).

Kingston, Maxine Hong, *The Woman Warrior* (1975; London: Picador, 1981).

Kirk, G. S., *Myth: Its Meaning and Function in Ancient and Other Cultures* (Cambridge University Press, 1970).

Kirwan, James, *Beauty* (Manchester University Press, 1999).

Kristeva, Julia, *Desire in Language: A Semiotic Approach to Literature and Art* (1980), trans. Thomas Gora, Alice Jardine and Leon S. Roudiez (Oxford: Blackwell, 1981).

——, *Powers of Horror: An Essay on Abjection* (1980), trans. Leon S. Roudiez (New York: Columbia University Press, 1982).

——, *Revolution in Poetic Language* (1974), trans. Margaret Waller (New York: Columbia University Press, 1984).

——, 'Women's Time', *The Kristeva Reader*, ed. Toril Moi (Oxford: Blackwell, 1986).

Larrington, Carolyne (ed.), *The Woman's Companion to Mythology* (London: Pandora, 1992).

Leach, Edmund, *Genesis as Myth and Other Essays* (London: Jonathan Cape, 1969).

Leach, Maria (ed.), *Standard Dictionary of Folklore, Mythology and Legend* (London: New English Library, 1972).

Lévi-Strauss, Claude, *Myth and Meaning* (London: Routledge and Kegan Paul, 1978).

Lochhead, Liz, *The Grimm Sisters* (London: Next Editions, 1981).

Lurie, Alison, *Don't Tell the Grown-Ups: The Subversive Power of Children's Literature* (Boston: Little, Brown and Company, 1990).

—— (ed.), *The Oxford Book of Modern Fairy Tales* (Oxford University Press, 1993).

Lykke, Nina and Rosi Braidotti (eds), *Between Monsters, Goddesses and Cyborgs: Feminist Confrontations with Science, Medicine and Cyberspace* (London and New Jersey: Zed Books, 1996).

Lyotard, Jean-François, *The Lyotard Reader*, ed. Andrew Benjamin (Oxford and Cambridge, Mass.: Blackwell, 1989).

Maack, Annegret, 'Translating Nineteenth-Century Classics: Emma Tennant's Intertextual Novels', *(Sub)Versions of Realism: Recent Women's Fiction in Britain*, ed. Irmgard Maassen and Anna Maria Stuby (Heidelberg: Universitätsverlag C. Winter, 1997).

Maassen, Irmgard and Anna Maria Stuby (eds), *(Sub)Versions of Realism: Recent Women's Fiction in Britain* (Heidelberg: Universitätsverlag C. Winter, 1997).

Makinen, Merja, 'Sexual and Textual Aggression in *The Sadeian Woman* and *The Passion of New Eve*', *The Infernal Desires of Angela Carter: Fiction, Femininity, Feminism*, ed. Joseph Bristow and Trev Lynn Broughton (London: Longman, 1997).

Malinowski, Bronislaw, 'The Role of Myth in Life', *Myth and the Modern Imagination*, ed. Margaret Dalziel (Dunedin: University of Otago Press, 1967).

Manton, G. R., 'The Making of Myth', *Myth and the Modern Imagination*, ed. Margaret Dalziel (Dunedin: University of Otago Press, 1967).

Marks, Elaine and Isabelle de Courtivron (eds), *New French Feminisms* (1980; Brighton: Harvester, 1981).

Milton, John, *Paradise Lost* (1667; Harmondsworth: Penguin, 1968).

Moi, Toril (ed.), *The Kristeva Reader* (Oxford: Blackwell, 1986).

Morris, Pam (ed.), *The Bakhtin Reader* (London: Edward Arnold, 1994).

Morrison, Toni, *Beloved* (1987; London: Picador, 1988).

Namjoshi, Suniti, *Feminist Fables* (1981; London: Sheba, 1990).

Nemerov, Howard, *The Quester Hero: Myth as Universal Structure in the Works of Thomas Mann* (Cambridge, Mass.: Harvard University Press, 1940).

New Larousse Encyclopedia of Mythology (1968; London: Hamlyn, 1975).

Olson, Alan M. (ed.), *Myth, Symbol and Reality* (London: University of Notre Dame Press, 1980).

Orr, Mary, 'Crossing Divides: *Miss X or the Wolf Woman*', *Tea and Leg-Irons: New Feminist Readings from Scotland*, ed. Caroline Gonda (London: Open Letters, 1992).

Ovid, *Metamorphoses*, trans. A. D. Melville (Oxford University Press, 1986).

Paglia, Camille, *Sexual Personae: Art and Decadence from Nefertiti to Emily Dickinson* (New Haven, Conn.: Yale University Press, 1990).

Peers, E. Allison (ed), *The Complete Works of Saint Teresa of Jesus*, vol. II (London: Sheed and Ward, 1946).

Pettazzoni, Raffaele, 'The Truth of Myth', *Sacred Narrative: Readings in the Theory of Myth*, ed. Alan Dundes (Berkeley, Calif.: University of California Press, 1984).

Pirani, Alix, *The Absent Father: Crisis and Creativity – The Myth of Danae and Perseus in the Twentieth Century* (1988; Harmondsworth: Penguin, 1989).

Propp, Vladimir, *Morphology of the Folktale*, trans. Laurence Scott (University of Texas Press, 1968).

Purkiss, Diane, 'Women's Rewriting of Myth', *The Woman's Companion to Mythology*, ed. Carolyne Larrington (London: Pandora, 1992).

Rice, Anne (written under the name A. N. Roquelaure) *Beauty's Punishment* (New York: Plume Books, 1984).

——, (written under the name A. N. Roquelaure) *Beauty's Release* (New York: E. P. Dutton, 1985).

——, *The Vampire Lestat* (New York: Alfred A. Knopf, 1985).

——, (written under the name Anne Rampling), *Belinda* (1986; New York: Jove, 1988).

——, (written under the name Anne Rampling), *Exit to Eden* (1985; New York: Dell Publishing, 1989).

——, *The Tale of the Body Thief* (New York: Alfred A. Knopf, 1992).

190 Bibliography

Rice, Anne, *Queen of the Damned* (1988; London: Warner Books, 1995).
——, (written under the name A. N. Roquelaure) *The Claiming of Sleeping Beauty* (1983; London: Warner Books, 1997).
——, *Interview with the Vampire* (1976; London: Warner Books, 1998).
Rich, Adrienne, *Of Woman Born: Motherhood as Experience and Institution* (1976; London: Virago, 1984).
Roberts, Bette B., *Anne Rice* (New York: Twayne, 1994).
Roberts, Michèle, *The Wild Girl* (London: Minerva, 1984).
——, *The Book of Mrs Noah* (London: Methuen, 1987).
——, *Impossible Saints* (1997; London: Virago, 1998).
——, *Food, Sex and God: On Inspiration and Writing* (London: Virago, 1998).
Roe, Sue, Susan Sellers and Nicole Ward Jouve, *The Semi-Transparent Envelope: Women Writing – Feminism and Fiction* (London: Marion Boyars, 1994).
Rose, Cronan, 'Introduction', *The Voyage In: Fictions of Female Development*, ed. Elizabeth Abel, Marianne Hirsch and Elizabeth Langland (Hanover: University Press of New England, 1983).
Rostas, Susannah, 'Mexican Mythology: Divine Androgyny but "His" Story, the Female in Aztec Mythology', *The Woman's Companion to Mythology*, ed. Carolyne Larrington (London: Pandora, 1992).
Rowe, Karen E., 'Feminism and Fairy Tales' and 'To Spin a Yarn: The Female Voice in Folklore and Fairy Tale', *Fairy Tales and Society: Illusion, Allusion and Paradigm*, ed. Ruth B. Bottigheimer (Philadelphia: University of Pennsylvania Press, 1986).
Ruthven, K. K., *Myth* (London: Methuen, 1976).
Sage, Lorna (ed.), *Flesh and the Mirror: Essays on the Art of Angela Carter* (London: Virago, 1994).
Said, Edward, *The World, the Text and the Critic* (London: Faber and Faber, 1984).
Schwartz, L. S., 'Quartet Plus Ghost', *Village Voice*, 3 January 1977.
Sellers, Susan, (ed.), *Writing Differences: Readings from the Seminar of Hélène Cixous* (Milton Keynes: Open University Press, 1988).
——, *Language and Sexual Difference: Feminist Writing in France* (Basingstoke: Macmillan, 1991).
——(ed.), *The Hélène Cixous Reader* (London: Routledge, 1994).
——, *Hélène Cixous: Authorship, Autobiography and Love* (Cambridge: Polity Press, 1996).
Sexton, Anne, *Transformations* (Oxford University Press, 1972).
Shelley, Mary, *Frankenstein or the Modern Prometheus* (1818; Oxford University Press, 1969).
Shields, Carol, *Larry's Party* (London: Fourth Estate, 1997).
Showalter, Elaine (ed.), *The New Feminist Criticism: Essays on Women, Literature and Theory* (1985; London: Virago, 1996).
Sjöö, Monica and Barbara Mor, *The Great Cosmic Mother: Rediscovering the Religion of the Earth* (San Francisco: Harper and Row, 1987).
Sontag, Susan (ed.), *A Barthes Reader* (London: Cape, 1982).
Spence, Lewis, *An Introduction to Mythology* (London: Harrap, 1921).

Stevenson, Robert Louis, *The Strange Case of Dr Jekyll and Mr Hyde* (1886; Harmondsworth: Penguin, 1994).
Stoker, Bram, *Dracula* (1897; Ware: Wordsworth Editions, 1993).
Stone, Kay F., 'Feminist Approaches to the Interpretation of Fairy Tales', *Fairy Tales and Society: Illusion, Allusion and Paradigm*, ed. Ruth B. Bottigheimer (Philadelphia: University of Pennsylvania Press, 1986).
Stone, R. G., 'Myth in Modern French Literature', in *Myth and the Modern Imagination*, ed. Margaret Dalziel (Dunedin: University of Otago Press, 1967).
Tatar, Maria M., 'Born Yesterday: Heroes in the Grimm's Fairy Tales', *Fairy Tales and Society: Illusion, Allusion and Paradigm*, ed. Ruth B. Bottigheimer (Philadelphia: University of Pennsylvania Press, 1986).
Tennant, Emma, *Alice Fell* (London: Cape, 1980).
——, *Queen of Stones* (London: Cape, 1982).
——, *Travesties* (London: Faber and Faber, 1995).
Tepper, Sheri S., *Beauty* (1991; London: HarperCollins, 1995).
Thompson, Alice, *Pandora's Box* (London: Little Brown, 1998).
Todd, Richard, *A. S. Byatt* (Plymouth: Northcote House, 1997).
Valdès, Maria J. (ed.), *A Ricoeur Reader: Reflection and Imagination* (University of Toronto Press, 1991).
Von Franz, Marie-Louise, *The Feminine in Fairy Tales* (1972; Boston and London: Shambhala, 1993).
Voragine, Jacobus de, *The Golden Legend: Readings on the Saints*, 2 vols, trans. William Granger Ryan (Princeton University Press, 1993).
Walker, Barbara G., *Feminist Fairy Tales* (New York: HarperCollins, 1996).
——, *The Women's Encyclopedia of Myths and Secrets* (Edison, New Jersey: Castle Books, 1996).
Wandor, Michelene (ed.), *On Gender and Writing* (London: Pandora Press, 1983).
Ward Jouve, Nicole, *Female Genesis: Creativity, Self and Gender* (Cambridge: Polity Press, 1998).
——, 'The Red Road', *The Semi-Transparent Envelope: Women Writing – Feminism and Fiction*, with Sue Roe and Susan Sellers (London: Marion Boyars, 1994).
Warner, Marina, *Monuments and Maidens: The Allegory of the Female Form* (London: Weidenfeld and Nicolson, 1985).
——, *Managing Monsters: Six Myths of Our Time* (London: Vintage, 1994).
——, *The Mermaids in the Basement* (1993; London: Vintage, 1994).
——, *From the Beast to the Blonde: On Fairy Tales and their Tellers* (1994; London: Vintage, 1995).
——(ed.), *Wonder Tales: Six Stories of Enchantment* (1994; London: Virago, 1996).
——, *No Go the Bogeyman: Scaring, Lulling and Making Mock* (London: Chatto and Windus, 1998).
Weldon, Fay, *Down Among the Women* (1971; Harmondsworth: Penguin, 1973).
——, *The Life and Loves of a She Devil* (London: Hodder and Stoughton, 1983).
——, *The Heart of the Country* (London: Hutchinson, 1987).
——, *The Cloning of Joanna May* (1989; London: Flamingo, 1993).

Wertenbaker, Timberlake, 'The Love of the Nightingale', *Timberlake Werternbaker: Plays* (London: Faber & Faber, 1996).
Weston, Jessie L., *From Ritual to Romance* (Cambridge University Press, 1920).
White, John J., *Mythology in the Modern Novel: A Study of Prefigurative Techniques* (Princeton University Press, 1971).
Whitford, Margaret (ed.), *The Irigaray Reader* (Oxford: Blackwell, 1991).
Whyte, Christopher (ed.), *Gendering the Nation: Studies in Modern Scottish Literature* (Edinburgh University Press, 1995).
Wilson, Emma, 'Hélène Cixous: An Erotics of the Feminine', *French Erotic Fiction: Women's Desiring Writing, 1880–1990*, ed. Alex Hughes and Kate Ince (Oxford: Berg, 1996).
Winterson, Jeanette, *Sexing the Cherry* (1989; London: Vintage, 1990).
Wolf, Naomi, *The Beauty Myth: How Images of Beauty are Used Against Women* (1990; London: Vintage, 1991).
Woolf, Virginia, *A Room of One's Own* (1928; Harmondsworth: Penguin, 1975).
——, 'Modern Fiction', in *The Crowded Dance of Life: Selected Essays*, vol. 2, ed. Rachel Bowlby (Harmondsworth: Penguin, 1993).
Zipes, Jack, *Fairy Tales and the Art of Subversion* (New York: Routledge and Kegan Paul, 1991).
——, *Breaking the Magic Spell: Radical Theories of Folk and Fairy Tales* (1979; New York: Routledge and Kegan Paul, 1992).
——, *Fairy Tale as Myth: Myth as Fairy Tale* (The University of Kentucky Press, 1994).
Ziv, Amalia, 'The Pervert's Progress: An Analysis of *Story of O* and the Beauty Trilogy', in *Feminist Review*, no. 46 (Spring 1994), pp. 61–75.

Index